THE
SAS

THE
SAS

The Savage Wars of Peace

1947 to the Present

Anthony Kemp

LONDON   NEW YORK   SYDNEY   TORONTO

Typeset in 11/13 pt Ehrhardt by Wearset, Boldon, Tyne and Wear
Printed and bound in Great Britain by
The University Press, Cambridge

'In retrospect it is a miracle that the post-war SAS survived, let alone flourish as it does today. Several times it was touch and go. Our salvation depended on a few, very few, dedicated visionaries and persistent champions in the right place at the right time.'

C.L.D. Newell
D.G.C. Sutherland
28 February 1987

Contents

Illustrations

The author and publishers wish to thank the following for permission to reproduce illustrations: 4, 5, 6, 8, 9, 10, The Imperial War Museum; 7, *Soldier*; 12, Pacemaker Press; 11, 13, 14, Press Association; 15, Military Picture Library

Foreword

Essentially, this book is the second part of a two-volume history of the SAS Regiment, and the reader who is interested in the Second World War period is referred to *The SAS at War, 1941–1945*, by the same author. Yet strangely enough there might well not have been a need to write this particular volume, as it is a miracle that the SAS survived after the war at all. The passage quoted as an epigraph, written in 1987 by two senior officers of the regiment, makes it quite plain that the whole idea of a small élite force was anathema to some within the British Army who were determined to abolish the SAS. The passage continues, 'Was it chance or destiny that guided the fledgling SAS safely through those anxious formative years? We will never know.'

Ever since a handful of black-clad men wearing respirators stormed the Iranian Embassy in London to free a group of hostages in May 1980, the SAS, much against its will, has remained firmly in the public eye. The more that the regimental establishment tries to fade into the background, the more the public's appetite for information is whetted and the more fanciful many of the written accounts become. No matter how mundane the unfortunate violent demise of someone in Ulster, the Republican propaganda machine routinely blames the SAS. When members of the regiment shot three Provisional IRA members in the busy streets of Gibraltar, acting needless to say under orders from their superiors, certain sections of the press inferred that the SAS were trained killers who were a law unto themselves.

Inevitably, as with so many things in Britain, opinions have become polarized along divisions of class and political opinion. For those who espouse strong left-wing views, the SAS is the hit-squad of the Establishment, maintained for the oppression of the lower orders and the ultimate defence of the status quo. For those at the opposite end of the political spectrum, members of the SAS are heroes. Their head-quarters was flooded with gifts of champagne after the lifting of the siege of the Iranian Embassy, and in the eyes of the right-wing newspapers, they can do no wrong.

Because of the nature of the work the SAS is called upon to perform, any potential author is under a number of constraints, both practical and moral. The earlier post-war colonial campaigns in which the regiment saw service are well within the public domain, documentation is available in the Public Record Office and anybody is fully entitled to write about them. Indeed, several distinguished ex-members have written books about their experiences during those end-of-empire campaigns, with official approval in the case of soldiers who were still serving at the time. The difficulty starts during the 1970s when the role of the regiment changed as a result of external pressures and circum-stances. During that period it acquired a counter-revolutionary warfare (CRW) role and found itself no longer a specialist infantry unit but in the forefront of the fight against international terrorism.

From then on, its activities and expertise had to be hidden behind a veil of secrecy and the identities of its members protected, which is perfectly fair and reasonable. We do, however, live in a free society with an independent press, and the SAS, as a part of the Army, is funded by the British taxpayer. As such, the press is entitled to comment, no matter how much that fact may irk the powers that be. If three people are shot dead in a public thoroughfare in broad daylight in Gibraltar, it is hardly surprising that the fact is of interest to the media which, after all, only reflects what its viewers and readers wish to see or read.

Recently there has been a spate of books about events in Northern Ireland, in the wake of the Stalker affair and the whole question of a 'shoot to kill' policy. Inevitably the SAS has been dragged into this, criticized by one section of opinion and warmly lauded by the other. Whether it likes it or not, the SAS is in the limelight and is likely to remain so, while the public appetite creates a healthy demand. At the time of writing, General Sir Peter de la Billière, the most distinguished member of the SAS still serving, has published his Gulf War memoirs which deal in considerable depth with the role of special forces in that conflict. Of course he has the right to do so, but in conversation with a recently retired member of the regiment, the latter made the comment that if he wrote his story, 'they'd throw the Official Secrets Act at me'.

Neither this book, nor the last one for that matter, is an 'official' history, written with the blessing of the Ministry of Defence or the SAS Regiment, and I take full responsibility for any opinions expressed. In the later chapters I have taken the greatest of care to secure the anonymity of regiment personnel and to avoid anything that might prove useful to a potential enemy.

My interest in attempting this history was originally sparked during a number of lengthy conversations with Sir David Stirling, the founder of the regiment, who sadly died shortly before the fiftieth anniversary of his creation. He spoke of the ethos of the SAS and the necessity of writing an unvarnished factual account, not only of the wartime years, but of the later campaigns as well. The late Major Dare Newell, affectionately known as the 'Father of the Regiment', was another responsible figure who spent a lot of time talking me through those early turbulent post-war years and the battles to keep the SAS in being.

Over the last few years I have had the privilege of meeting a considerable number of men who are serving or have served in the SAS. I have drunk with them, eaten with them and yarned with them. Throughout I have respected their confidence. Their secrets are safe, and it will be the task of my grandchildren to sift the public records for the documentation of their deeds during the last twenty years. This book is dedicated to those who served and are serving in the regiment, both regulars and volunteers.

One accusation often levelled by reviewers against those who have written about the SAS in the past is that they are 'groupies', battening on to the reputation of the regiment in order to sell books – and thus profit from the courage of others. I will cheerfully admit that I became fascinated, as a historian, during the 1980s when I wrote about the war crimes investigation team in *The Secret Hunters*, which was based on the highly successful television documentary of the same title. That whetted my appetite to undertake further research, and the present book brings the story to a close. I have great admiration for the regiment and what it stands for, and if that makes me a 'groupie', then so be it.

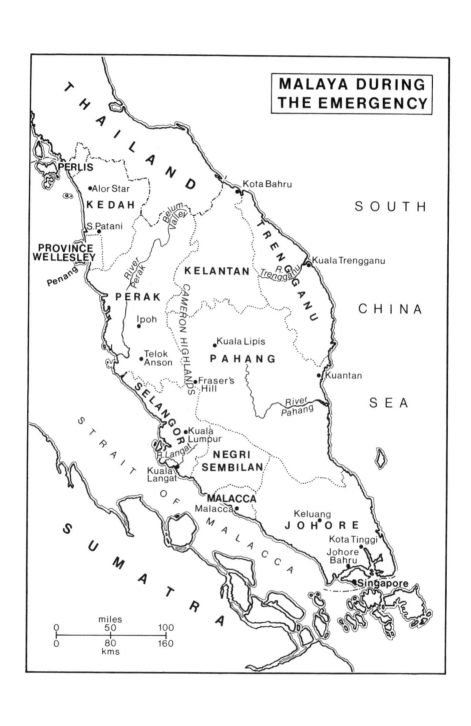

MALAYA DURING
THE EMERGENCY

THAILAND

PERLIS

KEDAH
•Alor Star

S.Patani

PROVINCE
WELLESLEY

Penang

PERAK

Ipoh

Telok
Anson

SELANGOR

Kuala
Lumpur

R.Langat

Kuala
Langat

Belum
Valley

River
Perak

CAMERON HIGHLANDS

Kota Bahru

KELANTAN

TRENGGANU

Kuala Trengganu

R.
Trengganu

Kuala Lipis

PAHANG

Fraser's
Hill

Kuantan

River
Pahang

NEGRI
SEMBILAN

MALACCA
Malacca

JOHORE

Keluang

Kota Tinggi

Johore
Bahru

Singapore

SOUTH

CHINA

SEA

STRAIT OF MALACCA

SUMATRA

miles
0   50   100
0   80   160
kms

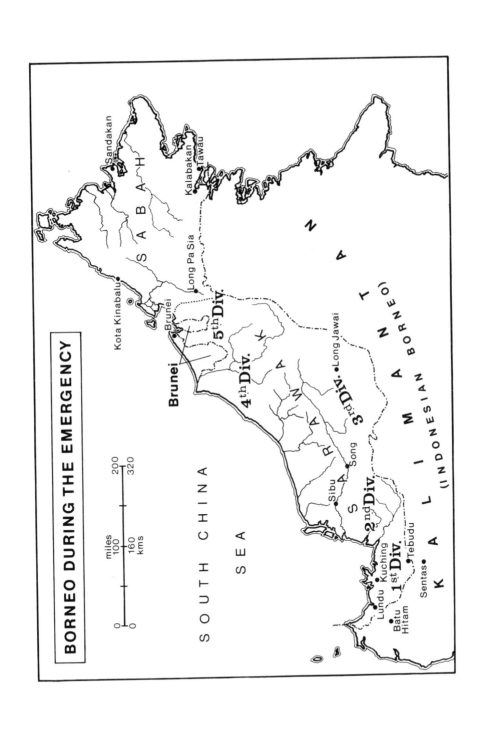

BORNEO DURING THE EMERGENCY

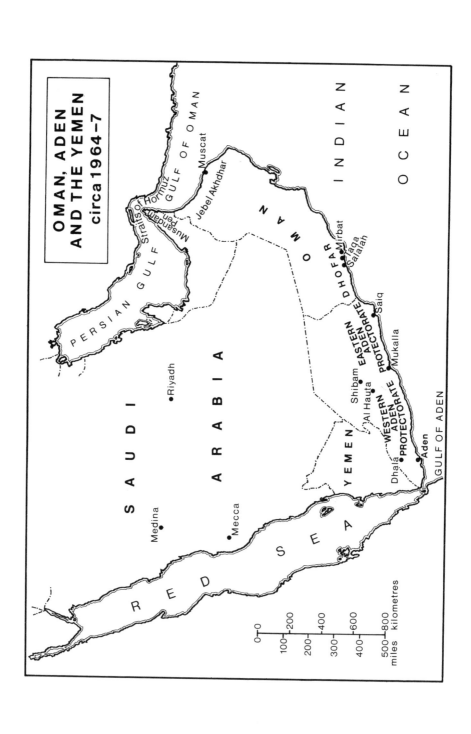

OMAN, ADEN AND THE YEMEN circa 1964–7

PERSIAN GULF

Strait of Hormuz

Musandam Pen.

GULF OF OMAN

Muscat

Jebel Akhdhar

SAUDI

•Riyadh

ARABIA

Medina •

Mecca •

OMAN

DHOFAR

Mirbat
Taqa
Salalah

Saiq

RED SEA

YEMEN

Shibam •
Al Hauta •

Dhala •

EASTERN ADEN PROTECTORATE

Mukalla

WESTERN ADEN PROTECTORATE

Aden

GULF OF ADEN

INDIAN

OCEAN

0
100 200
200 400
300
400 600
500 800
miles kilometres

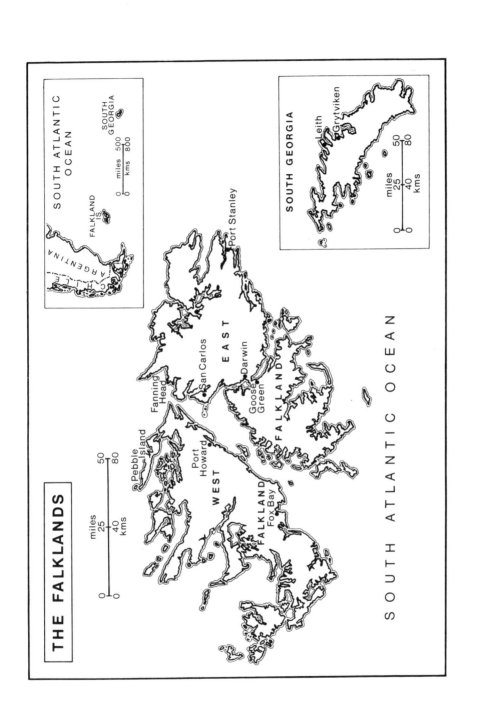

THE FALKLANDS

miles
0   25   50
kms
0   40   80

Pebble
Island

Fanning
Head

San Carlos

Port
Howard

WEST

FALKLAND
Fox Bay

EAST

Darwin

Goose
Green

FALKLAND

Port Stanley

SOUTH ATLANTIC OCEAN

SOUTH ATLANTIC
OCEAN

ARGENTINA
CHILE

FALKLAND
IS.

SOUTH
GEORGIA

miles
0   500
kms
0   800

SOUTH GEORGIA

Leith
Grytviken

miles
0   25   50
kms
0   40   80

I

Phoenix

By the end of the Second World War the SAS had increased in size to such an extent that it formed a somewhat unwieldy brigade, consisting of two British regiments, numbered as 1 and 2 SAS, two French battalions known as 3 and 4 SAS and the Belgian SAS Regiment. The last operational deployment of the British was to oversee the disarmament of the German forces in Norway. That was not a particularly onerous task, and for many of the officers and men it was a welcome holiday after the rigours of wartime service. At the end of August 1945 their future was very much in the balance; 1 and 2 SAS Regiments sailed back to their bases in the Colchester area of Essex.

Their brigade commander, 'Mad' Mike Calvert, had returned to the UK in June to start a strong lobbying campaign for SAS units to be employed in the Far East, where the war was still in progress. The official proposal was for a part of the brigade to be sent to join Lord Louis Mountbatten's South East Asia Command, but in the meantime the founder, David Stirling, had been released from Colditz and in April 1945 was back on the scene in London. While still imprisoned in the castle, his ever-fertile mind had dreamed up a plan which he called the Chungking Project. His intention was to form a brigade which he would command, consisting of 2 SAS Regiment, an OSS regiment (the American equivalent of Special Operations Executive: SOE) and a third regiment recruited from released prisoners of war, including several of his friends from Colditz.

It has to be borne in mind that at that time only a select few had been initiated into the secret of the atomic bomb, and it was generally assumed in the corridors of power that the war in the Far East would be a long hard slog to dislodge the Japanese from Malaya and to capture the home islands. Stirling's plan was to operate in China, thus cutting the Japanese supply lines into Malaya, to sabotage industrial centres in Manchuria and to secure beaches along the coast suitable for American amphibious landings. He had a meeting with Winston Churchill, who gave his blessing to the idea, and planning got under way during the spring of 1945. The following is a quotation from an undated and unsigned brief in the possession of the author.

> It is proposed that a force, consisting of approx 2 SAS Regts., should operate in Northern CHINA in an SAS role. The operation would initially be purely military. One Regt. will be British and the other probably American. This force will have a British Commander, but will be under the Theatre Command of the Americans. It is hoped that the British Regt. will be ready to operate by the beginning of Dec. 1945 and the American one about March 1946. Initially, operations will consist of small parties up to 1 or 2 Sqns. in strength, equipped on a jeep basis, which will be parachuted or glided into areas up to one thousand miles from the base, to attack Japanese Ls of C. They will be maintained by air, and when the operation has ended, may be withdrawn by sea or by land.

This was clearly a most audacious plan when one considers that the force proposed to operate a considerable distance from their base. The document went on to recommend the setting up of a base at Chungking where the theatre command was located, and discussed in detail the aircraft requirements for resupply as well as the insertion of the operating parties. The basic plan called for a force of 850 men, 800 tons of stores and 320 vehicles, all of which would have to be brought into China via the Burma Road.

In fact, the dropping of the atomic bombs in August put paid to any involvement in the Far East, and the regiments of the SAS Brigade found themselves still marking time. The end of the war against Japan gave those in the War Office who heartily disliked what they called 'private armies' the opportunity to press for the abolition of the various raiding forces that had grown up during the war. On 21 September the

Belgian SAS reverted to its own national command and on 1 October it was the turn of the French, who departed for a new base at Pau. On 5 October, after final parades, 1 and 2 SAS Regiments were officially disbanded and, except for a small party which remained behind to hand in stores, the personnel were dispersed. Those who were regular soldiers returned to their parent regiments where they often felt like fish out of water, while others had to make their way back into civilian life.

There, but for circumstances, the story of the SAS might well have ended. David Stirling went off to Africa to carve out a career for himself, and for many years lost contact with his creation. In order to keep the spirit of wartime comradeship alive, however, the SAS Association was formed in late 1945, with Winston Churchill as the patron and Stirling as president. The first dinner, held at the Connaught Rooms in London on 17 December 1946, was attended by some 500 men from the two regiments.

Yet in spite of the disbandment, odd little pockets of the SAS did survive for some years, on a strictly unofficial basis. One group was sent off to Greece to serve in the British Military Reparations Committee, where they continued to wear SAS insignia, and many of them subsequently became entangled in the Civil War in that country. One particular officer, who as a teenager before the war had served on the Republican side in the Spanish Civil War, ended up fighting for the Greek Royalist cause.

The most cohesive remainder of the SAS was a war crimes investigation unit that had been established by 2 SAS Regiment in May 1945 to discover the fate of thirty-two men who were missing at the end of Operation Loyton, which had been mounted in Alsace between August and October of the previous year. The regiment's commanding officer, Lieutenant-Colonel Brian Franks, had received information that some of those missing might have been executed by the Gestapo, and this was borne out by an officer whom he sent to the area in December. Franks decided to send his intelligence officer, Major Eric Barkworth, together with a small team to mount a full investigation. They established themselves in a requisitioned villa in Gaggenau in the French occupation zone of Germany, where they found the bodies of several of their comrades who had been murdered at the nearby concentration camp at Rotenfels.

By the autumn of 1945 Barkworth had built up an impressive dossier of evidence about the fate of the missing men and those who were culpable of their murder, as well as taking on responsibility for investigating other crimes committed against Allied personnel in the area. Franks, however, was fully aware of the threat of disbandment which was hanging over his regiment and he was determined to keep his team in existence, using political influence if necessary.

He enlisted the help of Captain Yuri Galitzine, son of a Russian prince, who had served as an intelligence officer during the war. In 1945 he was at the War Office, working for the Department of the Judge Advocate-General which was responsible for crimes committed against British and Commonwealth members of the armed forces. In September Galitzine went to Europe, and on his return wrote a comprehensive report, much of which was devoted to the efforts of Barkworth and his team. It was highly critical of the work being carried out by the official War Office group commanded by Colonel Leo Genn, who had been a well-known actor before the war. The latter had been sent down to help the SAS, but:

> The team was staffed with inexperienced and unenthusiastic personnel and seemed to have been under a misapprehension as to their task. Lt. Col. Genn stated that the team's task was [to] 'put into legal form already existing evidence'. Investigation was not recognised as a job of the team. No attempt was made to find bodies or to dig about for evidence, but they purely went over ground already covered or went after witnesses known to exist.

Galitzine, who wrote the above in a report, recommended that the Barkworth team be directly seconded to the War Office, and their base signals station was set up in the loft of his office in Eaton Square, which enabled an efficient level of communications to be maintained. When the investigations on the ground had been completed, the unit moved north into the British Zone and became involved with a series of trials before a military court which was convened in the administration buildings of the zoo at Wuppertal. All the missing men were accounted for and a number of the murderers were hanged at Hameln prison by Albert Pierrepoint, the official executioner. Although Barkworth was officially listed under his parent regiment, as late as 1948 he still signed himself on reports as Major, Commanding 2 SAS War Crimes Investigation Team, all the members of which continued to wear their regimental insignia and berets. The full story of the war crimes team has been told in my book, *The Secret Hunters*.

Following the disbandment, a number of influential people were determined to keep the SAS principle alive at all costs, and a rigorous lobbying campaign got underway. Brian Franks, who had returned to his civilian position as general manager of the Hyde Park Hotel, was in many ways the instigator and it was mainly due to his tireless efforts that the regiment was to be reborn. Mike Calvert, the last brigade commander, was informed that the Director of Tactical Investigation, Major-General Rowell, had been ordered to investigate the role of the SAS and to make recommendations for the future employment of such a unit in wartime. In October 1945 Calvert wrote a lengthy letter to a number of senior officers who had served with the SAS during the war, urging them to co-operate with the investigation, to ensure that the regiment's point of view was stated correctly. Behind the scenes, Franks wined and dined politicians and senior military officers with good effect and had the ear of Winston Churchill via his son Randolph, who had served briefly with the SAS in North Africa in 1942.

In November 1946 the War Office came to the conclusion that there was room for an SAS-type unit within the scope of the Territorial Army, which was in the process of reconstitution at that time, but the problem was to find a suitable unit on to which it could be grafted. While looking around, Brian Franks came across a unit called the Artists Rifles, which owned a drill hall in Duke's Road near Euston Station, and a fine hut on the shooting ranges at Bisley. The Artists was originally formed in 1859 as a volunteer unit at a time when the government feared an invasion from France, and in a rush of patriotic fervour, members of the artistic community in London banded together to volunteer, even buying their own uniforms. They took as their cap badge the emblem of Mars and Minerva, which has been retained as the title of the regimental journal today. The French threat never materialized, but the Artists Rifles remained in being as a volunteer battalion of the Middlesex Regiment. The unit served with distinction during the First World War, and in 1939 became an Officer Cadet Training Unit (OCTU).

The Artists were also casting around for a role in the post-war Army, and so a marriage of convenience was contracted, which in spite of minor quarrels has continued until today. The new regiment took on the title of 21 SAS (Artists) TA, for a fairly mundane reason. The two wartime British regiments had been numbered 1 and 2, and it would appear that the original idea was to call the new creation 12 SAS. There was, however, 12 Airborne (TA) Battalion already in existence, so it was decided to adopt the number 21, which is still the senior SAS regiment. It has to be remembered that when the new unit was formed its members wore the red beret of the airborne forces and it was subordinated to 16 Airborne Division (TA). The famous beige beret had been taken away in early 1944 when the regiments came back from fighting in Italy to be formed into a brigade as part of 1 Airborne Corps. They were not to regain their own beret until 1957.

Recruiting for 21 SAS started in the autumn of 1947 and many of the wartime members hastened to join up, supplemented by men who had served with the Special Boat Section (SBS) in the Mediterranean and by other volunteers from the Artists Rifles. Brian Franks was appointed commanding officer and had a regular officer, Major L.E.O.T. 'Pat' Hart, as his deputy. The latter, who had been serving in the Middle East, was a Rifle Brigade officer who had joined the staff of the SAS Brigade in 1944. The original establishment consisted of a headquarters, a signals unit and two squadrons, all based in London. Franks realized that he needed to spread his net more widely and cater for the wartime veterans who lived in the north of England. As a result he also formed a phantom SAS troop attached to the 10th Yorkshire Parachute Battalion, and to command it he recruited Johnny Cooper, who was one of David Stirling's original recruits and had ended the war as a temporary major commanding a squadron in 1 SAS Regiment.

Thus, like a phoenix from the ashes, the SAS concept arose. In 1947, however, it was a territorial unit and little more than an appendage of the Parachute Regiment establishment, which tended to regard 21 SAS with covetous eyes. It was up to that small group of largely amateur soldiers to forge a role for themselves and use all the influence they could muster to stop themselves from being absorbed elsewhere. At the time when the new unit was founded the Cold War was still in its infancy, and a non-nuclear-capable Soviet Union was not regarded as an immediate threat. It was envisaged that the unit would fight in a future Middle Eastern conflict and much of the early training was directed towards that end.

Behind the scenes, Brian Franks was locked in battle with the War

Office over the higher establishment of the regiment, the perennial problem being that nobody at that level had any true understanding of what the SAS was capable of and what special requirements were needed for them to fulfil their true role. War Office planners persisted in regarding them as an infantry battalion. The philosophy of the SAS had been laid down by David Stirling in 1941 when he founded the regiment and those principles still apply today. He insisted right from the beginning that his unit must be used strategically in support of the overall objectives of the commander-in-chief of a particular theatre and that his men should not be frittered away in localized actions of a purely tactical nature. Another point he emphasized was the basic four-man patrol as the operating unit at the sharp end. It is interesting to note that after Stirling was captured by the enemy in early 1943 and his powerful influence eliminated, those principles were steadily whittled away, to such an extent that in many subsequent operations the two regiments were unable to achieve worthwhile results. In addition, they became caught up in rivalries between different headquarters, including Special Operations Executive, so that resources were frequently duplicated and intelligence gathered was not properly pooled.

In August 1949 Brian Franks wrote a lengthy memo to the War Office and to 16 Airborne Division (TA), concerning their plans for the higher establishment (HE) of 21 SAS. He started off by defining the role of SAS troops as being able to undertake small-scale military operations of every type, from offensive to intelligence, far from the main battle area and using small numbers of men. They would approach their objectives by land, sea or air, and in view of the small size of patrols, a regiment would be capable of undertaking a variety of operations simultaneously, each controlled from the base. He went on to state that:

The fundamental difference between SAS 'units' and other units of the army, which must be grasped if the special needs of the SAS establishment are to be understood, is that the former are not 'units' in the sense generally accepted for the latter. The SAS regiments are NOT organised and can NOT be employed as *units*; all operations undertaken by SAS troops are carried out by parties especially picked and equipped for the occasion. The strength, composition, equipment and method of employment of each party depends on the exact circumstances of each operation and are only decided when the

7

operation is allotted and examined in detail.

It will be seen therefore that the term 'unit' is a misnomer in this case and that the SAS regiment is not a tactical unit. It is merely a force of SAS troops from which a large number of SAS operational parties can be found, controlled and maintained.

The man who founded 2 SAS Regiment, David Stirling's brother Bill, had resigned his command in the spring of 1944 because of plans by higher headquarters to use his unit tactically, committing it piecemeal to the immediate area of the battlefield on D-Day. He was replaced by Brian Franks, who had to fight the same battles throughout the rest of the war, and to continue them on behalf of the new territorial regiment. Essentially he was pleading for sufficient manpower, including a large number of specialists to build up a strong skeleton base organization, basing his justification on the following point: 'SAS troops are likely to be required in the earliest stages of the next war. The necessary organization to plan, prepare, mount, control and maintain their operations must be in being *before* the outbreak of war.' The manpower envisaged consisted of a base organization of 192 all ranks, supporting three operational squadrons each of 118 all ranks.

As established, 21 SAS was essentially a copy of one of the wartime regiments, with the same equipment and weapons. For mobility, it relied upon the armoured jeep fitted with twin Vickers K machine guns and in some cases the .50mm. Browning. Such vehicles could be dropped by parachute or landed by glider. Experience had shown that to maintain a number of parties in the field behind enemy lines, a sophisticated base organization was required as well as liaison with the RAF who supplied the aircraft. During the latter stages of the war, the SAS Brigade had its own stores and container packing organization, a squadron of specialist signallers supplied by 'Phantom', a separate liaison headquarters to handle the two French regiments, as well as officers detached to liaise with SOE, Supreme Headquarters Allied Expeditionary Force (SHAEF) and 21st Army Group. The individual regiments had their own pool of specialists to deal with equipment maintenance, medical matters, communications, resupply and so on. So Brian Franks was quite correct in putting a strong case forward for an adequate base establishment to enable his regiment to function immediately on the outbreak of hostilities.

The essential problem was that the small territorial unit, grafted on to an airborne TA division, suffered from lack of political influence. Its commanding officer, in spite of his enthusiasm and experience, was only a part-timer with important business commitments. His deputy, a regular major, lacked the rank to be able to exert any real control over the decision-making processes of higher headquarters, who insisted on regarding the SAS as simply a variety of parachutists, albeit exotic. The ultimate responsibility for the role of the regiment lay with the Directorate of Land/Air Warfare at the War Office, where none of the officers on the staff had had any experience of SAS methods.

The next chapter deals exclusively with the war in Malaya and the formation of the regular 22 SAS Regiment. What follows is therefore a chronological jump to continue the theme of the phoenix arising, until the time when an embryo regimental headquarters was established, finally giving a certain level of stability to the post-war development of the SAS. First, however, the enduring mystery of involvement in the Korean War will be discussed.

In June 1950 North Korean troops invaded the southern part of the country by crossing the 38th Parallel, an action that was condemned immediately by the United Nations, which authorized the use of force to repel the invaders. The war seemed to offer opportunities for the employment of SAS troops and there was a readily available pool of battle-hardened officers and men either serving with 21 SAS or on the special 'Z' reserve who were bored with civilian life and itching to get back into a fight. A squadron of volunteers, known as M Squadron, was raised by Major Tony Greville-Bell, to go to Korea, and Philip Warner, in *The SAS*, asserts that this was at the request of General MacArthur, the American Far East Commander-in-Chief. Greville-Bell had served in 2 SAS during the war, both in Italy and in north-west Europe, and was an officer of some experience in irregular warfare. In a remarkable feat of endurance, he and Sergeant 'Bebe' Daniels walked through Italy for seventy-three days before regaining Allied lines after an operation.

In Greville-Bell's appreciation of the employment of SAS troops in Korea he made the valid point that the existence of an oriental population meant that it would be difficult to maintain clandestine parties in the interior for lengthy periods. In addition, the mountainous terrain would restrict the number of suitable dropping zones for the insertion of personnel and their resupply. As the country was long and thin, bounded by sea coasts, he recommended insertion by sea as he felt that the enemy would be unable to divert sufficient forces to guard the entire coastline. His suggested targets for raiding included airfields, rail communications, bridges, petrol dumps and headquarters complexes. As an added bonus, alarm and despondency would be spread throughout the enemy rear areas and valuable intelligence could be obtained. At a later stage, when United Nations forces had gained the upper hand and the armour was ready to break through, SAS formations mounted on jeeps could penetrate deep behind the front line.

The report is undated but was probably written during the late summer of 1950. Attached to the copy in my possession is a handwritten letter from Greville-Bell to Brian Franks. In it he writes, 'I expect Pat is keeping you in the picture but I will keep in touch with you though I imagine you will probably know more and sooner than I will.' The 'Pat' referred to is Major Hart, the regular second-in-command of 21 SAS Regiment. Thus one can safely assume that both Franks and his deputy were fully aware of what was being planned.

Yet, in a report written by Pat Hart and dated 5 November 1951, concerning the organization and control of the SAS Regiment, there is a section dealing with undesirable matters that had occurred and could have been avoided. One of these was:

> The carrying out of operations in KOREA by so-called SAS parties, about which neither the War Office nor 21st SAS had any knowledge until after the event, and which had no SAS approval. M Indep Sqn, which had been intended for KOREA, was withdrawn as a matter of policy; yet an officer of only slight SAS experience, who had been turned down for the Sqn, subsequently was permitted to operate as SAS.

I have been unable to determine who that officer was and to what extent 'unofficial' SAS activities were mounted during the Korean conflict. It is a matter of record that M Squadron was diverted to Singapore and subsequently formed B Squadron of the Malayan Scouts, later to become 22 SAS Regiment. That will be dealt with in the next chapter, which is exclusively concerned with the role of the SAS Regiment in the Malayan 'Emergency'.

By 1950, 21 SAS (TA) had found its feet but still lacked a specific role and was little more than an appendage of the Parachute Regiment, complete with the red beret. It consisted of only two squadrons plus a signals detachment and training was based on wartime methods. Brian Franks finished his stint as commanding officer and was replaced by Colonel Newman, VC, a highly decorated wartime Commando officer. He in turn handed over in 1952 to Lieutenant-Colonel Ian Lapraik who had served with the SBS in the Mediterranean during the war as a squadron commander, being decorated with the DSO, the OBE and two MCs. On top of that he was mentioned in dispatches six times, wounded six times and captured and escaped three times. He was associated for most of his SBS service with the Greek detachment known as the Sacred Squadron which mounted a series of daring raids from a flotilla of caiques based in Turkish waters. The training major at the time was Major Anthony Marsh, DSO, who had commanded C Squadron of 1 SAS in France, Holland and Germany.

The first really important development was in January 1951 when the ad hoc unit that was raised in Malaya by Mike Calvert (see next chapter) was incorporated as 22 SAS Regiment, and as a result the SAS became a corps in the British Army – admittedly the smallest but ranking in seniority directly after the infantry. The new regular unit, however, had only been raised for the duration of the Malayan Emergency and answered direct to the Commander-in-Chief Far East Land Forces rather than to the War Office.

The report prepared by Pat Hart in November 1951, alluded to above, set out in some detail the still precarious position of the SAS, in spite of its apparently more permanent status. The author was making the point that there were no co-ordinating or supervisory arrangements for the SAS other than the recently authorized Regimental Headquarters (RHQ) and the Directorate of Land/Air Warfare. The latter, a War Office directorate, was concerned with such matters as co-operation between the Army and the RAF, and airborne policy in general. It was dominated by personnel from the Parachute Regiment and there was no officer with SAS experience on its staff. The author's plea was based on the need for co-ordination of all aspects of SAS activity, including 'role, employment, establishment, training methods, staff teaching etc.'. The RHQ post authorized was for a major, who would not have had the necessary authority to negotiate on the regiment's behalf with higher headquarters and was anyway outranked by the commanding officer of the TA unit, who was a lieutenant-colonel. Major Hart went on to recommend that action was needed under the following headings:

(a) formulate, crystallise and propagate, SAS teaching and policy.
(b) ensure that the SAS is accepted and understood as a permanent and valuable part of the Army.
(c) ensure a proper common standard among SAS units, and standardisation of training, establishments, equipment and techniques as far as possible.
(d) propose, and/or advise on, the use of SAS units as and when situations arise in various parts of the world, both in peace and war.
(e) ensure a proper standard of recruits, including the training of reserves.

The report concluded by calling for an officer to be appointed to RHQ having no other responsibilities and equipped with sufficient seniority to be able to act as the War Office channel for all dealings with the SAS. He would have to be a full colonel so as to outrank regimental commanding officers, and ideally should have had command of an operational SAS unit. That was of course common sense, as otherwise any SAS unit raised for whatever purpose in the future would develop its own identity and characteristics, a factor the War Office was determined to avoid as a result of the 'private armies' that had been created during the Second World War.

It may seem surprising to the reader that in the early post-war years the SAS existed on little more than a wing and a prayer, but at the time such élite units were still regarded with hostile eyes. The recommendations contained in the report quoted above were only implemented in a hesitant way in May 1954, almost three years after it was written, when Major Clarence Dare Newell, who had been serving with 22 SAS in Malaya, was posted back to England. His job, which carried the title of RHQ SAS, was 'in limbo, unattached to any formation, although in theory, it reported to DL/AW at the WO'. His office consisted of a desk in the officers' mess at 21 SAS headquarters, and from this he was meant to organize the raising of standards of recruits being sent out to the regiment in Malaya and to supervise those on leave in the UK.

Dare Newell had served with distinction during the war as a member of Special Operations Executive. He had parachuted into Albania to organize the resistance in that mountainous country, and later went out to the Far East as part of Force 136 which operated behind the Japanese lines in Malaya. He was one of those recruited by Calvert into the Malayan Scouts right at the beginning of the campaign, and has justly been referred to as 'the Father of the Regiment' by subsequent generations of the SAS. His devotion to the ideal was of paramount importance in getting the SAS accepted by the Army and ensuring its survival to the present day.

Finally, it is worth considering how the fledgling SAS saw its role in warfare at the time. As we have seen, David Stirling had always contended that its role must be strategic rather than tactical: a force available to the theatre commander for specific operations carried out by small parties of men. He had also strongly emphasized that the SAS should plan and control its own operations rather than being subject to a staff body that had no knowledge of its specific capabilities. When the TA unit was formed, the threat was seen as being situated in the Middle East, but Soviet acquisition of a nuclear capability in Europe caused the scenario to be radically changed. The additional war task of deep penetration raids in support of the NATO northern flank was assigned to 21 SAS, and this was practised at the annual summer camps. Penetration was envisaged as being either by parachute or from the sea, followed by an approach on foot or by Land Rover. It is interesting to note that during the early 1950s there was no real cross-fertilization between 21 SAS based in England and the regiment serving in Malaya. The former remained wedded to the wartime experience of its senior officers and it was not until experienced men began to return from Malaya that new ideas began to circulate. The same lack of co-ordination was evident in the selection of recruits. 21 SAS applied its own criteria, yet towards the end of 1952, 22 SAS sent Major John Woodhouse back to England to organize the first course for potential regulars which was carried out at the Airborne Forces Depot at Aldershot. This was the forerunner of the system still in use today.

An essay written in 1952 examined in detail the possibilities for employment of SAS troops both in north-west Europe and in the Middle East, and was a valid contribution to the role discussions then taking place behind the scenes. As far as the former area was concerned, the author felt that the use of SAS would initially depend upon the ability of NATO to stem a westward advance by Soviet ground troops.

In other words, he was not envisaging any attempt to disrupt the enemy concentrations by mounting raids behind his lines, which is perhaps strange to our way of thinking today. Even when a static front was established, attacks behind the lines should be limited to targets of such importance that the high risk involved in exfiltrating the raiders could be justified. The whole text of the essay strikes a distinctly pessimistic note: the conclusion reached is that the only real opportunity for useful employment of SAS troops is in the case of a total evacuation of the European mainland, as in 1940. The author envisaged the formation of 'stay-behind' parties around which a nucleus of resistance forces could be built up, and the mounting of raids by sea from the British coast. 'The plan for north-west Europe should therefore be: first, no commitment of special units unless Allied countries are overrun; secondly, tactical raids and organization of resistance until an Allied offensive is possible; thirdly, long term SAS operations in conjunction with Resistance, and Commando assault in conjunction with the main forces, when Allied invasion eventually takes place.'

The Middle East, on the other hand, was viewed as 'likely to afford the finest possible opportunities for carrying out practically every kind of special operation of the types studied. If successful Communist advances into the Balkans, Turkey, Persia and Iraq are visualised, the situation in those countries would be ideal from the point of view of SAS ... operations.' In the event of a general Soviet advance into the area, the assumption was that it would be held to the north of Syria and between the Jordan and the Tigris/Euphrates Delta. Operating from a base in Egypt and using the aircraft then available, the author posited that up to six squadrons of SAS could be profitably employed both on land and in attacks on enemy shipping.

The core of the essay was special pleading: for a proper SAS headquarters to be set up in peacetime and for adequate communications equipment. 'Planning on the creation of a unit when the war starts is not realistic, and will inevitably miss some early opportunities for operations.' In future chapters we will examine how long it took for such an eminently practical suggestion to be realized, until the point when 22 SAS was able to react incredibly rapidly both to the invasion of the Falkland Islands and to the decision to send a United Nations force to the Gulf.

2

Emergency

Having examined the rebirth of the SAS after its temporary eclipse at the end of the Second World War, we now move on to the regiment's first operational assignment and the formation of a regular unit. The long-drawn-out campaign in Malaya was to be the first of a series of conflicts in which the SAS became involved as Britain gradually withdrew from its overseas colonies. Although the SAS contribution in terms of numbers involved and enemy killed was minuscule, it was in the jungles of Malaya that the foundations of the modern regiment were laid down by an enlightened series of officers who came to the fore during that early period. Another factor to be borne in mind was that a completely new set of skills had to be learnt the hard way, by practical experience. Although many of the officers and men had had experience with the regiment during the war, the SAS had never before been called upon to fight in jungle conditions. Nor were the men who served in Malaya involved in a declared all-out war against a uniformed enemy. Instead, they found themselves locked in combat with what was essentially a terrorist force motivated by Communist ideology. Such a conflict could not be resolved by force of arms alone, and the Army was forced to adapt to the political realities of a situation in which it frequently assisted the civil power in controlling the insurrection. That factor was to set a pattern for the future development of the regiment's skills in deployments around the world's trouble spots.

Within the scope of the present book it is impossible to give a blow-by-blow account of the regiment's eight years in Malaya. Much of the time was spent in long patrols through the jungle and in the mundane yet vital work of gaining the hearts and minds of the aboriginal inhabitants of the interior. The SAS involvement in Malaya is worth a lengthy book in its own right, but this chapter will outline some of the more important aspects of the campaign.

At the beginning of 1942 Malaya and the island state of Singapore at the southern tip were overrun by Japanese invaders, who totally outfought the garrison of British and Commonwealth troops. Trailing a limp Union Jack affixed to a pole, General Percival and his ADC in their baggy khaki shorts walked up the Bukit Tima Road in Singapore to a humiliating surrender, condemning most of their men to three appalling years in the Japanese camps. The pathos of that scene was not lost on the indigenous peoples who saw a white European power defeated by an Asiatic one. Before the war, local defence had been a matter for the British masters, who had consistently refused to arm the local population until it was too late, yet the large Chinese community in Malaya was endowed with a bitter hatred of the Japanese who had overrun their homeland. The paradox is that after the defeat a number of courageous British officers stayed behind in the jungle to organize resistance, and were supplied with weapons by Force 136, an arm of Special Operations Executive. The most effective resistants were Chinese members of the Communist Party of Malaya which had been in existence since 1930, and when the Japanese in turn surrendered in 1945, they quietly greased and buried their weapons in the jungle – for future use.

The Malayan peninsula is a pear-shaped 500-mile-long stretch of land south of Thailand, divided down the middle by a mountainous spine, which restricted settlement to the coastal areas on either side. Four-fifths of the land area is covered with dense jungle, with trees of up to 200 feet in height blocking out the light with a dense canopy of lush foliage. On the ground, visibility is limited to such an extent that two people can pass within a few yards of each other unaware of each other's presence. Anyone penetrating into the jungle has to cope with extremes of heat and humidity, swamps, hordes of vicious mosquitoes, hornets, snakes and leeches.

In 1948 that beautiful fertile country was home to a mixed population of native Malays, aboriginal tribesmen, Chinese and Tamil Indians, all of whom lived in relative harmony with each other. The 12,000 British were made up of civil servants, professional people, rubber-planters and those working in the tin-mining industry. Politically, Malaya was a federation of states ruled by hereditary sultans who governed as constitutional monarchs aided by British advisers, and it was the stated aim of the government to prepare the country for independence. The start of a Communist-led insurrection came as a surprise to most of the inhabitants. On the morning of 16 June 1948 three British rubber planters were murdered on their estates in the start of a campaign of violence and intimidation also directed against local people who worked for overseas companies. The response to the threat was hesitant, to say the least, as the CTs (Communist terrorists) as they became known, had the initiative and the advantage of surprise. Their leader was a man in his mid-thirties, Chin Peng, who had fought for the British against the Japanese and dreamed of a Communist take-over in Malaya. From the outset he deployed some 5,000 well-armed troops hidden away in prepared camps in the jungle, complete with the apparatus of political indoctrination. It was an almost entirely Chinese force although there was a token Malay unit to enable the Communists to claim that they were fighting a war of liberation for all races. The Malays themselves remained largely uninvolved in the fighting.

After some delay, a state of emergency was declared, in spite of the fact that open warfare was in progress. The reason for this was concerned with insurance: the London market paid out for losses incurred as a result of civil commotion but not through acts of war. The Army and the police lumbered into action but were largely powerless against the hit-and-run tactics of the guerrillas, who seemed to be able to murder with impunity, fading away into their jungle hideouts. One tentative counter-insurgency method put into practice in those early days was the formation of Ferret Force, which was recruited from civilian volunteers who had served with Force 136, as well as some regular soldiers. Guided by a small number of trackers from the head-hunting Iban tribe brought in from Borneo, Ferret Force made forays into the jungle and destroyed several CT camps. Their efforts, however, were only a drop in the ocean and the killing continued. In 1949, 344 civilians were murdered, 229 members of the security forces lost their lives, and a further 247 men were wounded.

Early in 1950 General Sir John Harding who was the commander-in-chief Far East, decided that he needed independent advice from an expert. He called in 'Mad' Mike Calvert, who was cooling his heels in

Hong Kong. Calvert had become something of a legend, immensely tough, hard-fighting, and with considerable experience of jungle warfare. He had spent three years during the war in Burma with Wingate's unorthodox Chindit formations, much of it behind enemy lines, and in December 1944 he had taken over command of the SAS Brigade from Rod McLeod. Calvert, one of the prime movers at the end of the war in ensuring that the SAS ethic did not die out, had a reputation for leading from the front. Although he had ended the war as a brigadier, he had had to revert to his substantive rank as a major. Calvert went to Malaya with an open brief to come up with fresh ideas; he spent several weeks touring the country talking to planters, civilian officials and soldiers.

Coincidental with Calvert's mission, the British government sent out another highly experienced man as Director of Operations. Lieutenant-General Sir Harold Briggs, who had also fought in Burma, agreed to come out of retirement to take on the assignment in Malaya as a civilian appointee, and in many ways he was to prove the architect of the final victory over the CTs. This was based on what became known as the Briggs Plan, although several people's input, including that of Calvert, was incorporated. Essentially the Briggs Plan proposed a policy of food denial, cutting off the guerrilla bands from their sources of supply and intelligence by moving Chinese squatters into protected new villages – which entailed the resettlement of 600,000 people over a period of two years. Calvert's contribution was a proposal to set up a force of troops who could live in the jungle for lengthy periods, and by winning the confidence of the aboriginal tribes, control the movement of the insurgents in areas where they had previously felt safe. His aim was to force them out into the open where they could be dealt with by the police and regular army patrols.

Calvert was authorized to form his special force as quickly as possible and was given the necessary support. It must be stressed that this was to be for the duration of the emergency only, came directly under Far East Command and had nothing to do with the SAS territorial set-up in Britain. The new formation was called the Malayan Scouts (SAS). Under the shoulder titles on their olive green jungle uniform they wore the green patch and yellow kris of the local command. Even today the reputation of the Malayan Scouts remains an unsavoury one among certain elements of the SAS establishment, and this needs to be looked at before their operational achievements are discussed.

Calvert's initial step was to trawl for volunteers in the Far East; this produced the original 100 men who formed A Squadron. There was no selection process, and many of the volunteers were quite unsuitable for special forces work, yet a few of them were to become outstanding members of the SAS. Calvert cast his net more widely in his search for top-class officers and attempted to recruit Roy Farran, who as a squadron commander in 2 SAS during the war had been one of the most successful SAS operators of all time. After the war, Farran had gone to Palestine, where he became involved in the clandestine struggle against Jewish terrorists. He was tried for the murder of a suspect and acquitted, but his brother was killed by a parcel bomb that had been sent to him in England. A signal was sent to Farran on 10 August 1950, offering him command of a squadron. He accepted, but shortly afterwards Calvert was forced to withdraw. He signalled on 17 August:

> Most unfortunate official view is that your presence here however desirable from military point of view which is accepted would be considerable source of embarrassment as large number of government and police including GURNEY and GREY are from PALESTINE. Therefore C-in-C suggests any other theatre. Regret and best wishes for the future....

The two men referred to in the signal were Sir Harold Gurney, the High Commissioner, and Colonel Nicol Grey, the Commissioner of Police.

The second source of recruits for the Malayan Scouts was the group of wartime reservists mentioned in the previous chapter who had been formed to fight in Korea. They were commanded by Major Anthony Greville-Bell and among their number were Alastair McGregor and Bob Bennett. Bennett, one of David Stirling's 'originals' in the North African desert in 1941, had ended up as a sergeant-major, but after the war had had to revert to corporal in his parent regiment. He remembers meeting Greville-Bell on Aldershot station and being told: 'Get those tapes off and put up your crowns.' These highly experienced men arrived in Malaya in January 1951 and formed B Squadron. C Squadron came from Rhodesia, where on a quick visit Calvert had picked them from 1,000 volunteers.

The Malayan Scouts set up a base camp at Kota Tinggi near Johore and a somewhat ad hoc induction programme was started under Major John Woodhouse who later stated that the training of A Squadron was 'not extensive. Subsequent squadrons, almost literally, were trained on operations.... Apart from the not entirely relevant experience of veterans of the Burma war we had no skilled instructors and very largely taught ourselves.' Calvert was an enthusiast for practice using live rounds and was under pressure from his superiors to get results; quickly. The new arrivals from Britain were not impressed, and sent back reports to 21 SAS of indiscipline and excessive heavy drinking, which have since marred the reputation of A Squadron and its founder. It must be pointed out, though, that Calvert had to work largely single-handed, supervising training in the south, starting up an operational headquarters in Ipoh, forming an intelligence cell and wheedling the necessary equipment from obstructive staff officers. His experience was almost parallel to that of David Stirling in the summer of 1941: he too had to walk roughshod over many of the military niceties – but was not criticized for doing so.

Operationally, Calvert's idea was to insert patrols of fourteen men into the jungle around Ipoh, accompanied by a few local police and Chinese liaison personnel, to set up a temporary base camp with a radio. From there, four-man sections would fan out to explore the jungle and interdict known CT approach routes. Previously it had been standard doctrine that an army patrol could not exist in the jungle for more than seven days, yet one of Calvert's groups managed to stay for 103 days, resupplied by helicopter: the Malayan campaign marked the first use by the Army of that new form of transport. Those early patrols made contact with aboriginal tribes and began the painstaking process of gaining their trust and friendship, to wean them away from supporting the enemy. Medical clinics, staffed by SAS personnel, were established in the jungle villages for the first time.

In the autumn of 1951 Mike Calvert was invalided back to England, suffering from a variety of ailments and the stress of several years of almost continuous warfare. The verdict on his period in command of the Malayan Scouts will probably always remain open, but John Woodhouse, one of his most gifted officers, surely has the best right to comment. In the letter quoted above, he wrote:

Numerous widely publicised, sensational and mainly true stories circulated for years, and very nearly led to the disbandment of the unit. [Calvert's comparison was that a building site can be a rough and mucky place until construction is finished!]

But if Calvert must accept much of the blame he deserves credit too, for his far-sighted perception of the broad strategy and tactics of counter-insurgency, which I learned mainly from him. . . .

Another cause of the bad start in Malaya was the woeful inadequacy of the administrative and 'Q' staff. Malaya Command should have known that a strong staff was essential, but they failed to appoint one, and Mike Calvert did not insist on replacements.

Blame us by all means for our failings, but learn from them too. Most of us had our hearts in the job and if we had not made a start perhaps no-one else would have done so!

The new commanding officer was Lieutenant-Colonel John 'Tod' Sloane, a regular Argyll and Sutherland Highlander who had no background in special forces. He was, however, ideal for the job at that time in the development of the unit, as he brought in a strong measure of discipline and normal military order. One of his first tasks was to pull the squadrons back out of the jungle and institute a period of solid retraining for all personnel, after which they were committed only on the fringes in late 1951 and early 1952, backing up ordinary police patrols. Another of Sloane's valuable contributions was to persuade a number of officers to stay on after several had decided to leave, fearing that their promotion prospects might be blighted by their association with a 'cowboy outfit'.

A worthy new recruit rejoined the SAS at that time. Johnny Cooper, also one of Stirling's 'originals' and his navigator in North Africa, had ended the war as a temporary major commanding a squadron in 1 SAS Regiment. Finding civilian life far too tame he contacted Greville-Bell and was offered a short service commission as a lieutenant, at the age of 29. He arrived in Singapore at the beginning of 1952 and was posted as a troop commander to B squadron, commanded at the time by Alastair McGregor, a wartime comrade. As far as jungle acclimatization was concerned, he was trained 'on the job' by accompanying his troop on short patrols. In his memoirs he described one of the main problems graphically.

Apart from the enemy, leeches were our main adversary. They would fall off the leaves and latch onto one's softest areas, around the neck, behind the ears, under the arm-pits, and on a long patrol they would even find their way to one's private parts. You couldn't feel them, but as they slowly sucked blood they enlarged into horrible black swollen lumps. If you were a smoker, it was easy to get rid of them – just a touch with a burning cigarette and they would fall off.

The SAS returned to deep penetration into the interior in February 1952 when all three squadrons took part in Operation Helsby. The resettlement of squatters in the new villages had deprived the enemy of a valuable source of food and they had been forced to start growing their own in jungle clearings. One such was located in the remote Belum valley close to the Thai border and Helsby was designed to flush out the terrorists and destroy this base. A mixed force was formed from the SAS, Malayan Police and a Royal Marine Commando, with B Squadron dropping in by parachute to form a 'blocking force' until the foot patrols could arrive on the scene. B Squadron was the only one with sufficient men who had been parachute trained, but most of them had not jumped since the war. As there was no training facility for airborne forces in the Far East at the time, the SAS decided to improvise their own. A collection of scaffolding poles, ropes, planks and pulleys was 'borrowed' from the garrison engineer and the men built a series of gantries from which practice descents could be made.

Having relearnt the basics, they had to persuade the RAF to lay on the aircraft from which to make some actual drops. The mainstay of RAF Transport Command was then the Valetta, a military version of the twin-engined Viking civil airliner. Known affectionately as the 'flying pig', it could carry twenty parachutists at a cruising speed of 170 miles per hour. The Valettas in Malaya, however, were not equipped for the dropping of parachutists, and no qualified RAF instructor was available. Major Jeff Douglas, whom Sloane had put in charge of the training scheme was lucky: the air officer commanding, Air Commodore Fullergood, was prepared to slash through red tape. He provided three Australian Dakotas and an instructor was discovered, who was immediately transferred. The trusty old Dakotas took up twenty men at a time to make basic jumps, then practice dropping as a stick and with kitbags. Shortly afterwards the Far East Parachute School was established on a permanent footing at Changi airfield in Singapore.

Operation Helsby started with a long and arduous approach on foot by A and C Squadrons together with detachments from the Royal Marine Commandos and the local police. As they approached the heart of the Belum valley where some one hundred CTs were located, fifty-four members of B Squadron were dropped into a jungle clearing without suffering any serious injuries. This was the first operational jump carried out by the SAS since April 1945. Conditions for jumping in Malaya, however, were vastly different from those in wartime Europe. Dropping zones in the jungle were few and far between. Those landing ran the risk of being spiked on bamboo or drifting into the surrounding trees, and where the RAF had made clearings by dropping bombs, the tangled tree trunks and craters were an equal hazard. The operation achieved nothing more than to destroy the enemy's vegetable patches: by the time the troops arrived on the scene after crashing through the jungle for a week, the birds had long since flown. The use of large bodies of men on such an operation was quite unsuitable as the noise they made easily warned the CTs of their approach. Over the years the SAS went on to prove that stealth was the only way to catch anybody in the jungle.

The fact that during the drop into the Belum valley a number of men had landed unscathed in trees prompted the start of a series of experiments which were carried out by the regiment in the spring of 1952. During the operational drop, each man had been issued with a 100-foot length of rope with which to lower himself to the ground if his canopy became snagged on the foliage, and that idea was the basis of a series of trials. The theory behind such efforts was the belief that the only way to cut off retreating CTs was to drop as close to them as possible, or even right on to their camps. Major Alastair McGregor was placed in charge of the programme and he chose Johnny Cooper, Freddie Templer and Peter Walls as his team. Templer was the nephew of General Sir Gerald Templer, who in 1952 had replaced Gurney as High Commissioner in Malaya, and Peter Walls was to become famous as the commander of Rhodesian forces under the regime of Ian Smith.

The first experimental drop into the jungle, in the Bentong Gap in Selangor, ended in near disaster. Each of the three men had a 150-foot coil of rope knotted at 18-inch intervals; the idea was that when they landed in a tree they would tie their Bergen rucksacks to one end of the rope, and the other end to a stout branch. Lowering the rucksack, they could then climb down to the ground. A troop of SAS was deployed on the drop zone to assist the jumpers to descend and the team took off into the unknown. When the green light went on, Templer exited, followed by Walls, who knocked his head on the door. He was given a shove forward by Cooper, who tumbled out immediately afterwards, not realizing that Walls's static line had become wrapped around his left arm. When the parachute opened he felt a violent stab of pain and became aware that his arm was broken in several places. Cooper crashed into the jungle canopy, tore through the branches and came to rest dangling between two tall trees with a thicket of bamboo directly below him. If he had not become snagged on the branches he would have been neatly impaled.

Cooper passed out for a while from the pain. When he came to he heard shouts from below that he had been found. After a while, Freddie Brunton, the unit doctor, arrived and took command of the rescue operation. He shouted that he was going to climb a neighbouring tree and that Cooper should try to free the rope with his good arm and drop it. Brunton clambered up about seventy feet and Cooper swung his rope so that the doctor could catch it. The end of the rope was lowered to the ground and a water bottle was attached. Cooper managed to pull this up and used the contents to wash down some Benzedrine tablets which had been issued before the jump. This kept him sufficiently awake and free of pain while the doctor climbed back up the tree to attach Cooper's rope to an iron piton. Cooper then had to cut the right-hand lift webs of the parachute so that he could swing nearer to Brunton in the neighbouring tree. With his one good hand he hacked through the harness and started to swing like a pendulum, but failed to make contact. The doctor told him that his only hope lay in cutting himself entirely free and dropping until the rope brought him up short.

Obeying the doctor's instructions, I cut the final web and started to drop. I must have fallen about fifty or sixty feet before the rope brought me up and I began to swing. I went past the doctor, and on the return I also missed the tree. On the third swing, which by then was considerably slower, my back brushed against the trunk and almost brought me to a halt. By then Freddie had climbed back down to the ground and they started to lower me. At about fifteen feet above the floor of the jungle I passed out, as the harness was strangling me through the weight of the rope. Realising this, Freddie shouted out, 'Let him drop!' I tumbled down in a heap, but luckily my fall was broken by the huge bulk of Roger Levett [Sergeant R. Levett, Life Guards] as he tried to catch me.

Johnny Cooper was given a shot of morphine, and had a lengthy spell in hospital before he was able to return to duty with the regiment, and Freddie Brunton was awarded the MBE for the gallant rescue. Both Templer and Walls had had heavy landings, but despite the mishaps the experiments continued. A form of abseiling device was developed which was more effective than climbing down a rope, and this was used on operational drops with some success. But there were a considerable number of casualties, including three fatalities, and the advent of larger helicopters eventually made tree dropping redundant in Malaya.

While those experiments were in progress, Major John Woodhouse departed for England to set up a selection course based at the Parachute Depot at Aldershot, with the endurance stage carried out in the Brecon Beacons in Wales. During the first intake, Woodhouse was suffering from severe malaria which he refused to acknowledge. He stayed in England for three years and the methods he instituted during that early period form the basis for the selection process used today by the SAS. Although his approach was often unorthodox, the regiment regards him as one of their finest trainers of men. David Stirling, with typical generosity, ranked Woodhouse as one of the co-founders of the SAS.

In the background, General Templer was rapidly stamping his personality on the conduct of the campaign as a whole. In appointing him to the post of High Commissioner the government had made an inspired choice as Templer was a man of action with a powerful intellect. He brought an often unconventional air into the dusty colonial administration, demanded results and got them. The numbers of troops available had been built up to a total of 40,000, but he remained convinced that overall the struggle had to remain a civilian one controlled by the police and government. He instituted a number of far-reaching measures, including a system of rewards for CTs who defected and the building up of a powerful special branch capable of gathering intelligence. It was Templer who coined the well-known phrase 'hearts and minds': he understood that the key to winning that type of war was to gain the moral advantage over an enemy that was difficult to defeat by conventional military action. In the war on the ground, the policy of food denial was expanded and jungle forts were built in the aboriginal areas to enable army and police patrols to operate for long periods. A disadvantage of this was that it forced more and more of the enemy to base themselves north of the Thai border where they could live in relative safety.

The next major sweep in which the SAS participated was Operation Hive in the jungles of the state of Negri Sembilan. This lasted for nearly two months from November 1952 and also involved a company of Fijian infantry and two battalions of the 2/7th Gurkha Rifles. The aim was to swamp an area with troops to disrupt the CTs' way of life and to kill as many of them as possible in ambushes. Inevitably though, there were not enough men available to contain some one hundred enemy in an area of 600 square miles, and the whole effort resulted in just sixteen dead terrorists.

That may seem unspectacular, but in those early operations in Malaya the fledgling SAS was learning a lot of important lessons. The essential problem was that they were still being used as a tactical arm of the wider military effort rather than being employed for specific strategic roles, which is where that type of unit achieves its best performance. The most important discovery was that they had the ability to live in the jungle in small parties quite independently, thanks to the development of a 14-day ration. This meant that a patrol could operate for a lengthy period without its presence being revealed by the noise of regular helicopter supply drops. The individual components of the ration were mainly dehydrated, which did away with the need to carry heavy tins, and rice was used to provide bulk. New weapons, too, were tested and approved, including shotguns: these proved extremely effective in ambushes, where a rapid reaction was required. The short-barrelled American M1 carbine which had been used by the SAS during the Second World War remained a favourite personal weapon.

In 1953 Lieutenant-Colonel Sloane handed over command of what had become 22 SAS Regiment to Lieutenant-Colonel Oliver Brooke. Towards the end of that year the Rhodesian C Squadron departed for their home, although they were to retain their title and SAS identity. They had made a great contribution to the early development of the regiment, despite a relatively high level of sickness whilst serving in

Malaya. To replace them, D Squadron was raised locally from volunteers, its first commander being Johnny Cooper, who had recovered fully from his parachuting accident. He was given a leavening of experienced men to form a cadre and set up his own training programme. For the rest of the regiment the emphasis during that period was on building jungle forts and gaining the confidence of the aboriginal tribes. Once construction of a fort was finished, it was turned over to the Malayan police and a security detachment of normal troops.

The fort-building programme really marked the start of the SAS involvement with Templer's 'hearts and minds' campaign, a skill which they perfected in subsequent campaigns in Borneo and Oman. To win over the aborigines, the men had to share in their lives, learn their language, eat their food and understand their customs. Officers and men could not set up a separate camp with a neat row of tents, a cookhouse, a mess and a flagpole. Medical care of their new charges became of paramount importance and SAS men began to master the skills of basic midwifery and dental surgery.

A typical operation was the first patrol of D Squadron. In October 1953 it set off to found Fort Brooke, the site of which had been determined by air observation. Accompanied by a number of trackers from the Iban tribe, Cooper and his men marched into the jungle in Pahang, following the Sungei Brok river, slashing their way through the thick undergrowth until they reached their destination. The first job was to make a small clearing, and to radio for an aircraft to fly over and confirm that they were in the right place. After that came the hard work of blowing up the huge jungle trees to clear an area large enough for helicopters to land, and the construction of a bridge across the river. The squadron then started active patrolling into the jungle, to make contact with the aborigines and to attempt to locate CT camps. One gang was dispersed, but in another contact two squadron members were killed in an ambush. During the 122 days that the unit remained in the jungle, half of the original complement had to be evacuated on account of disease – jungle fever, leptospirosis and general fatigue. On 7 February 1954 the remaining forty men of D Squadron, emaciated and with their uniforms in tatters, were relieved by a police detachment, their mission accomplished.

In Operation Sword in January 1954, the regiment suffered three dead as a result of a parachute drop into the jungle in Kedah, but in July all three operational squadrons dropped in Perak with only negligible injuries. Operation Termite was designed to wrest control of a considerable area of country along the central mountain spine from the terrorists and to work with the aborigines in the area. Several new forts were set up and the last troops did not withdraw until November, having killed fifteen of the enemy. This may appear a very small number in contrast to the forces employed, which included several infantry battalions, but as an overall figure it has been reckoned that in Malaya it took 1,800 man-hours of patrolling for one kill. Much of the time on operations was consumed simply by the battle for survival and men lost on average 10 lbs. in weight over a fourteen-day period. Their clothes rotted on them, they suffered from appalling jungle sores, grew pale in the perpetual twilight and often succumbed to heat exhaustion. A daily diet of Paludrine tablets kept malaria at bay, but much time was expended in removing leeches from the more vulnerable parts of the men's anatomy. And despite the privations of life in the jungle, where the only progress was on foot and heavily laden, there was no moment of relaxation. At any second a contact could be made or a patrol could find itself in an ambush where it was the man who shot first who emerged alive. Care of weapons became of prime importance, bearing in mind the constant rain and humidity.

Oliver Brooke badly damaged his ankle in a parachuting accident and was replaced at the beginning of 1955 by Lieutenant-Colonel George Lea, who later rose to the rank of lieutenant-general. On taking over command, he weeded out a number of unsuitable officers and cast his professional eye over the operational methods of the regiment.

That particular year was an important one for 22 SAS on the personnel front and was marked by a considerable, if short-lived, expansion in numbers. John Woodhouse returned from England to a short tour of duty in Regimental Headquarters and then took over command of D Squadron. He left behind him a properly established selection set-up based at Dering Lines in Brecon. Johnny Cooper, who had been serving as operations officer at headquarters, was promoted to major and took over B Squadron, known as Big Time Bravo. One of the newcomers to the regiment was a certain young lieutenant by the name of Peter de la Cour de la Billière, whose name will feature with some regularity as this book progresses. It is interesting to note that a number of national servicemen spent their time with the regiment in Malaya.

In the summer of 1955 a squadron of SAS was raised in New Zealand, and after rigorous selection and basic training they arrived in Malaya towards the end of the year, where they carried out their parachute course. Total strength was some 140 men, a third of whom were Maoris who found it easy to work with aborigine tribesmen. Commanded by Major Frank Rennie, after a brief shake-down period in jungle patrolling they went on to make a valued contribution to the ranks of 22 SAS. Also towards the end of 1955, a further squadron was added to the strength. Formed from volunteers from the Parachute Regiment in Britain, this was known simply as the Parachute Regiment Squadron and was commanded by Major Dudley Coventry. These additions brought the strength of 22 SAS up to some 560 men of all ranks, divided into five squadrons each with four troops of sixteen men, plus headquarters personnel and attached specialists. Not all of the squadrons were out on operations all of the time. After a lengthy spell in the jungle the men would find themselves with up to three months' pay to spend and plenty of opportunities to do so agreeably in Malaya. There was a regular rotation of personnel, with some being posted to other jobs in the Army and others departing for home leave in Britain. The normal pattern for a squadron was two months out in the jungle, two wild weeks of leave, two weeks of retraining and then back out again. There were courses to be taken, and in keeping with SAS policy, training was continuous. New skills had to be mastered, parachuting knowledge refreshed regularly and recently joined men had to be integrated into their squadrons and troops. From its somewhat inauspicious beginnings, 22 SAS Regiment had developed into a highly professional unit with a well developed *esprit de corps*, and those in charge, realizing that the war in Malaya would come to an end, were already looking to the future. Training for warfare in other parts of the world was instituted and courses in such counter-insurgency skills as resistance to interrogation. There was small boat training with instructors from the Royal Marines SBS, demolitions and mock attacks against RAF airfields. Foundations were being laid which would enable the regiment to survive as a vital part of the British Army.

In the wider context of the conflict, by 1955 the back of the Malayan terrorist campaign had been broken and murders of civilians were down to five or six a month. The leadership had fled over the Thai border and it was reckoned that Chin Peng's forces were reduced to around 2,000 men scattered around the jungle in small groups. The policy of offering rewards for those prepared to give up had paid off as a steady trickle of disillusioned insurgents handed themselves over to the security forces. Those still in the jungle were contacted by low-flying aircraft equipped with loudspeakers over which tempting offers of money and food were broadcast in Chinese. The security forces were taking a steady toll of those who refused to give up, which added to the general demoralization of those bands who could no longer rely on terrorizing the aborigines to provide them with food and shelter.

George Lea instituted a radical rethinking of operational policy. Lea, who thoroughly understood the value of stealth and patience, concentrated on putting individual squadrons into a jungle base and leaving them there for three months to thoroughly familiarize themselves with the terrain and to get to know the aborigines. Using the skills of their Iban trackers, small patrols moved silently through the jungle to entrap their elusive prey in ones and twos, thus contributing to the erosion of enemy morale. There were no great set-piece battles to be won; just patient detective work, observation and the setting of ambushes. Great inter-squadron rivalry over the body count developed and success was marked by what became known as the 'kill to contact' ratio.

Johnny Cooper took over B Squadron, Big Time Bravo, in the spring of 1955, after a spell as operations officer in RHQ. At that time there was hard intelligence information that the CTs were operating a clandestine radio transmitter in the jungle just south of the Thai border and his orders were to eliminate it. The approach was a lengthy one, involving a trip in native craft up the river from a starting point on the east coast at Kota Bahru, where the Japanese had landed in 1941. The squadron then had to cross the Akik Ring range of mountains on foot and descend into what was known as the Valley of no Return where the transmitter was thought to be located. It took eight days of hard slogging to reach the mountain crest, where Cooper split his squadron into its four troops for the descent into the valley. It fell to 'Punchy' McNeil's men to discover the target, as so often in Malaya, quite by accident. They stumbled into a clearing where they saw a water-wheel suspended in a fast-flowing stream, which was turning a dynamo. Launching an attack they drove the enemy into the jungle, then destroyed the radio. Cooper ordered all four troops to pursue the terrorists but permission to cross into Thailand was refused. That was frustrating, but during the following weeks the squadron accounted for two individual terrorists and encountered a group of aborigines who had never seen white men before.

During the same period the Parachute Regiment Squadron was operating in the Ipoh area. They hit the headlines in a big way when they killed a woman terrorist, only to discover that she had a six-month-old baby, which they 'captured' and took care of. One of the great characters in D Squadron was Sergeant Bob Turnbull, who became particularly friendly with the Ibans from whom he learnt the skills of tracking, to such an extent that he became their equal. He led his patrol of three men in a classic pursuit after they picked up some enemy tracks in the jungle. Painstakingly, they followed these for several days until Turnbull finally heard voices in a clump of bushes, went on ahead to locate the inevitable sentry and then sat down to wait. After a while, heavy rain caused the man to withdraw to the camp and he was silently followed. The patrol then opened fire and killed all four occupants of the camp. Turnbull's favourite weapon was the pump-action shotgun, with which he shot Ah Tuck, a prominent member of the Communist leadership, when the two of them quite literally bumped into each other in the jungle. Ah Tuck, who was reputed always to carry a cocked Sten, was not quite quick enough and Turnbull loosed off three shots so rapidly that the shotgun made a continuous roar instead of successive detonations, according to a witness.

The years 1956 and 1957 saw the beginning of a wind-down in the campaign, and in the SAS itself. The regiment had played a major role in winning the battle in the jungles: at the end of 1956 its official score was 89 terrorists killed and nine captured. The momentum of patrolling had to be maintained, however, and all five squadrons took their turn on operations which often proved fruitless in terms of enemy contact but served to maintain the pressure on the remaining terrorists. John Woodhouse took D Squadron into the jungle on foot to patrol an area around Fort Brooke, where they spent two months without sighting the opposition. They were replaced by the New Zealanders. Woodhouse took over the Headquarters Squadron in March and handed D over to Major Teede. Major Slim, son of the Field-Marshal who had commanded 14th Army in Burma during the war, was promoted to command A Squadron. In April the regiment had a prominent visitor: Brigadier Fitzroy Maclean who was serving as Under-Secretary of State for War at the time. One of the first officers recruited to the SAS by David Stirling in 1941, Maclean had taken part in several of the early raids behind enemy lines and later parachuted into Yugoslavia as head of the mission sent by Churchill to organize assistance to Tito's partisans.

In April 1957 the Parachute Regiment Squadron returned to England, where they were required by their parent unit. The New Zealanders also left at the end of that year, having accounted for fifteen of the enemy during their two-year tour. At the same time, George Lea departed to command an infantry brigade in Britain and was replaced by Lieutenant-Colonel Anthony Deane-Drummond. Lea was awarded a well-deserved DSO, the first such decoration for the SAS since the war. The citation included the following words: 'He personally directed the operations of his men, was parachuted with them into thick jungle, descended by rope from helicopter aircraft and shared every hazard, danger and discomfort inherent in jungle operations against a ruthless and fanatical enemy.' Deane-Drummond was an excellent choice as commanding officer. Although he had not served with the SAS during the war, he had considerable experience of small-scale raiding and had a reputation for escaping from captivity. In addition he was a world-class glider pilot.

The last major action in Malaya in which the regiment participated was Operation Sweep which started in February 1958. This was designed to encircle and eliminate a small band of terrorists commanded by the notorious Ah Hoi, whose nickname was 'baby-killer': he had once sliced open the stomach of a pregnant woman whose husband had allegedly been a police informer. Ah Hoi was known to be holed up in the Telok Anson swamps along the Tengi river to the north-west of Kuala Lumpur. D Squadron was selected for the job under its then commander, Major Harry Thompson, a Royal Highland Fusilier, six feet five inches tall with a shock of red hair 'and a boxer's nose'. He decided on insertion by parachute, to maximize the element of surprise. Don 'Lofty' Large, who had just joined the squadron, commented in his memoirs: 'Hardly anyone in the SAS liked parachuting; we looked upon it as a necessary bind.' One of the first Blackburn Beverley aircraft was in Malaya on a demonstration trip and it was arranged to use this as a practical experiment. The Beverley, a large unwieldy-looking four-engined machine, could carry seventy fully equipped parachutists who could exit from a tail ramp, which was far more practical than the usual method of scrambling out through a narrow side door. In fact, the thirty-seven men of D Squadron left the aircraft in only eighteen seconds, which meant that they arrived on a far more concentrated dropping zone. One man, however, got his canopy snagged in a tree. It failed to catch and he fell to the jungle floor, breaking his back. A helicopter had to be brought in to evacuate the casualty, which alerted the enemy.

Harry Thompson decided to follow the course of the river and split his force into two groups to track the terrorists' passage through the swamps. The SAS found themselves in what were probably the worst conditions they could possibly encounter in Malaya. Most of the time the men had to slosh through leech-infested muddy water, at times up to their necks, and then cut their way through clumps of sword grass. The rain pelted down incessantly, dripping from the tall trees, and mosquitoes attacked without respite even biting through shirts and trousers. The men's boots simply rotted away and they ended up walking barefoot. At night, the only way to sleep was to sling hammocks in the trees to get away from the perpetual swamp.

Peter de la Billière's troop followed the trail left by the terrorists for ten days through the mud, keeping in touch by radio. At the same time the other troop, led by Sergeant Sandilands, moved to head them off, constantly alert for signs of human presence. A supply drop brought in some rubber dinghies which Sandilands used to move his patrols along the river at night, their noses alert for the smell of enemy camp-fires. One of those waterborne patrols made the first contact when they came across a small group of the enemy who were cooking on the riverbank. The patrol was armed only with shotguns and as the range was too great, the terrorists escaped, leaving their equipment behind. A day or so later, however, an aborigine who made contact with Sandilands told him that he had seen a man and a woman standing by the river. The sergeant was suspicious, but arming himself with a rifle and taking Corporal Finn with him, he set off to investigate. They crept up silently and hid behind a log, where they saw the two terrorists who seemed quite unaware of the danger. Sandilands fired two rounds, killing the man outright, but the range of Finn's Patchet carbine was too short; he missed the woman and she fled back into the jungle.

A pursuit was mounted immediately. The woman's trail was easy to follow and the patrol found evidence of two camps that had been evacuated in a hurry. In the meantime the Army and police had thrown a tight cordon around the whole swamp area. Harry Thompson had his reserve troop helicoptered in as he felt he had pinned down the terrorists, who were operating in two distinct groups. By the ninth week of the operation the net was being closed although the enemy remained as elusive as ever. The breakthrough came when a woman, Ah Niet, came out and approached a patrol saying that her group was almost out of food. Initially she imposed conditions which the authorities refused to meet, but the following day she returned and said that she would bring out the rest of the terrorists that night. Harry Thompson, who took the surrender, was surprised to see that one of the group of five, who appeared to be a woman, was in fact the 'baby-killer' wearing a hat and a blue silk jacket. Ah Niet then led a patrol back into the jungle and within a couple of days three more terrorists had surrendered.

That operation was more or less the end of the war, although the SAS continued to patrol in Johore, co-operating with the security forces in winkling out the remaining hard-core resisters in the jungle. All three remaining squadrons kept up their training and many wondered what their future would be in the light of expected government policy on the armed forces, the background to which is covered in Chapter 3 of this book.

The Malayan campaign had lasted longer than the Second World War and was essentially different in nature. It was the first of a series of small-scale conflicts that Britain fought during the period of disengagement from Empire, in which the role of the armed forces was basically that of operating in aid of the civil power. The regular SAS Regiment that emerged at the end of it was in many ways different from those that had served with distinction between 1941 and 1945. After a distinctly inauspicious start, a series of excellent commanding officers, all of whom came from outside the SAS tradition, moulded a unit which was able to demonstrate conclusively that the SAS had a valid role in the post-war Army. John Woodhouse laid the foundations of the present-day regiment through his system of selection and training as well as his insistence on returning to the original principles laid down by David Stirling, including the self-sufficient four-man patrol as the basic element. Woodhouse was to be the first commanding officer of 22 SAS who had been produced from within the regiment, but his system ensured a future supply of officers for the regiment. Future COs who cut their teeth in Malaya included Peter de la Billière, Tony Jeapes, Mike Wingate-Gray and John Watts. The same system also produced a supply of top-class senior NCOs who provided the backbone of the regiment for years to come.

In 1958, 22 SAS was a regiment highly trained to operate in jungle conditions, and the only officer remaining with wartime service in the SAS was Johnny Cooper. Many new lessons had had to be learnt, including the need to co-operate with the civilian authorities and the value of winning over the hearts and minds of native peoples. New weapons and new tactics had been evaluated and absorbed. The training for warfare in general, and the adaptability that had been inculcated into all ranks, had prepared the regiment for assignments elsewhere.

3
The Creation of a Regiment

In writing a book of this sort it is necessary from time to time to interrupt the narrative of the various campaigns in order to keep up to date with the development of the structure of the SAS as a whole, as well as to examine its dealings with what Tony Geraghty has called the 'Whitehall jungle'. In the first chapter I discussed the new formation of a territorial regiment in London with its relative lack of influence *vis-à-vis* the army authorities as well as its search for a viable role in post-war military planning. This was further complicated by the formation of a regular unit in Malaya which was answerable to the local command structure in the Far East rather than to an SAS headquarters – which did not exist at the time. All of these anomalies were further complicated by the fact that in the early 1950s the SAS was little more than a dependant of the Parachute Regiment, which wished to absorb it.

When John Woodhouse returned to England in 1952 he set up the embryo selection system for 22 SAS, based initially at the Parachute Regiment depot at Aldershot. As a major, he answered to the lieutenant-colonel commanding his regiment in Malaya and had little to do with the civilian CO of 21 SAS, which had its own selection system. Although in theory 21 SAS was the senior regiment of the corps and commanded by a veteran of the Second World War SAS, this commander was a businessman serving as a part-timer. He could hardly exert influence on a regular officer without an SAS background who was fighting a war with his unit several thousand miles away.

The major factor which was to change that decidedly nebulous situation was the decision to post Major Dare Newell back from Malaya in May 1954. His task was to raise the standard of volunteers reaching 22 SAS, in conjunction with the selection programme instituted by John Woodhouse, and to supervise members of that unit while on leave in the UK. Before his appointment, men from Malaya who were in transit through the depot at Aldershot had been subject to petty chicanery on the part of Parachute Regiment personnel, which was naturally bitterly resented. Initially, Dare Newell found himself somewhat of a lone voice, answerable in theory to the Directorate of Land/Air Warfare at the War Office, which ignored the many letters he sent them over a period of eighteen months. In his battle for official recognition for the SAS, however, he had one very solid ally: Lieutenant-Colonel David Sutherland who had taken command of 21 SAS in 1954. Sutherland had served with both the SAS and the SBS during the war and had ended up in charge of the latter. While Newell was fighting for the survival of the SAS as a whole, Sutherland was establishing a new role for the territorial unit as an integral part of British Army of the Rhine (BAOR) forces in Germany.

After much lobbying, in early 1956 Dare Newell was allocated a desk at the Directorate of Land/Air Warfare (DL/AW) which gave him direct access to staff officers and the chance to spread SAS ideas within the War Office itself, a task made easier by the fact that the regiment's reputation had by now recovered from the Malayan Scouts period. It was during that year that the ill-fated Suez operation was mounted, the repercussions of which forced a radical reappraisal of the future role of Britain's armed forces worldwide. A special commission set up in 1954 by the War Office had spent some time examining the record of various raiding forces during the war, in the light of their possible employment in a general European conflict, and it concluded that there was a need for the SAS in a long-term deep penetration role.

On 24 January 1957 a special army order placed the Special Air Service in the order of battle of the regular Army, which was an important step in removing the SAS from the grasp of the Parachute Regiment. As a direct result, the SAS could revert to wearing the beige beret which they had adopted in North Africa, and get rid of the hated maroon one. That may seem trivial, but headgear was important both in terms of status within the Army and for morale within the unit itself. In July 1957 the Army Council laid down a list of requirements for future

SAS employment:

> the collection of intelligence by active and passive means;
> small-party offensive operations;
> co-operation with foreign partisan and guerrilla groups;
> assistance to combat survivors and escaped prisoners of war.

During the war, intelligence-gathering had been a very minor part of SAS activities at a time when the regiment had seen itself as a strictly offensive organization. The other three requirements, however, had formed very much a part of its role between 1941 and 1945, when valuable precedents had been established.

For the territorial arm, the 1950s was also a turbulent period, but, as mentioned above, the appointment of David Sutherland to command was an inspired choice. When he took over, the role of 21 SAS was to operate either on the NATO northern flank in Norway, or in the Middle East. All his most experienced officers and men were veterans from the two wartime regiments who naturally tended to allow their wartime service to colour their views on training and operations. In the 1950s they were faced with earning their living as civilians and inevitably began to drift away, owing to age and increasing responsibilities outside the TA. The Suez crisis in 1956 meant that the regiment's annual camp, due to take place in Libya, had to be cancelled. Instead the men camped on Salisbury Plain in pouring rain. There were, however, thoughts of possible operations. Sutherland was asked by the War Office to explore the possibility of mounting a raid from Libya on aircraft at Cairo airport. That idea had to be abandoned as it would have violated Britain's treaty relationship with the Libyan kingdom. Also abandoned was a scheme to attack airfields in the Canal Zone; this was overtaken by the decision to cancel the Suez operation. During the uprising in Hungary in the same year, the government proposed to send in parties from 21 SAS to gather intelligence, but this was forestalled by the rapid Soviet invasion.

In the aftermath of such disappointments, Sutherland foresaw that the future of 21 SAS lay in Germany in direct support of BAOR. He spent three years in formulating a whole new doctrine which became the basis for subsequent operational development of the territorial units. The use of 'units' is not a slip of the finger on the keyboard, but a reference to the fact that a second territorial regiment was born at the time and 21 SAS started to expand out of London.

Sutherland, foreseeing the need for new blood, was able to add a complete new detached squadron to his unit in 1956, when the Portsmouth-based company of a TA parachute battalion was faced with disbandment. They joined up with the SAS lock, stock and barrel, providing a welcome source of expertise and enthusiasm. In 1959, 23 SAS Regiment was formed as part of the Territorial Army, based in the Midlands and the North. This opened up a valuable recruiting area which had hitherto been untapped. There was in existence at that time a unit entitled the Joint Reserve Reconnaissance Unit (JRRU), commanded by Colonel Hugh Gilles, which had inherited the tradition of the wartime M19. This organization, in which the late Airey Neave MP had served, had been tasked with assisting escaped Allied prisoners of war and shot-down aircrew to escape back to Britain. It is interesting to note that the above-quoted list of requirements emphasizes assistance to escapees and combat survivors.

The idea of merging the JRRU with the SAS had first been considered by the War Office in 1957, and as usual there was much lobbying behind the scenes. JRRU came under the wing of the Director of Military Intelligence, who naturally wished to retain control, while the SAS insisted that all men must conform to their standards as well as being parachutists. It was not until 1959 that the new unit, 23 SAS, was born, and it transferred its allegiance to the DL/AW. It brought with it a wealth of experience in intelligence-gathering work as well as considerable knowledge in the field of communications.

It was obvious by that time – in view of the fact that 22 SAS would be returning to the UK after the end of the conflict in Malaya and that there were two TA regiments as well – that a more sophisticated headquarters set-up was required. A post for a full colonel was created and a number of clerical staff were attached. It was decided to reduce 22 SAS to only two operational squadrons when the unit returned from Malaya. As we shall see in the next chapter, A and D Squadrons were sent to the Sultanate of Muscat and Oman at the turn of 1958–9, while B Squadron was disbanded and its remaining personnel distributed among the other two, which were under-strength. The first location for 22 SAS was Merebrook Camp at Malvern, a wartime emergency hospital consisting mainly of Nissen huts.

The late 1950s and early 1960s were a time of stark retrenchment within the British Army as units were merged and famous regimental names disappeared from the order of battle. After the Suez débâcle, strategic policy was to concentrate on Britain's role within NATO and to withdraw from entanglements in the Far East. The regular SAS was reduced in strength because it was assumed that there would in future be less need for it to operate in the Third World, and the remaining squadrons began to concentrate on training in Germany. The same applied to the TA regiments as they studied their role of co-operation with BAOR. One of the tasks set them in a war situation was to locate and destroy Soviet mobile tactical nuclear weapons, but the densely populated German countryside did not lend itself to traditional SAS raiding tactics. New emphasis began to be placed on infiltration, concealment and observation, with units radioing back suitable targets for artillery and air bombardment. Such skills had been acquired the hard way in Malaya by members of the regular regiment, but for the territorials, imbued with the wartime tradition of gung-ho raiding, there had to be a change of attitude.

At the start of the 1960s the capabilities of the SAS had been realized and the various units had been accepted as being both valid and useful. During its service in Malaya 22 SAS had produced a number of extremely able officers who were fit to take command in future years, which ensured continuity of the regimental ethic. The wartime tradition had not been completely thrown overboard, but new skills had been absorbed which were more in keeping with the nuclear age. The regulars were all professional career soldiers who, although wedded to the army 'system', had taken on the vital SAS *esprit de corps* which is so essential to any élite unit. There was no longer any trace of the wartime amateurism that had characterized the original British regiments. The only difficulty was the relationship between 22 SAS and the TA regiments, which was to bedevil the SAS as a whole for a number of years. Regular NCOs were not keen on being posted to a TA unit as staff instructors as they felt that they were being sidelined and might miss out on promotion. There was also a tendency for regulars to look down on the 'amateur' soldiers who served as territorials, although today that attitude has largely been eliminated.

4
The Green Mountain

We left the three remaining squadrons of 22 SAS winding up the long campaign in Malaya and wondering what, if anything, the future had in store. Unknown to them, trouble was brewing in a totally different part of the world – the Sultanate of Muscat and Oman – which would give the regiment a chance to prove its versatility once and for all to the sceptics in Whitehall.

The Oman, as it is commonly called, is an independent sovereign state on the south-east corner of the Arabian peninsula, ruled by a hereditary Sultan. By its very position it has immense strategic importance for Western interests: to the north it overlooks the Straits of Hormuz, the bottleneck in the Persian Gulf through which oil tankers have to pass; the other coast being held by the volatile Iranians. In the early 1960s the Shah was on the Peacock Throne and sympathetic to Western interests. Oman's inhabitants are mainly Arabs belonging to a bewildering variety of tribes, who at the time were all armed and mainly engaged in the arms trade, when not feuding with each other. Britain, which had a treaty of friendship with the Sultan, regarded the area as very much a part of its sphere of influence, its importance having been increased since the Suez disaster of 1956.

The terrain broadly speaking consists of a relatively narrow coastal strip, parts of which are quite fertile, backed by a high range of mountains which in turn give way to the desert, known as the Empty Quarter, bordering on Saudi Arabia. Put simply, the climate is terrible. In daytime there is an almost constant wind and baking sunshine that

43

can drive the temperature towards 60° centigrade, yet on the high mountains in winter it is well below freezing point at night. There is virtually no shade and the rough rock shale can wreck a good pair of boots in a couple of days.

The political background to the arrival of the SAS was highly convoluted. In addition to the Sultan there was an Imam, or religious leader, who at the time was a certain Ghalib bin Ali, and the two men were sworn enemies. In 1954 Ghalib launched a rebellion, backed by his warlike brother, Talib, and one of the local tribal leaders. They in turn were supported covertly by American oil concerns, which had a vested interest in weakening the British-backed Sultan. The Egyptians became involved by supplying weapons, as they were keen to export Nasser's brand of Arab nationalism, and for reasons of their own the Saudi government also provided money and arms. The Sultan won the first round of the conflict by capturing Talib's base, but in 1957 the rebels had occupied the mountain plateau known as the Jebel Akhdhar or Green Mountain because of its comparatively lush vegetation. The Jebel is part of the mountain spine of Oman, which rises to an average height of 6,500 feet. Its sides are quite sheer with few tracks leading upwards, making it an almost impregnable stronghold; this was held by a force of 600 well-armed rebels.

The Sultan's armed forces, led by British officers, consisted of only a few hundred men, and Britain sent in a battalion of infantry and a few aircraft from the RAF to back up the local levies. They succeeded in bottling up the rebels but it was quite obvious that the only way to defeat them was to capture the Jebel Akhdhar, for which infantry were clearly unsuitable. A stalemate ensued until the arrival in 1958 of Colonel David Smiley who had been appointed Chief of Staff to the Sultan's Army. Smiley had fought with SOE in Albania during the war and was no stranger to clandestine warfare. He asked for an assault force of a Royal Marine Commando or a battalion of the Parachute Regiment to be sent by the government; which found itself in a cleft stick owing to opposition in parliament to the involvement of large numbers of British troops. There was also the problem that the sending of a large force would lead to accusations of neo-colonialism both in America and in Third World countries.

Serving under the Director of Military Operations at the time was a Major Frank Kitson, later a general and the author of the definitive work on counter-insurgency warfare. It was his idea to use the SAS. Kitson had served in Kenya in the fight against the Mau Mau guerrillas where he had successfully 'turned' groups of enemy prisoners and sent them back against their erstwhile comrades. His intention was to try the same tactic in the Oman by capturing any of Talib's men who ventured down from the mountain and bribing them into serving as guides for small groups of British troops who would then infiltrate the plateau. Anthony Deane-Drummond was flown from Malaya to Aden, where he had a conference with Kitson and Smiley in October 1958, and he paid a brief visit to Oman to study the terrain. It was decided to use a squadron of SAS, and Deane-Drummond flew back to activate the move of D Squadron, which was in the jungle to the north of the Malay peninsula. What followed was a superb example of the SAS tradition of versatility and improvisation. Within forty-eight hours the seventy men of the squadron had been extricated from their operational area and brought back to Kuala Lumpur where they were re-kitted, rearmed and briefed. Commanded by Major John Watts, they were flown to the Oman where they arrived early on 18 November. The squadron was considerably under-strength and could muster only about forty men carrying weapons, the remaining twenty-odd being support elements – cooks, armourers, signallers, mechanics, and so on.

Initially they confined themselves to patrolling the base of the Jebel, cutting off the routes used by Talib's raiding parties. The total area of the plateau itself was about thirty square miles and the base little more, so any ascent would mean an almost vertical climb. The few existing tracks up the side could easily be blocked by a handful of determined enemy well protected among the rocks. The squadron soon discovered that movement in daylight was extremely hazardous owing to the total lack of cover and the clarity of the air, which allowed visibility over vast distances. Life in the Oman was a great contrast to life in Malaya, where visibility was measured in yards rather than miles. The SAS rapidly learnt to patrol by night, which gave them a distinct advantage over their opponents who, feeling themselves secure after dark, often left their positions unmanned to retire to sleep. One hazard was the opposition's American-made mines, which were liberally sown along the desert tracks, causing both casualties and frequent damage to vehicles.

Deane-Drummond was under pressure to get results, and quickly. He had a certain amount of support from a detachment from the

Household Cavalry, men from the Trucial Oman Scouts and service units such as the Royal Electrical and Mechanical Engineers (REME) and Royal Engineers to deal with mine clearance. He ordered John Watts to institute a series of active patrols to endeavour to gain a foothold on the plateau. A local tribal leader was persuaded to guide a party up an ancient pathway known as the Persian Steps; the Persians had also attempted that route in ancient times in an abortive attempt to capture the plateau. The steps, worn smooth by centuries of traffic, were so narrow that the men had to walk in single file. Two troops (16 and 17) under the command of Captain Roderick Walker, known as 'Red Rory', who had already distinguished himself in Malaya, together with Lieutenant Tony Jeapes, made the steep ascent at night, carrying loads of up to 60 lbs. per man in their Bergen rucksacks. They had to move fast to cover the 6,000-foot climb before daylight to avoid being caught on the bare mountainside. As silently as possible and in bitterly cold temperature they managed to gain the summit undetected, where they found the enemy *sangars* (rock shelters) unmanned. The two troops rapidly occupied them and sighted their weapons: they were only 3,000 metres away from a well-established rebel position. Yet during the first day on the Jebel there was no sign whatsoever of the opposition, and 17 Troop headed back down the mountain to bring up more ammunition.

During the next few days the two troops took it in turn to descend and then clamber back up laden with sleeping bags and equipment, assisted by donkey handlers they had managed to recruit to carry jerry cans of water. Walker pushed out patrols to establish command of the territory, until inevitably the first contact was made with the enemy. Sergeant Herbie Hawkins won a well deserved DCM when with only nine men he brought down such a hail of fire that a rebel force of thirty was compelled to withdraw with heavy losses; an action that entered SAS legend as the Battle of Hawkins' Hump. He withdrew his men without sustaining any casualties and the opposing side failed to follow up their attack.

While Red Rory was busy to the north of the plateau, the rest of the squadron was not idle. The other two troops kept up the pressure to the south of the plateau, which created a useful diversion. A patrol had discovered a cave that was being used both as a guard post and a store for weapons and ammunition and it was decided to mount a concerted attack from two directions. One troop, led by Peter de la Billière, made a ten-hour night climb lugging with them a rocket launcher as well as their normal loads of weapons and ammunition. Before dawn they were in position facing the mouth of the cave, and when the first rebels came out still groggy from sleep, the troop opened up. Immediately there was a hail of fire from the surrounding hills that were honeycombed with small caves and enemy *sangars*. Many of the troop's rockets failed to go off and had to be extracted from the launcher tube while still potentially live. Meanwhile a flight of RAF Venom fighters was hovering overhead. Summoned by radio they swept down and launched their rockets at the enemy positions, enabling the SAS to conduct an orderly withdrawal from a position they could not have held on to indefinitely. Involved in that action was one of the best known of the SAS veterans, 'Tankie' Smith, who manned a machine gun to give vital covering fire. Unfortunately, a popular survivor of the Malayan campaign, 'Duke' Swindells, was killed by a sniper.

By now the forty-odd men of D Squadron had been operating on the supposedly impregnable Jebel for about a fortnight and Cairo Radio was boasting that thousands of British parachutists had been wiped out by the intrepid freedom fighters. Local headquarters in Bahrain could hardly believe what had been achieved by the handful of SAS men, and sent an aircraft to overfly the given position to check that they were really there. Although they had managed to have their sleeping bags brought up, the men were suffering from monotonous ration packs and having to take cover in their *sangars* from the occasional stray mortar rounds that were lobbed at them, armed only with their rifles and Bren light machine guns. In those days there were no lightweight portable radios available and the only method of communication was a battery-powered Morse set which operated back to squadron headquarters. They had no means of communication with the fighter aircraft that were on call for strafing attacks. With hindsight it seems incredible that the enemy failed to realize just how few men there were and did not launch an all-out assault. The only supply line was via the steep climb up from the base which a few determined men could easily have severed.

Walker was under strict orders to keep casualties to an absolute minimum, which hampered his offensive capability; nevertheless, he moved his two troops forward and kept up the momentum of active patrolling by night and day. Browning machine guns were brought up to increase the firepower as well as a 3-inch mortar and several rocket launchers. The problem was the supply of bombs for the mortar, which were to be delivered by airdrop. The local RAF, obviously inexperienced in such matters, dropped the loads from far too high and most of the parachutes drifted over the cliff. Those that did arrive on the dropping zone (DZ) simply exploded, sending shrapnel flying all over the place. Lofty Large commented: 'We salvaged all we could. A few brave souls rushed in and out of the exploding DZ trying to get the mail, the decent rations (the rum ration?) and anything else they could. Like most of the others, I got behind a good sized rock, lit a cigarette and waited for the shrapnel to stop screeching past before venturing out into that lot.'

To free the SAS for an attack on the enemy base, a company of Omani troops was brought up to defend their original position. About 4,000 yards away was a cliff known as the 'Akbat' which barred the way to any advance towards the centre of the plateau. This was honeycombed with caves in which the enemy could shelter and the approach was over boulder-strewn ground fissured with deep ravines, or wadis. Many of the men were suffering from lack of suitable footwear: marching over the jagged, rocky Jebel had wrecked their issue boots. With the limited force available, Walker could stage no more than a raid, so he decided to use one troop to mount a diversionary attack while the other assulted the Akbat position frontally. Detailed planning of the route was impossible as the only map showed a blank white area, and without portable radios, support fire had to be based on accurate timing. The first night of the operation, 16 Troop moved up to about 600 yards from the target area, while 17 Troop moved away to the north flank. They lay up the following day in the open under the glare of the sun, but luckily were unobserved. The following night as the twelve-man assault party moved forward they found themselves confronted by a deep wadi with almost sheer sides. Scrambling down they realized that their fire-support timings were going to be way out; while still at the bottom they heard the sound of the 17 Troop attack starting. Climbing up the other side they came under fire from their own rockets and when they finally reached the target area a vicious firefight started up in pitch dark. 'Blurred shadows, a couple of half-seen, split-second silhouettes and a glinting cartridge belt' was all Lofty Large remembered. Firing at enemy muzzle flashes and lobbing grenades into dimly seen cave mouths, they suppressed the opposition and then beat a retreat, having suffered no losses.

When they stumbled exhausted into the base position, they discovered that it was Christmas Day and that some kind soul had provided a fine ration of spirits as well as tinned chickens. In the inimitable style of the SAS, the few men isolated on top of the Jebel ate and drank their fill around the fire, entertained by Red Rory's bagpipes which had some-how found their way up to the top of the mountain. A severe mortar attack was regarded as a minor nuisance.

It had become clear to John Watts that a larger force was necessary to exploit the toehold on top of the plateau. The enemy, despite consider-able losses, remained as determined as ever and were well established in strong, easily defended positions on the commanding high ground. After discussions between Deane-Drummond and Smiley, it was decided to withdraw A Squadron from Malaya and to get them to the Oman as rapidly as possible. The squadron, commanded by the ubiquitous Johnny Cooper, was patrolling on the Thai border and had to be whisked out of the jungle by helicopter. None of them had any idea of where they were going and were surprised to be issued with Arctic-quality anoraks and sleeping bags. Missing any chance of a Christmas break, they were flown out by Transport Command via Ceylon and deposited on a small airstrip at Azaiba near the Jebel Akhdhar on 9 January 1959.

After only a few days' acclimatization, it was decided that A Squadron should relieve the elements of D Squadron who were holding the position on the plateau, which was dominated by a twin-peaked mountain, the Akbat al Dhofar. As that was far too much of a mouthful, the mountain was promptly christened Sabrina by the SAS after a bosomy pin-up of the period, a fifties version of the modern Page 3 girl. Sabrina was a key feature as it dominated a pass along a narrow ridge which was the only route to the rebel stronghold at Saiq. Cooper handed over to his second in command, Warwick Deacock, a well-known mountaineer with experience in the Himalayas, who would lead the ascent via the Persian Steps. Bent double under their heavy Bergens, the squadron trudged upwards until somewhat exhausted they stumbled into the D Squadron positions. The defenders, after six hard weeks, were glad to take a short break at the SAS base at Bait el Falage.

The regimental commander, Deane-Drummond, left Malaya shortly after Christmas and flew to Oman to take overall command of the two squadrons for an all-out assault on the main enemy position at Saiq. He was joined by Cooper and Watts for a thorough recce and, after overflying the area, decided to mount a series of deceptions while at the same time capturing features which would give his men good jumping-off points. Cooper was ordered to use A Squadron to capture Sabrina, leave a troop there to create a diversion and lead the opposition to believe that the attack would come from that direction. D Squadron was to mount an assault to the south on to the Tanuf plateau, a vast slab of rock about three miles long, and also to leave one troop there. The remaining six troops would then descend to the base of the Jebel and join up for a combined attack via two features known as Vincent and Pyramid. To crown the deception, the intelligence officer leaked information to the local donkey handlers that the attack would come from the direction of Sabrina, knowing full well they would sell that to the Imam's spies within a matter of hours.

Back up on the plateau, Johnny Cooper ordered a flight of Shackleton bombers to soften up the enemy positions and had a forward air controller who could speak directly to the pilots of Venom ground-attack fighters equipped with rockets. On the night of 26 January 1959 A Squadron attacked Sabrina with three troops while the fourth was held in reserve to give covering fire with machine guns. By dawn they had secured the twin peaks in spite of stiff opposition and controlled the Akbat ridge which had previously been assaulted by Walker's men.

D Squadron after their short rest made the stiff climb up to the Tanuf Slab and established themselves there, although they were overlooked by the enemy who had longer-range weapons. John Watts also had a forward air controller, who brought down a successful Venom strike on a heavy machine gun hidden in the entrance to a cave. Two days of active patrolling stirred up the opposition to such an extent that they were forced to withdraw into cover. This enabled three troops to withdraw down to Tanuf where they met up with Johnny Cooper's contingent. After a break for a meal and the usual weapon check, all six troops were loaded into trucks for a hair-raising ride over rocky tracks along the base of the Jebel. They travelled in broad daylight, clearly visible to everyone who cared to watch, but as dusk fell the convoy abruptly changed direction. Driving without lights they headed south and approached the start point after a detour out into the empty desert. As silently as possible the men clambered stiffly out and set off to climb the Jebel by a route that had not previously been tried. The loads each man carried were immense, consisting mainly of ammunition. Lofty Large weighed his Bergen and belt equipment: together they amounted to 120lbs. – not including his rifle.

The men had to climb some 8,000 feet to reach Vincent, starting at 2030, and it was vital that they were on top and in cover by dawn. This was not a scramble up a defined track, but an actual climb where ropes had to be used for one section, and at that time the SAS had not really been trained for mountaineering. What they achieved was a truly remarkable feat. Led by de la Billière's troop, D Squadron were the first to arrive, and in the dim half-light set to work to build *sangars*, only to find they were in the middle of an enemy position that had been left untended for the night. Moving forward, one troop cleared a number of caves, while the rest of the squadron advanced to occupy the feature known as Pyramid. In view of the need for speed they left their packs behind, carrying only their rifles and as much ammunition as could be stuffed into pockets and pouches. Had they been caught in the open, the operation could have ended in disaster. Thus far, however, there had been little opposition and an airdrop of supplies was successfully brought in. A Squadron moved on through Pyramid, but lost two men, killed when a stray sniper's bullet hit a grenade in a man's pack. It exploded, taking with it the man behind him. A further man was wounded.

Those moves brought the SAS force on to the plateau proper and within view of Saiq, the main rebel base. At that point, probably as a result of seeing the supply parachutes floating down and imagining a full airborne assault, the Imam commandeered camels and fled with a few of his retinue over the border into Saudi Arabia. With his departure the rest of the opposition melted away, and the SAS marched into Saiq in open order. A total of eighty men had conquered the Green Mountain, for the first time in recorded history. The town itself had been abandoned, shimmering in the heat haze and bearing the scars of RAF bombing raids. Even the civilians had fled, but a thorough search of the surrounding caves revealed a large cache of weapons, documents and even valuables.

The operation was a textbook example of the application of minimum force to achieve the desired ends. For a loss of three men killed, a troublesome rebellion had been brought to an end, which earned the gratitude of the Sultan in an area vital to British interests. Before that, the SAS had been a small part of the vast operation in distant Malaya, but their success on the Jebel brought them to the direct notice of Whitehall, at a time when overall defence planning was in a state of flux. The political masters showed their gratitude with a veritable shower of decorations. Deane-Drummond was awarded the DSO for his planning and command of the assault. MCs went to Rory Walker, Jeapes, Watts and de la Billière, and Hawkins was given a richly deserved DCM. A Military Medal went to Trooper Cunningham and the list was topped off with six mentions in dispatches.

For many of the men, the aftermath was a bit of an anticlimax. Deane-Drummond flew back to Malaya to finish off the regiment's move to England and to oversee the orderly disbandment of B Squadron. As the senior officer, Cooper took command of what was known as Vector Force, with orders to deploy patrols throughout the Jebel to flush out any remaining pockets of resistance. The men had to map the tracks, count the population and 'show the flag'. There was quite a lot of moaning as they had been told that they would be going back to England, and resented having to undertake chores that could easily have been carried out by the local infantry. A further worry was that many men who were married did not know if their families were still in Malaya, in England or in transit between. Johnny Cooper seized the initiative and, circumventing the normal channels, made an appeal to the senior RAF officer in the Persian Gulf. Although he received a mild reprimand, the ploy worked and the force was airlifted back to England in early March 1959.

The Jebel Akhdhar campaign marked the end of active soldiering for quite some while. Reduced to only two sabre squadrons the SAS installed itself in a wartime hutted location, Merebrook Camp at Malvern, where they were to spend a frustrating year. Remaining B Squadron personnel were distributed between A and D, and officers surplus to requirements had to return to their parent regiments. Johnny Cooper finally left the regiment and went to serve in Oman under Colonel Smiley. For the men, there was a full programme of training, starting with driving, as few of them had licences. Parachuting had to be brought up to date and everyone made the acquaintance of the Brecon Beacons.

Although there was to be a four-year pause for the SAS as far as active combat was concerned, many of the principles upon which the regiment operates today were laid down during that period of relative calm. At the helm was John Woodhouse, promoted to lieutenant-colonel in command of 22 SAS. Training in Malaya had mainly concentrated on preparing the men for the job in hand – jungle survival – and the brief interlude in Oman was purely a combat situation. In view of the changed situation, both squadrons were sent to Germany at regular intervals to familiarize them with their new role in support of NATO forces. When the men arrived back from Oman few had had any experience of training for warfare in Europe and only a few old hands with wartime service remained in the regiment. In 1960 a regular exchange programme with the US Army was instituted. A captain and a sergeant were sent for a year to work with 7th Special Forces Group, and Americans trained with 22 SAS.

There was a divergence of philosophy within the regiment. One school of thought favoured concentration on tasks with NATO in Europe, yet that brought the still present threat of absorption by the Parachute Regiment. Others saw the role of the regiment essentially as that of 'fireman' in Third World countries threatened by Communist insurgence. At last there was the inevitable compromise, with the two TA units concentrating on the long-range reconnaissance task in Europe while the regulars trained on an ever-widening selection of different terrains.

Overseas secondments became a feature of regimental life, as men were sent in small groups to friendly countries to train their troops in SAS methods. Whole squadrons were sent to the Oman and North Africa to learn desert navigation and to Kenya to become accustomed to bush conditions. There were courses to be taken, and new skills such as free-fall parachuting to be learnt. Foreign-language study became institutionalized for all ranks, and men were given training in quite advanced medical techniques, far in excess of normal army first aid. In 1960 the regiment made the move to Bradbury Lines in Hereford, which was to become its permanent headquarters. On the organizational side, the early 1960s saw the introduction of troop specialization within each squadron which resulted in a free-fall troop, a mountain troop, a boat troop and a desert mobility troop. These may have been specialities but cross-training ensured that every man in the squadron had an ability in the skills of the others.

During that period far less secrecy surrounded the regiment than today, although in keeping with their basic philosophy, a low profile was maintained. Their role within the Army was a specialist one, but international terrorism had not yet reared its head. The SAS regularly parachuted on to Hereford racecourse, for example, and paraded in uniform. Essentially, 22 SAS was a small, air-portable shock infantry unit, which if fully deployed could have put about 160 fighting men in the field anywhere in the world – from the icy mountains of Norway to the jungles of Malaysia. The vital component was still the four-man patrol and the heaviest weapons available were machine guns and mortars. In 1964, with ever-growing commitments in Aden and Borneo, B Squadron was reformed by John Watts, and in 1965 G Squadron, recruited from the Brigade of Guards, joined the regiment to give it its present four-squadron line-up.

5
The Return to the Jungle

The period between 1963 and 1966 is a confused one. 22 SAS was faced by simultaneous commitments in Borneo and Aden in addition to the normal training routines and absorbing the new squadrons. Only one squadron at a time was committed to action in those two theatres respectively and in this book they will be described separately as a matter of convenience. The two geographically isolated and very different campaigns during the end-of-empire phase certainly proved just how versatile the regiment had become as a result of its intense training and the inspired leadership of John Woodhouse since the return from Oman in the spring of 1959.

The large mountainous island of Borneo is mainly covered by primary jungle and swamps. In 1963 three-quarters of the land, lying to the south, was the Indonesian province of Kalimantan, from which the Dutch colonists had been expelled in 1949. The northern coastal strip comprised three territories: the British colonies of Sarawak and Sabah, and the British protected Sultanate of Brunei. In September 1963 Sarawak and Sabah joined the Malay states and Singapore in the new Federation of Malaysia. Indonesia was ruled by President Ahmed Sukarno, a charismatic demagogue who dreamed of uniting his territories with the Philippines and Malaysia to form an Asian great power. In pursuit of that illusion he instituted a campaign of propaganda, intended to force the fledgling Malaysia to close down the remaining British bases there. The Malaysians had no intention of doing so as their eyes were fixed upon the threat of further Communist subversion from the north.

Trouble in Borneo served only to cement their resolve to keep British garrisons in place, without which the new state would have been virtually defenceless.

At the end of 1962 a revolt broke out in the Sultanate of Brunei. This was a strictly local affair although it had undoubtedly been fomented by Indonesia, which had provided weapons and training facilities. The insurgents attacked police stations, government buildings and industrial targets and took a number of European hostages. As there were no British troops present at the time, a rescue operation from Singapore was hastily mounted, using Gurkha troops and a Royal Marine Commando. Order was swiftly re-established, but it was clear that a credible force would have to remain in order to deter any further outbreaks of trouble. Major-General Walter Walker, who was appointed Director of Operations in Borneo, was convinced that it was only a matter of time before the Indonesians decided to inspire further sections of the population to revolt. There was already a sizeable Clandestine Communist Organization (CCO), with a mainly Chinese membership. Walker's strategic dilemma was to keep order in the interior while preventing Indonesian troops from crossing the 700-mile-long jungle border. Walker had spent much of his service career with the Gurkhas, had fought in Burma during the war and in Malaya during the emergency, so he had unique experience in controlling operations in a jungle environment. Often abrasive by nature, he was a tough fighting general, yet also understood that the prime need was to win the support of the indigenous population.

Initially no SAS component was envisaged for service in Borneo, but individual commanding officers can be extremely tough lobbyists when they feel that their men have been left out of a potential fight. John Woodhouse was no exception. He took himself off to the War Office in London, where he pointed out that his regiment was immediately ready for service and had vital jungle experience to offer the commander on the spot. Moreover, the regiment had also benefited from advances in communications technology to obtain several new long-range radio sets. The War Office agreed to place an SAS squadron on the list of units available to Walker, who sent for Woodhouse to fly out to see him at the beginning of January 1963. The general had little idea of the capabilities of the SAS; it seems that initially he wanted them as a reserve airborne unit as he remembered from Malaya that they could parachute into trees. The eloquence of Woodhouse, who knew full well the casualties involved in tree-jumping, persuaded Walker that his men would be far more valuable in patrolling the long frontier. Many of them spoke Malay, which was understood in the area, and by living among the natives they could provide a vital source of intelligence.

Walker agreed. A signal was sent back to Hereford for A Squadron, under the command of Major John Edwardes, to be prepared to move. They were brought down from winter training in the Brecon Beacons, rekitted with tropical gear and put on to aircraft within three days; not even their wives knew where they were going. They were left hanging about in Singapore for several days, and even when they arrived in Borneo nobody had any clear idea of what to do with them. This was anathema to the SAS, who traditionally dislike being left to cool their heels anywhere. The log-jam was broken when Woodhouse suggested that his men should move up to the frontier, which in many places was ill defined, to act as an early-warning screen with small patrols living with the local native population. The SAS were particularly well suited to the task after their long apprenticeship in Malaya. They were trained to stay out in small groups for long periods, were experienced in treating a whole range of ailments and had enough Malay speakers to make themselves understood. General Walker accepted the suggestion: it enabled him to concentrate his forces as a mobile reserve, ready to move to any area where an incursion was threatened.

So A Squadron shouldered their Bergens and set off into the unknown, charged with patrolling 700 miles of frontier and acting as the eyes and ears of the British force commander. They took with them their new lightweight radios to transmit warnings back to base. The forces available to General Walker consisted of five battalions divided up into two brigade commands, a small naval detachment to patrol the coastline and an RAF component which at first lacked helicopters. The SAS divided up into patrols of two to four men, each of which had to cover a front of some 10,000 yards, basing themselves across a natural area of approach such as a river or a mountain pass. Clearly they could not cover every foot of their area but they were able to use the local people as scouts, reporting on any hostile movements. The frontier was largely an arbitrary one established by the colonial powers, so that tribal areas straddled the border which was crossed by hunting parties at will.

One of the main tribes were the Iban who had served the SAS well in

Malaya as scouts and whose skill in following a trail was uncanny. The local tribespeople lived in small villages in communal longhouses spread out along the riverbanks and hills. They tended small fields and hunted the plentiful wild animals in the jungle. Largely untouched by Western civilization and the activities of Christian missionaries, they welcomed the soldiers into their villages. Head-hunting, a traditional pastime derived from religious beliefs, had last been engaged in seriously during the Japanese occupation of the island. In many ways that first tour by A Squadron was an idyllic one. They made friends with their hosts, were entertained to feasts and dispensed medical care. Gifts were exchanged, offers of girls tactfully refused – at least that was the official line – and much intelligence-gathering was undertaken.

John Edwardes inserted his patrols into the communities where they were to stay for the following three months. With only four troops at his disposal the men were spread thinly on the ground. No. 3 Troop, commanded by Sergeant Ian 'Tankie' Smith, was given responsibility for the border between Sabah and Indonesian territory in the north-east of the island, which was inhabited by the Murut tribe. Large sections were uninhabited and virtually unexplored but there were several obvious crossing points where two or three men were positioned to watch and wait. Each small patrol had to take a census of the local population and prepare an account of their way of life, health condition, and names of their leaders.

Moving south-west along the frontier, Captain Bill Dodds and his No.2 Troop were given the task of covering the mountainous area of northern Sarawak leading on southwards from the Kelabit Highlands. The sixteen men of the troop were divided into four patrols placed about twenty-five miles apart. No.1 Troop, commanded by Captain Ray England, was in charge of a stretch of border roughly the same length as that between England and Wales. He set up a base where he left his signaller, and spent his time walking from patrol to patrol. The squadron commander too walked the entire frontier, carrying only a light pack and an Armalite rifle.

As there was no trouble, the patrols could get on with their tasks of intelligence-gathering and map-making, which would be vital when the campaign started in earnest. They made many friends in the local area, and a genuine contribution to general health standards, all of which were to be crucial when the fighting began. British soldiers, instead of being viewed as colonialist oppressors, were welcomed and assisted rather than sniped at with blowpipes. No SAS heads decorated the doorposts of longhouses in Borneo.

A Squadron was due for relief in mid-April by D Squadron, who were on the way out from training in Norway and Germany to replace them. The powers that be in Singapore, however, had decided that armed incursion by Indonesians was not imminent and decided to pull General Walker back. Fearing that the Vietnam War might spill out into other areas of the Far East, they preferred to concentrate their forces at the main base. Walker was saying his farewells when news came of an attack by Indonesians on the police station at Tebudu in Sarawak, not far away from the border. As it could be reached by road from the coast, it was not an area where an SAS patrol had been stationed. One policeman was killed and the post looted, before a troop of Royal Marine Commandos arrived on the scene. That minor hit-and-run raid caused an immediate rethink. Walker was ordered to stay put and reinforcements were sent, including helicopters, which were vital for moving troops in to seal off further raiding parties.

Walker was certainly converted to the SAS ideal and warmly thanked the departing squadron for their assistance. D Squadron at the time was commanded by Major Tom Leask, with Bob Turnbull as Squadron Sergeant-Major. On arrival Leask found his men were to be responsible for training tribespeople as Border Scouts; the Scouts were not a militia as such but were used to patrol the frontier and to guide regular infantry units. General Walker moved companies of troops up into fortified posts not far back from the frontier and relied on air mobility to move them rapidly into action. On the political front, Brunei decided against joining the Malaysian Federation, preferring to remain under British protection, and the general set up his headquarters there. The Sultan placed a residence known as the Haunted House at the disposal of the SAS. The house had gained its name because the Japanese version of the Gestapo, the Kempetai, had used it during the occupation. John Woodhouse set up a tactical regimental headquarters there and spent a lot of time in Borneo, where the action was. An interesting sidelight is that when the Federation of Malaysia was proclaimed on 16 September, Major Roderick 'Red Rory' Walker, who had served with such distinction at the storming of the Jebel Akhdhar, was the assistant military attaché at the Embassy in Jakarta. The Indonesians whipped up a rentamob estimated at 5,000 screaming men who had every intention of sacking the embassy building. In a scene reminiscent of the film *Carry on up the Khyber*, Walker, wearing his SAS beret, calmly marched up and down playing his bagpipes, totally ignoring a hail of stones and brickbats.

The D Squadron tour was largely uneventful in terms of contact with the enemy. Besides training the irregulars, they engaged in active patrolling over wide areas, adding to their store of local knowledge. The technique they developed was to sleep out in the jungle, cache their rations and approach villages only during the day, bringing gifts of medical supplies. Every seventh day a resupply mission was flown in by helicopter. The worst encounters were with the local wildlife – the odd angry elephant, vast boa constrictors and the ever-present leeches and malevolent insects. Leask's period of attachment to the SAS came to an end, and he left for home, handing over command of the squadron to Major Roger Woodiwiss.

The tour was marred by a tragic accident. On 4 May the second-in-command of the regiment, Major Ronald Norman, accompanied by the operations officer, Major Harry Thompson, and Corporal Murphy, took off in a helicopter for what was a routine visit to patrols near the border. The aircraft crashed, killing all nine occupants. It was a serious loss for 22 SAS, as Woodhouse had envisaged Harry Thompson as his replacement in command at the end of 1964.

A Squadron returned to Borneo in August 1963, temporarily commanded by Captain Bill Dodds, and with only three troops initially available. These were deployed to cover the main approach routes to Brunei, but there was still a stand-off with the Indonesians. It was known that they were reinforcing border areas with their regular troops, but politically, the orders were not to intervene. The troops established their respective headquarters at isolated airstrips, and, stiffened with groups of infantry, engaged in active patrolling along the border, keeping in contact with the local Border Scouts whom they continued to train. The tactical aim was that if an incursion took place the men on the spot would be reinforced by helicopter. At the start of 1964 A squadron was relieved by D in relays. There had been the odd contact, but in none of them had SAS troops been involved. Woodhouse was present during the handover, assisting Woodiwiss in positioning his troops across likely access routes.

Standard dress for the SAS in the jungle then consisted of the ordinary-issue olive green (OG) shirt and trousers and the men still carried the wartime-pattern water bottle. Other items were often unsatisfactory and the men tended to improvise their own carrying equipment. According to Lofty Large:

> Our belts fell to bits. Our magazine carriers were locally made in the Far East, and in short supply, so that the ones we had were repaired time and time again. Belt pouches were a 'hodge-podge' of allsorts. Spare water bottle carriers were a favourite type of belt pouch. Issued ammunition pouches had to be modified and strengthened to be of any use.

He went on to remark that personal equipment was generally repaired with parachute cord and masking tape, and that if anyone had invented a method of destroying those two trusty items the SAS would have fallen to pieces.

Tactically, the situation was fraught with a variety of complications, mostly political. As war had not been declared and as Whitehall feared repercussions from the vociferous group of non-aligned countries at the United Nations, the SAS had to stay on their side of the border, in theory at least, and retaliate only if attacked. John Woodhouse knew that he had to avoid SAS casualties at all costs, owing to sensitivity about the regiment's presence in the area and his chronic lack of manpower. His orders were: if involved in a fight, 'shoot and scoot' rather than hang about to slug it out. To have to explain away a lot of dead heroes would have handed a propaganda victory to the opposition. At the time, however, Walker did authorize reconnaissance patrols to cross the border and gather information about the build-up of Indonesian troops and to locate their camps. If caught they were to claim that they had made a map-reading error.

In March 1964 the tacit truce was broken when the Indonesians staged a series of raids over the frontier, using well-trained regular troops, and for the first time the SAS were involved in direct combat. The area was the Long Pa Sia Bulge where Sabah and Sarawak abutted on to the Indonesian frontier, consisting of mountainous, trackless and unpopulated jungle. Sergeant 'Smokey' Richardson was ordered to take his four-man patrol through the area to meet up with Sergeant Creighton's patrol on the River Plandok. He was accompanied by

'Lofty' Allen, a corporal who had seen service in Malaya, a young Scot named John Allison and the patrol signaller, Paddy Condon who had been loaned from A Squadron. Equipped with rations for three weeks and with each man carrying about 70lbs. in weight, they set off at the end of April into the unknown on what they thought would be a routine patrol. Seldom managing more than two miles a day and hampered in their navigation by almost total lack of visibility, they struggled on for nearly two weeks until they found a clearing that could be expanded enough for them to receive a helicopter resupply on 10 March. Two days later they reached the river and discovered fresh tracks, which led them to two large camps that had obviously just been abandoned. Richardson radioed back to base and Major Woodiwiss alerted local army units to concentrate on the Bulge, telling his patrol commander to follow the track leading from the camps and observe.

The four men spent the night huddled in undergrowth and the following morning stealthily set out, hoping to avoid contact with what was clearly a large force as well as colliding with Gurkha troops sent to intercept the same enemy. By evening they were unsure whether or not they were on the wrong side of the border, so decided to lie up. The squadron commander himself was also unsure of their position. Unfortunately they ran into a group of the enemy and in a shoot-out, Condon, and the radio, became separated from the patrol. Several miserable days were spent looking for him and dodging Indonesian patrols. The men were now completely out of touch with their base. Woodiwiss, convinced that he would find them, personally led a search by helicopter which eventually recovered the hungry and exhausted survivors. It was later discovered that Condon had been killed by the Indonesians.

The incursions were defeated and in April the Indonesians retreated across the border. D Squadron, exhausted after four months in the jungle, had expected to be home for Easter, but were due for a disappointment. Woodhouse had to tell them that their tour was to be extended until June, as A Squadron had been sent to Aden and the embryo B Squadron was still engaged in training new recruits. This illustrates just how thinly the regiment was stretched at the time, although it was decided that the Guards Independent Parachute Company was to be trained up to SAS standard; subsequently they became G Squadron of 22 SAS. In the background, Colonel Woodhouse had been lobbying hard for the commitment of an Australian SAS squadron during a visit to Perth in July 1963, and this was agreed in principle. Walker, who by then was completely 'sold' on the value of the regiment in fighting his unofficial war, is reported to have said at the time: 'I regard 70 troopers of the SAS as being as valuable to me as 700 infantry in the role of hearts and minds, border surveillance, early warning, stay behind, and eyes and ears with a sting.'

The temporary lull in activity on the part of the enemy enabled the tired men of D Squadron to take it in turns to have ten days of leave in Singapore, but then it was back to the routine of border patrolling, day in, day out. At the end of May Woodiwiss led an enlarged patrol, including Richardson and Allen, back to the area of their last operation in the Bulge, to determine if the camps they had found were actually on Malaysian territory. They found the camps still in use, although empty, but there was evidence that a strong enemy patrol had headed into Sabah. Splitting his patrol, the squadron commander set off with three others to follow the route taken by the enemy, and radioed for an infantry step-up unit to be flown into the area. A unit from the 2/7 Gurkhas joined the patrol and together they set off to trap the Indonesian force, still following their trail, with Sergeant 'Buddha' Bexton in the lead. All that Woodiwiss heard was a shout, followed by a burst of fire. That was all; no further contact was made and a good man lay where he had fallen.

D Squadron pulled out at the end of June, to be replaced yet again by A Squadron, then under the command of Major de la Billière with Lawrence Smith as his sergeant-major. A new second-in-command of the regiment was also in the area at the time: Major Mike Wingate-Gray, who had been selected to replace Harry Thompson as commanding officer designate. A Squadron came hot from a four-week stint in Aden where they had been involved in an action which will be described later. The immediate problem they faced was the fact that the frequent Indonesian incursions had unsettled the border villagers, who were no longer as friendly as they had been the previous year. They could hardly be blamed as they had to continue living there, whoever won, but A Squadron had to rebuild contact with a reopening of the 'hearts and minds' campaign. A valuable reinforcement was the arrival of the Guards Independent Parachute Company, which had completed its training in SAS methods.

The Bulge continued to worry the high command, so Sergeant

Maurice Tudor took the four patrols of his 4 Troop into that area. Trooper Billy White was killed after one patrol stumbled on a party of the enemy. For his action in killing one of the enemy before being cut down himself, he was awarded a posthumous mention in dispatches. Other troops were preparing to take the war over the border, as General Walker had received authority from the government to institute cross-border operations up to a depth of 3,000 yards. The aim was to unsettle the Indonesians on their own territory and to win back the initiative in a form of active defence. Denis Healey, Secretary of State for Defence in the newly elected Labour government, was a firm supporter of measures to bring the confrontation to a close by proving to the Indonesians that the British were determined to support the Malaysian Federation. The new operations were given the name Claret and the SAS role was to provide the reconnaissance capability for Gurkha troops to be guided to enemy concentrations. They were given strict orders not to reveal their presence and to leave nothing behind in hostile territory.

Stealth was the key as patrols were sent over the border to locate the river routes the Indonesians were using to move supplies and men. The weight the troops carried in their Bergens had to be reduced to a minimum, 30lbs., which brought with it problems of malnutrition. Three weeks on low-calorie dehydrated food led to considerable loss of body weight. Steps were taken to disguise the standard tread pattern of issue boots which might have revealed the fact that British troops were at large on the wrong side of the border, and all the men involved had to be expert navigators. No sign that might indicate a human presence could be ignored – a broken spider's web, scuffed bark on a tree, the faintest whiff of tobacco smoke. The men had to learn to blend into the jungle, to smell like it and to take on the sensual abilities of animals, living in almost total silence for days on end and never allowing their concentration to slip.

The first of the cross-border recces was carried out by Captain Ray England's patrol which was tasked to explore the River Sembakung and report on traffic. He took with him as fourth man, a Gurkha officer, whose job was to guide in a strike force if necessary. They travelled incredibly light as England succeeded in reducing the ration load per man per day to 16 ounces and 2,000 calories. A normal fit and healthy man would need 5,500 and previous SAS patrols had been making do with 3,600. A further weight-saving tactic was to provide patrols with the

American Armalite rifle which was destined to become a firm favourite with the SAS. Even so, the signaller still had to carry the radio, spare battery and the Sarbe, a search and rescue beacon, with which they had at last been issued, and another man was responsible for a full medical pack. Once over the border they managed only one and a half miles a day, creeping steadily towards the river and leaving no trace of their passage – every disturbed leaf had to be replaced. Once in position they kept watch in pairs during daylight hours before retiring into the jungle for a meagre meal and to sleep. Emerging from the jungle they looked like emaciated scarecrows, bearded, smelly and with their clothes in tatters.

That first patrol sighted very little military traffic on the river. Other patrols carried out similar recces, and on one, Sergeant Tudor was stricken with leptospirosis, a particularly vicious tropical disease, and very nearly died. As his patrol was over the border he could not be brought out by helicopter, and with a temperature of 105, he had to march back to the crossing more dead than alive. On another occasion the patrol had to be aborted after a wild boar, being chased by a hunting party, charged through the observation post on the riverbank.

At the end of October 1964, B Squadron, which was already acclimatizing in Borneo, took over from A Squadron. John Watts and his 'new boys' had to prove themselves in battle and earn the respect of their comrades in the two 'old' squadrons. To blood the four troops gently they took on the task of regular patrolling and got to know their territory, practising the skills they had learnt mainly on the hills in Wales. In December the squadron was moved to Kuching in Sarawak which intelligence felt was threatened by a considerable Indonesian force of division strength that was reported to be assembling along the border. The area of the Bulge was handed over to the Guards Parachute Company while Watts pulled his patrols out and had them flown down to Kuching, where their first accommodation was a long room over a brothel and bar.

There were changes too at the top, as John Woodhouse left the Army at the beginning of 1965, handing over command of 22 SAS to Mike Wingate-Gray. David Stirling regarded Woodhouse as the founder of the modern SAS and he was the first home-grown officer to command the regular regiment. Sadly for the Army, higher rank was barred to him and he was compelled to retire to civilian life; his years of experience in counter-insurgency warfare could surely have been put to better use. It was he who laid down the selection procedure that is still broadly in use today and he stamped his own qualities of leadership on the regiment.

Authority had been given for the depth of penetration to be increased to 10,000 yards and B Squadron was to have the job of finding targets for the infantry to attack. Watts instituted an aggressive patrolling routine all across his area of the frontier, but although signs of enemy activity were found in a number of places and much useful intelligence was collected, no really worthwhile targets were located. This was not the fault of the squadron, however, and they finished their tour having proved their abilities in jungle tracking and survival. It is difficult to maintain a narrative of a typical squadron tour, as it split into sixteen four-man patrols who spent much of their time sitting silently in observation posts. Although it sounds somewhat mundane, as the eyes and ears of the infantry brigade who were behind them, the patrols' work was invaluable.

In February 1965 D Squadron, still commanded by Major Roger Woodiwiss, returned to Borneo for the fourth time and immediately threw themselves into the routine of patrolling all along the Sarawak border with Indonesian territory. One of the initial patrols of the tour, led by Sergeant Eddie 'Geordie' Lillico, consisted of eight men including a number of new recruits to the squadron who were being introduced to life in the jungle. Lillico's task was to observe traffic on the River Sekayan, but once over the border they came across an old enemy camp which appeared deserted. Lillico decided to recce the camp the following morning as it was a legitimate intelligence source, and left the bulk of the patrol at their overnight lying-up position.

Lillico set out with four men, not expecting trouble. They left their Bergens behind and took only their belt equipment and personal weapons. Ian Thompson, a trooper from Fife in Scotland, carrying an Armalite was the lead scout as they closed in silently on what they assumed was the deserted enemy camp. They reached the perimeter, watched for a while well concealed, and convinced that the coast was clear, Thompson stepped out from behind a clump of bamboo. Immediately there was a burst of fire and he was hit in the thigh. Dropping to the ground he rolled sideways almost on top of another Indonesian soldier who was fumbling with his rifle. Thompson managed to grab his Armalite and kill the man, noticing that blood was pumping out of a fair-sized wound. The initial burst had also severely wounded Lillico, who lost the use of his legs but could still fire. He loosed off several rounds in the direction of the enemy; this seemed to discourage them from following up the contact.

Hearing the shots, the two rear members of the patrol, both recently joined recruits, obeyed the 'shoot and scoot' standard operating procedure and made their way back to the rendezvous, where a signal was sent to squadron headquarters. They then made their way back to the border to gather an infantry patrol with which to institute an armed search for the missing men. In the meantime Thompson applied a tourniquet, injected two syrettes of morphine and set out to crawl away from the danger zone, dragging his wounded leg. Lillico padded his wounds with shell dressings and also set out to crawl back in the direction of the border, conscious only of the pain and the fear of being captured by what was regarded as a barbarous enemy.

Back at base, the squadron commander obtained permission for helicopters to cross the border for a rescue mission, but had very little idea where the men might be, or even if they were alive. Thompson and Lillico, moving separately and painfully on their bellies away from the contact point, laid up through the night, trying to conserve their strength, even at the risk of letting their lives slip away. When Lillico woke up he found himself hidden in the midst of a group of enemy soldiers and then heard a helicopter overhead. As he had the Sarbe he could have switched it on, but the descending aircraft would have made an easy target for the opposition. At the same time, Thompson crawled back into the rendezvous and found his Bergen. Weak and hardly able to move, he was finally discovered by a Gurkha patrol who cared for him during the night. The helicopter which had been sent to rescue Thompson failed to find the spot where he lay with the Gurkhas but did hear the bleep of Lillico's Sarbe. In a brilliant feat of airmanship the pilot manoeuvred close enough to the tops of the trees to lower a strop and winch him to safety. Thompson was brought out the following morning. Both men survived the ordeal and Lillico was justly awarded the Military Medal.

At about the same time, the SAS mounted their first overtly offensive patrol into enemy territory at the behest of the intelligence people who wished to obtain documents known to be carried by a certain person who would be at a certain place. For many of the regiment it was a welcome change from the passive patrolling that had been their lot since the confrontation had begun. Captain Mackay-Lewis commanded two patrols, backed up by a company from the Scots Guards. They crossed the border and located the position of the hut they had to raid. Surrounding the camp they moved in, firing from the hip and killing several of the enemy. The documents were found and the detachment retired without loss back to their starting point.

On 12 March Major-General Walker was replaced as Director of Operations by Major-General George Lea, who had once commanded the regiment in its early days in Malaya. A squadron of the Australian SAS and a half-squadron of New Zealanders also arrived as welcome reinforcements. By that stage of the confrontation, British forces in Borneo had reached a peak of 15,000 men from all three services. The Claret operations, which remained strictly a state secret, were being regularly mounted but the Indonesian forces across the border still represented a very real threat. The SAS component was as yet a very small element in the overall forces employed but nevertheless enjoyed a high reputation. One squadron at a time could not win the war, but by acting as the eyes and ears of the infantry it was greatly valued by the commanders on the spot. Wingate-Gray lobbied hard with General Lea and obtained permission for a more offensive role for his men, reasoning that such raids might force the Indonesians into a more static role. The high command was situated on Labuan Island, and Wingate-Gray set up an SAS tactical headquarters there manned alternately by himself and his second-in-command, John Slim.

During April the patrols roved beyond the border, gathering information and with permission to kill any enemy troops they might find, which probably served to create a sense of alarm and despondency within the ranks of the Indonesians. Captain Robin Letts was awarded the MC for a typical patrol in which he and his three men successfully ambushed boats carrying Indonesian troops, shooting them and retiring in good order. Sergeant Don 'Lofty' Large was dispatched to the Koemba river. He was one of the regiment's most experienced trackers, a huge man who was totally at home in the jungle. He led his three men over the border in search of the river, but for several days their way was barred by swamps. When they reached the Koemba they discovered that it was a main supply route with a regular flow of launches flying the Indonesian flag. They got into the firing position to attack one smart-looking vessel when they noticed a woman on the deck and Large aborted the ambush – both because he did not wish to shoot a woman and because such a vessel might be owned by a senior political figure. Shooting someone at that level would certainly have broken the unwritten rules of engagement and provoked consternation in Whitehall.

They finally dispatched a 30-foot launch and its crew, then beat a timely retreat. On the way back Large had a near brush with death in the form of a king cobra poised to strike. It was an eyeball-to-eyeball confrontation. Lofty, a crack shot with rifle at the ready, knew it was not a good idea to fire, as that might alert the enemy. Luckily, the snake backed down and slid away behind a log, leaving the patrol commander's heart thumping.

During the tour, Roger Woodiwiss had had to return to England for personal reasons and his place was taken by Major Glyn Williams. D Squadron had carried the war into the enemy's camp with enthusiasm and with pinprick raids had unsteadied the scattered Indonesian posts. When de la Billière arrived with A Squadron in May 1965, all his four troops were commanded by sergeants, with the veteran Maurice Tudor still in charge of No.4. This illustrates the problem often faced by the SAS at the time: shortage of good junior officers. A tour with the SAS was not necessarily seen as a useful career step for an officer and very often parent regiments actively tried to hinder their best men from volunteering for selection. But de la Billière did have three suitable candidates assigned to him who were to join the squadron shortly. Even his sergeant-major, Lawrence Smith, doubled as second-in-command and operations officer.

Much of A Squadron's initial patrolling was taken up with an abortive search for a Communist camp which intelligence knew was there, somewhere, called Batu Hitam. They worked in close conjunction with a unit of Iban trackers known as the Cross-Border Scouts which had been raised by John Edwardes when earlier in the campaign he had been in command of A Squadron. De la Billière, however, was looking for action and struck up a profitable partnership with the commander of a newly arrived Gurkha battalion. With parties of SAS attached to act as guides, the Gurkhas carried out a series of raids into enemy territory, which kept the opposition so busy that they were unable to cause much trouble on the British side of the border. Towards the end of the tour the commander himself led three troops in a massive sweep in search of

69

the elusive Communist camp, again without success. De la Billière was awarded a bar to his MC for his exemplary leadership, and another MC went to Lawrence Smith who as a warrant officer would not normally have received that decoration. He was given it for doing an officer's job consistently and well for so long. One of the original Malayan Scouts, he had joined in 1950, seeing service in Malaya, on the Jebel Akhdhar and in Aden. Maurice Tudor was awarded a mention in dispatches for command of his troop and went on to take a commission.

B Squadron's second tour started in October. John Watts had moved on to other duties and his place had been taken by Major Terry Hardy. There had been a failed Communist *putsch* in Jakarta which had weakened the position of Sukarno. When General Suharto assumed the reality of power the British ordered a halt to offensive patrolling until the new man's attitude became more apparent. Patrolling went on unabated to gain intelligence of enemy activity, but shooting and scooting was not encouraged. This unofficial truce was broken by an Indonesian incursion, and the green light for action was given. The British forces as a whole were far more active right along the border at that stage of the campaign, with company-size attacks regularly being mounted into enemy territory. The SAS tactics also changed; they now tended to operate as a squadron rather than split into individual troops and patrols.

Major Hardy took his entire force into the jungle to mount an ambush against a track known to be used by the enemy. After four days they placed themselves in a favourable position and sat down to wait. But, human nature – in the form of the soldiers' love of baked beans – intervened and nearly wrecked the operation. A number of local tribespeople on the track had not noticed the SAS lying in wait, but when a man and a boy passed by, someone farted, loudly. The natives halted and found themselves face to face with the squadron commander, who was in a dilemma. Killing local people was not good form and it was hardly practicable to take prisoners, so he silently motioned them to move on. As they rounded a bend they were seen to carve a large notch in the bark of a tree: it was obvious that they would inform the enemy of the presence of the ambush.

The enemy mounted a serious attack in the afternoon and the SAS opened fire. Several Indonesians were blown apart when they triggered a claymore mine that had been sited to protect the flank; others were dropped by well-aimed shots. By then Hardy decided that discretion was the better part of valour as his party was being mortared, and gave the order to disengage. Firing off final bursts to keep enemy heads down, the troops moved back in turn and all crossed safely into Sarawak. It was later reported that they had accounted for twenty enemy dead.

There was a temporary lull in December 1965 while the authorities tried to guess the outcome of the struggle in Jakarta, but then it was decided to resume the search for the elusive Chinese Communist camp at Batu Hitam – on the assumption that even if the Indonesians called a halt, a Communist terrorist threat would remain. Several patrols were mounted, again without success. At the end of January a more tempting target presented itself after the intelligence people predicted that an attack would be mounted by Indonesians from a village called Sentas, just over the border. An offensive sweep was ordered and the job was given to three troops of B Squadron reinforced by Australians and New Zealanders, and a back-up force from the Argyll and Sutherland Highlanders. Hardy led the raiding force in person, and after successful penetration and the crossing of a river, he prepared to attack. 6 Troop was allotted the task of neutralizing what was thought to be a small farm but which proved on close inspection to be a strongly held advance post. A short but vicious battle developed and yet again the whole unit had to withdraw.

One or two further patrols were carried out, but when B Squadron returned to Britain in the early spring the conflict, as far as the SAS was concerned, was over. D Squadron was sent back to Borneo in the summer of 1966, but saw no action. The Indonesians settled their differences with the Malaysians, and apart from minor Chinese Communist agitation, peace descended on that beautiful country – which is still, however, a popular jungle training ground for the squadrons today. One thing is certain. Had Britain not been prepared to stand by its allies, the Indonesians could well have overrun large chunks of Malaysia and destabilized the entire region.

The non-military reader of this chapter may be tempted to wonder if all the effort by the SAS had been worth while. Squadron after squadron had rotated through the theatre, patrolled busily, lost some good men and eliminated comparatively few of the opposition. There had been no really spectacular raids and in the end the campaign had simply fizzled out. Colonel Anthony Farrar-Hockley, who was General Lea's principal staff officer, made the disparaging remark that the SAS contribution was 'small beer'. To accept that, however, is to ignore the political realities of the conflict as well as the terrain in which it was fought. All the forces involved had their hands tied by the prohibition of waging open warfare on the enemy; otherwise the jungle camps could have been bombed and rocketed by the RAF. The aim was to persuade the Indonesians that the territory of Malaysia would be defended and that attacking it would not be worth their while in the long run. It was only towards the end that the SAS was even allowed to cross the border, yet at the same time their presence there would be denied in public. They were fighting a cat-and-mouse type of war in impenetrable jungle for most of the time.

The imposition of political restraints on their activities was henceforth to form a major part of the history and development of the SAS Regiment. Gone were the glorious days in the Western Desert when David Stirling, Paddy Mayne and the lads could swan around free to shoot anything that moved and then return in triumph to beat up the bars in Cairo. By 1966, 22 SAS was a highly professional force of dedicated men that had found a new ethos and role in life. Although air portable, it was still essentially an infantry unit trained to operate anywhere in the world. In sixteen short years the regular regiment had mastered the arts of fighting in jungle and desert as well as preparing for the ultimate war in Europe. In Borneo they learnt the skills of patient tracking, the silent gathering of intelligence and the need for constant watchfulness. Without them, the higher commanders in the theatre would have been blind in a country where there were few maps and air reconnaissance was useless in penetrating the jungle canopy.

6
Keeni-Meeni and the Radfan

Parallel to the campaign in Borneo, 22 SAS Regiment was involved in fighting in the Arabian Peninsula, specifically the Aden Protectorate, at intervals between 1964 and 1967. The terrain of the two areas could hardly have been more different, yet the same men in the same squadrons and troops coped equally well with both. Many of the SAS had cut their teeth in the Jebel Akhdhar battle, and desert training was standard practice for everyone on a regular basis. It was in pursuit of such training prior to a stint in Borneo that Peter de la Billière's A Squadron was tasked to fly to Aden in May 1964. Before detailing how they became embroiled in fighting the local tribesmen, it is worth briefly examining the background to the situation, which was part of a wider political vacuum in the area.

The Aden Protectorate, as it was then known, lay at the southern tip of Saudi Arabia strategically placed at the entrance to the Red Sea; directly to the north was the Yemen. British interest in the area started at the end of the nineteenth century in the age of the coal-fired steam-propelled battleship. The opening of the Suez Canal had considerably shortened the lines of communication to British colonies in India, the Far East and Australasia, and the need for imperial defence made it necessary to establish coaling stations strategically placed along the main sea routes from Britain. Aden was annexed in 1839 as a colony administered from India, and by the turn of the century a large naval base had been established there. It became a crown colony in 1937, when Britain also assumed a protectorate over some 100,000 square miles of the inhospitable volcanic hinterland. In 1959 the status of the latter was changed to that of a federation of Arab emirates to which the colony of Aden was added in early 1963. As Aden's strategic importance had waned with the decline in seaborne trade, Britain intimated that it would pull out by 1968 to leave behind a stable independent state within the Commonwealth. What followed was the usual tragic saga of muddle and incompetence that characterized Britain's withdrawal from empire during the 1960s.

In the background lurked the spectre of Egyptian pan-Arab nationalism which came to the fore after the débâcle of Suez in 1956. Colonel Nasser's propaganda machine exhorted Arabs everywhere to revolt against both their colonial masters and their traditional rulers. One result was the overthrow of the Imam, the hereditary ruler of the Yemen, in September 1962 by a group of left-wing army officers. As will be seen in the next chapter, a mercenary force led by ex-SAS members successfully brought in support for the Imam, who maintained a civil war in the territory for several years. The immediate effect, however, was the arrival of Egyptian troops in the Yemen together with considerable supplies of weapons.

Inevitably the war spilled over into both the protectorate and Aden town itself. In December 1963 a state of emergency was declared after a grenade attack on the High Commissioner. The military authorities knew that to stabilize the situation they had to gain control of the tribes in the Radfan mountains in the interior, to stop the flow of weapons over the Yemeni border. That was more easily said than done. The tribes were completely at home in that desolate, scorching trackless waste of volcanic rock and their nomadic way of life made them difficult to find. They had been fighting the British for years and even regular bombing by the RAF during the 1930s had failed to subdue them. As warriors they were akin to the Pathans of the North-West Frontier in India and the present-day Afghani guerrillas. There was no possibility of a 'hearts and minds' campaign as all concerned heartily wished to be rid of the British, who by stating their intention to withdraw made it impossible for any locals to co-operate with them.

Attempts to subdue the tribes with the local forces available were doomed to failure and were restricted to demonstrations of force, before which the enemy simply loosed off a few rounds and melted away. The subsequent British withdrawals were hailed on Cairo Radio as magnificent victories for the mountain warriors. Following appeals for help from the Federal government, a motley force was strung together and sent out to Aden. Under the title of Radforce, it consisted of one troop from the 16/5th Queen's Royal Lancers with armoured cars, a troop of Royal Engineers and a Royal Horse Artillery battery, in support of the three battalions of the local Arab infantry under British officers. To them was added a Royal Marine Commando and a company from the Parachute Regiment. The RAF provided a squadron of Hawker Hunter ground-attack jets, some Shackleton bombers and sundry transport aircraft. The aim was to seize control of the Radfan mountains once and for all.

Peter de la Billière was in Aden in April 1964 preparing for a squadron training exercise. He offered the assistance of his men for the planned operation, which was eagerly accepted by Middle East Command. The Ministry of Defence authorized the deployment and the squadron was flown out a month earlier than planned, arriving on the scene in mid-April. They moved up to Thumier, sixty miles to the north of Aden where they established their base for operations and almost at once set out into the surrounding hills to gather intelligence. The object of the campaign was to dominate the commanding heights and thus control traffic along the trackways leading from Yemen. As an immediate aim it was decided to occupy two such heights, known in military jargon as 'Cap Badge' and 'Rice Bowl'. The latter was to be assaulted in a night attack by the Marines while the former was reserved for the Paras, who were to drop into the valley below.

The problem was that the Paras would have to drop blind into undefended territory so it was resolved that the SAS would capture the dropping zone (DZ) in advance. 3 Troop under Captain Robin Edwards was given the task. Selecting a patrol of nine men to accompany him, Edwards set out at dusk on 29 April with some eight miles to cover in twenty-four hours: they would have to lie concealed from enemy patrols during daylight. At dusk the following day their job was to light torches on the DZ and signal in the Paras.

For the first part of the way they were given a lift in Saracen armoured cars up the Wadi Rabwa, but when these came under fire from the commanding heights, the patrol slipped quietly away in the confusion and melted into the night, climbing steadily upwards. Each man was carrying around 60 lbs. in weight including a lot of water, which was vital to stave off dehydration during the vicious daytime heat that could climb as high as 120° Fahrenheit. As they steadily gained height, however, it was discovered that Trooper Warburton, the patrol signaller, was quite seriously ill with a stomach complaint. In spite of assistance from the others who took the radio, he began to fall more and more behind, and it was decided that instead of continuing to a lying-up point near the objective, they would halt for the night in the hope that a rest would get Warburton on his feet. They would stay in hiding in the hills during the day and at dusk walk downhill to the DZ with plenty of time in hand to carry out their mission.

They discovered two aged stone *sangars* (rock shelters) and concealed themselves inside, sending a message back to base informing the squadron commander of their position. Also at Thumier at the time was Mike Wingate-Gray, then second-in-command of the regiment. At dawn the patrol stood to and although there was a village some distance below their position, they were undisturbed. Disaster struck in mid-morning when they were seen by a goatherd, who gave the alarm. He was dispatched with a single shot but the damage had been done and soon a crowd of tribesmen were in position to open fire. The members of the patrol were well protected and they managed to call in an air strike by Hunter jets that strafed the ridge behind the *sangars* with accurate cannon fire. The real problem was that the enemy were bringing in increasing numbers of warriors; the patrol was severely outnumbered, and when dusk fell their air cover would cease. Eventually their ammunition would run out. An attempt was made to fly in a second patrol to relieve them by helicopter but the machine was so badly shot up that it had to return to base.

As Edwards saw it, the only chance was to try to make a run for it and get back to Thumier on foot. The first member of the patrol to be wounded was Lance-Corporal Baker, who was hit twice in the thigh, and shortly after one of the troopers took a stray round. The patrol sergeant, 'Geordie' Tasker, firing a bren from the hip and ably backed by the wounded Baker, dispersed a crowd of the enemy who tried to rush the *sangars*. It was only a matter of time before they would be overrun and any attempt to mark the DZ for the Paras was out of the question. The patrol began to destroy any equipment that they could not carry and the decision was made to break out at 7.30 p.m. under cover of a friendly artillery barrage that had been laid on by base. The intention was to split the party into two groups that could give each other covering fire, but just before leaving they discovered that Warburton was dead, killed outright at his radio set.

The four survivors in one of the *sangars*, led by Edwards, left at the run covered by the remaining four men concealed in the surrounding rocks, Geordie Tasker still blazing away with the bren. In that first headlong rush for cover, Edwards was hit and killed outright, but the other three managed to get behind some rocks, Baker hobbling on his injured leg. Unable to carry the bodies with them they crept silently, hearing the crash of the artillery barrage around the *sangars* they had just left. Their march that night was a heroic feat of endurance. The men were all suffering from extreme fatigue, post-action shock and lack of water, and the two wounded had a hard time trying to keep up. On two occasions they detected parties of tribesmen following them and had to mount ambushes. Clambering over rocky outcrops in the moonlight, dropping down into gullies and ascending steep ridges, constantly on the alert, they finally made it to the wadi where they were met by an armoured car at dawn. By then Baker had collapsed, but his bravery was recognized by the award of the Military Medal.

The general attack on the Radfan had to be somewhat modified and it took several weeks of hard slogging by the main force to impose some sort of control on the area, which at most was tenuous. The tragic sequel to the Edwards patrol was that the bodies of the troop commander and the signaller were decapitated by the exultant tribesmen and the heads publicly exhibited on poles in the Yemeni town of Taiz.

A Squadron assisted for a few weeks in the general operation, seeking out targets for air and artillery strikes, and then departed for the UK prior to redeploying to Borneo. One of their last patrols was in mid-May in an intelligence-gathering role in support of the regular forces, lying up six days in the searing heat without resupply. Once again, the comparatively small force of an SAS squadron had proved its worth to higher command by the value of the information they provided at little cost. The affair of Edwards and Warburton made the headlines in the press, which caused distress to the families of the men and displeased the regiment with its traditional dislike of publicity. The tribesmen were nicknamed the 'Red Wolves of Radfan' by reporters. The regiment reckoned that it had a few scores to settle with them, but it had to wait nearly a year and a half to do so. Borneo took priority, and the SAS still had only two operational squadrons to deploy as well as the normal momentum of training to maintain. Once B Squadron was operational, however, the SAS returned periodically to the area in 1966 and 1967.

A further aspect of the conflict was the insertion of trained Yemeni killer squads into Aden city, where they acted as an urban guerrilla force, assassinating local politicians suspected of being friendly towards the British administration. Foreshadowing to a certain extent the activities of the SAS in Ulster, the regiment became involved for the first time in counter-insurgency warfare in an urban setting. British forces had had a tradition of waging clandestine warfare in plain clothes against terrorists using many techniques that had been developed after the war in Palestine, notably by the redoubtable Roy Farran who had served with 2 SAS Regiment in Italy and Europe. Techniques were further refined during the conflicts in Cyprus and Kenya and documented by General Frank Kitson in *Bunch of Fives*.

In early 1966 A Squadron was back in Aden, ostensibly for training, and Peter de la Billière set up a so-called close-quarters battle school which taught accurate pistol-shooting. He selected a group of his men who, disguised as Arabs, were to sally out in small groups into the town, looking for targets. If prisoners could be taken and interrogated that was a bonus, but essentially the purpose was to meet terrorism by terrorism. These squads became known as keeni-meeni, from the Swahili word for the slithering movement of a snake through the grass. During the early 1960s the SAS had recruited a number of excellent Fijians and they proved particularly suitable for the work as their skin colour was similar to that of the local population. Others who had black hair and swarthy complexions were also chosen.

In all some twenty men were employed on keeni-meeni work, yet the results were meagre. Operating in civilian clothes brought with it the possibility of confusion with the other army and police special squads which were formed at the same time. On one occasion an SAS patrol mistakenly fired on some armed members of the Royal Anglian Regiment.

D Squadron arrived in Aden in January 1966, tasked to patrol the Radfan in an attempt to halt the caravans bringing weapons in from the Yemen. The aim was to establish covert observation posts on the commanding hills to observe movement and then to call down artillery or air strikes on the insurgents. Part of the squadron had been in Libya training for desert navigation with long-range Land Rovers. On arrival they were based at a small outpost called El Milah on the road leading north to Dhala, the traditional trading route from the Yemen. The base consisted of a few tents, a vehicle park and a helipad for the attached flight of Scout helicopters which were to give them limited air mobility. Such was the precarious nature of the British hold on the area that the camp was regularly mortared, and bullets whipped through the screen during one open-air film show.

Operational patrolling was limited to five days: the limit set by the amount of water one man could carry as well as his weapons and equipment. Lofty Large described it as a terrible routine.

> Lying up during daylight, watching for armed bands of rebels in the mountains, then spending all night in an ambush on a likely track ... sleep was practically impossible during the day due to the intense, baking heat and hordes of flies. Then at night, lying in the cool ambush position, sleep tried to overcome us, just when we had to remain alert.

On account of the thirty-year rule, no documentation about the Aden period is yet in the public domain. Lofty Large, however, has given an account of one such patrol in the Radfan as part of a squadron action, seen from the eyes of a troop sergeant. Like many NCOs and troopers in the SAS, he tends to regard most young officers as 'clowns'. In the chapter on Borneo we saw that the regiment found difficulty in recruiting suitable subalterns and that at one time all four troops of A Squadron were commanded by sergeants. From Lofty's account of the patrol one gains the impression that the whole operation was a cock-up from start to finish, yet its CO, Major Glyn Williams, was awarded the MC due to his good work.

During the night of 1 February, two troops were taken up the road in armoured cars and dropped off to make their way up into the hills. Lofty's troop took off on their own to their lying-up position, but through an element of confusion, the other unit was caught in daylight on low ground and had to be helicoptered out. When daylight broke, a third troop spotted a party of twelve armed rebels at too great a range to engage them, and the squadron commander had the previously evacuated unit flown in to intercept. According to Large they were landed too close and got into a scrap in which their sergeant was severely wounded. Trooper Brian Dodd rescued the situation, eliminating two of the enemy with his rifle and turning on another group with a grenade-launcher, an action for which he was awarded the Military Medal. The squadron commander, seizing the initiative, repositioned his remaining two troops by helicopter to cut off the fleeing enemy. Again according to Large, they could not achieve anything as they were not allowed to engage independently, and at dusk they were withdrawn. His final comment was:

I expect the decision to hold us back was more political than military as usual. The whole scene was typical of the situation in Aden at the time. We were committed to pulling out of Aden in the not too distant future. It seemed pointless to put us into operational situations just to build up enemy morale by making us look useless.

Later he wrote: 'What we were doing in Aden remained a mystery to all of us. Ours not to reason why.'

D Squadron remained in the area patrolling in the hills for the best part of two months, before they were sent out to Borneo as the last tour in July 1966 when the war was virtually over. They were replaced in Aden by B Squadron. In April 1967 D returned to the regular grind of patrolling. As the British withdrawal became imminent, the rebels moved closer and closer to the base at Thumier, and the remaining troops were simply holding the 'thin red line'. The brunt of the action fell to 45 Commando, Royal Marines, who were quite capable of operating outside the protection of the base. The SAS had a vital role to play in warning of attacks as they sweated it out in the mountain observation posts.

At the end of June 1967 the British flag was finally hauled down and a very disgruntled D Squadron left for home. Nobody had had much of a chance to cover themselves with glory, least of all the politicians. The squadron had lost a man killed by a sniper, which did little to improve morale. The grim darkness of a vicious Marxist state fell on the local people and the Russians gained a fine naval base. But the SAS had done what was required of them and had sharpened their patrolling skills in a harsh desert environment, which a few years later would stand them in good stead in Oman.

7
Extra-Curricular Activities

In the previous chapter I alluded to an operation that was mounted to assist the Yemeni royalists who took up arms against the Egyptian forces in their country. As the few accounts of this are incomplete it is worth a closer study, especially in the light of recent adverse publicity in the media about ex-members of the SAS raiding people's dustbins. A word often bandied about is 'mercenary' and it is that field of work that is most often considered reprehensible by critics of the SAS. A mercenary is one who serves in the armed forces of a country which is not his own, a typical example being men of the French Foreign Legion. Many ex-SAS personnel have taken service, and still do serve, in the forces of the Sultan of Oman, which is done with the full approval of the British government. The prevailing image, however, is of the 'Dogs of War', and this has some basis in fact, as will be described below. But there are grey areas. A private security firm can be engaged by a foreign power to provide a training team to teach certain skills to members of its armed forces. That is fair enough, and the British government frequently provides such teams from serving members of the Army.

In every society there has always been and always will be a group of soldiers who will hire themselves out to the highest bidder. When one reads about a failed coup or some botched revolution one is almost sure to find an allegation that ex-SAS men were behind it. Yet the number of men from the regiment who have become involved in such enterprises is remarkably few. The problem is that so many professional mercenaries like to claim they have served in the SAS or some other élite force, to boost their importance. Where there is a genuine connection with the regiment, the man concerned has often been thrown out for unsuitability or has come from the pool of Rhodesian SAS who found themselves unemployed when the Ian Smith régime collapsed. 22 SAS Regiment and SAS Group frowns on ex-members of the 'family' getting involved in such activities and those serving in the TA regiments are expressly prohibited from taking paid employment with private security companies.

Until the early 1960s, during the period when the SAS had been exclusively involved in colonial campaigns, there had been no real requirement for mercenary employment, but that era saw the start of the age of the political coup in many Third World countries, as imperial masters handed over their colonies to ill-prepared governments. 'Mad' Mike Hoare's Commando in the Congo was the first white mercenary force to achieve notoriety and it is a fact that his successor, John Peters, had served in the Rhodesian C Squadron of the SAS in Malaya. To understand just how the British SAS became involved and is still frequently blamed for engaging in mercenary exploits, we will examine the career of the founder of the regiment, David Stirling.

In Chapter 1 I discussed Stirling's role in the plans to send an SAS force to China, which was aborted by the dropping of atomic bombs on two Japanese cities. He was made president of the SAS Association when it was founded in 1946, but took very little part in its affairs as he went off to Africa at the same time. It was only during the latter part of his life that he became actively involved, attending reunions and making speeches at functions. During his period in Africa he was the motivating force behind an organization known as the Capricorn African Society which was devoted to achieving harmony between the black and white races and creating a politically stable environment within which the various countries could expand commercially. As in so many of his projects he was far ahead of his time and Capricorn, which had the potential to heal many of the tensions in Black Africa, came to naught.

During his life after the war, David Stirling made, and lost, considerable sums of money, had a great amount of fun and was always an inspiration to his wide circle of friends. As a businessman he was a disaster, but was always intensely patriotic and often vilified, especially by the press, which regarded him as a latter-day Colonel Blimp. He fought and won a number of libel cases, notably against the *Sunday Times*, which in his own words, 'helped to top up his sporran from time to time'.

His first foray into running a mercenary operation got underway in the spring of 1963, when he met a number of old friends who had been involved with SOE during the war and had operated in Albania, as also had Colonel David Smiley who had latterly been commanding the Sultan of Oman's forces. All had also been involved with the Chungking Project in 1945.

This group had become interested in the affairs of Yemen, the large rocky and sparsely populated country that lay between Saudi Arabia and what was then the Aden Protectorate. Yemen was a hereditary monarchy, but in September 1962 a group of officers had seized power, inspired by the pan-Arab brand of nationalism and revolution sponsored by Colonel Nasser in Egypt. The royalist forces and the Imam sought refuge in the mountainous north of the country from where they conducted a spirited resistance against the Egyptian troops who had been poured in to support the rebels. The situation in Yemen was of great concern to the British government, firstly on account of the base in Aden, but more importantly there was the worry that the revolution might be exported north, threatening the oilfields in Saudi Arabia. In conjunction with the Foreign Minister, Sir Alec Douglas-Home, it was agreed that something should be done to help the royalist cause, but that it would have to be on an unofficial basis. French support was enlisted, as the French were keen to clip Nasser's wings.

Stirling got in touch with Brian Franks, the Colonel-Commandant of 22 SAS Regiment, who introduced him to Lieutenant-Colonel Jim Johnson who had until recently been in command of 21 SAS. Johnson was a Lloyd's insurance broker, but he agreed to set up a London base and organize the recruitment of a small force to conduct a reconnaissance on the ground. In fact he set up his office in the basement of Stirling's office in Sloane Street. As leader, they chose Major Johnny Cooper, MBE, DCM. He had finished his career in the SAS in 1960 and had taken up a contract position with the Sultan of Oman at the time when David Smiley was still commanding the forces there. Cooper was summoned to a meeting in Bahrain where he was briefed by the medical officer of 21 SAS and Smiley, who told him to go back and arrange a month's leave of absence from his duties and then to travel to London.

He arrived there on 5 June 1963 and met Johnson and his old commanding officer, David Stirling, who told him that he was to lead a reconnaissance mission of four British and four French soldiers into Yemen to determine the degree of Egyptian involvement. The following day they flew to Paris and had a meeting with French officials at the house of a member of the princely family of Bourbon-Parma, to organize the French side of the operation. The whole affair was mounted extremely rapidly. Cooper was provided with three men from 22 SAS who had been given 'leave' to take part – a weapons expert, a trained medical orderly and a man skilled with mortars. John Woodhouse was commanding the regiment at the time, and Stirling always acknowledged him as the founder of the post-war SAS.

The money to pay for all this came from Saudi sources, which was paradoxical, as Johnny Cooper had spent a lot of time fighting Saudi-backed insurgents in Oman. David Smiley, who had made a study of the situation for the Saudi government, remained the field commander of the mission. Although the team's assignment was ostensibly one of reconnaissance, Stirling naturally wanted action: he came up with the idea of destroying the Egyptian fighters on the ground, in true desert warfare style. He flew off to Aden to organize the discreet infiltration of the team with the aid of the Governor-General, and when the men arrived they were whisked off the airport without having to go through customs or immigration checks. There was a last-minute hitch when the government, enmeshed in the Profumo scandal, told Stirling to call off the mission, orders which he ignored as firm promises had already been made to the Yemeni royalists.

Johnny Cooper and his team of three SAS members and four Frenchmen, disguised as local Arabs, infiltrated the mountains around the capital San'a, travelling by night to avoid the prying eyes of Egyptian aircraft and negotiating minefields. They safely delivered their cargo of arms and ammunition, and met up with the royalist commander, Prince Abdullah bin Hassan, who gave them a warm welcome. He was not too keen, however, on the idea of blazing MIGs littered all over Egyptian air bases; he wanted training and weaponry to do the fighting himself. Cooper and his three SAS colleagues threw themselves into the task with great enthusiasm, finding that the Yemenis made apt pupils in spite of the language barrier. The bren proved to be a popular weapon and the pupils, as natural guerrilla fighters, had a feel for moving over the mountainous terrain.

Their first engagement was a definite victory in an ambush planned and set up by Cooper. He and the team had discovered that the Egyptians dominated only the low ground around the capital San'a and were unwilling to penetrate into the mountain strongholds held by the royalist forces, restricting themselves to air raids. The training team had been harassing the opposition by laying mines and sniping, which provoked a strong response from the enemy. Cooper led a force of his trainees into an excellent ambush position in a wadi and with his men well concealed, waited patiently. Sure enough, a packed column of Egyptian infantry of battalion strength backed by field artillery and T-34 tanks moved into the wadi. Excellent fire discipline ensured that the irregulars waited until the enemy were packed into a pre-selected killing ground before they opened up. Their machine guns cut down the packed ranks of infantry, who promptly panicked. This was com-pounded by the fact that their tanks and then the artillery fired on their own side. The carnage was complete: nearly a hundred bodies were left behind on the battlefield together with a valuable haul of weapons and equipment.

Another operation was a spectacular mortar attack on an Egyptian outpost that was overlooked from higher ground. Cooper and two of his lads loaded a mortar and a good stock of bombs on to camels and during the night slipped into a suitable position. When dawn broke they opened fire, causing such panic that the garrison started firing in all directions. The bombs exhausted, the raiders slipped contentedly away, having helped to damage Egyptian morale and boost that of the royalists.

By that time, however, all the members of the team had outstayed their 'leave' and had to make their way back south into the Aden Protectorate, bearing with them a list of equipment needed by Prince Abdullah, as well as much valuable intelligence. On arrival in London, Cooper was debriefed and asked to return in command of a larger force that Stirling and Smiley were trying to assemble. Eventually almost fifty men were sent in small parties into the Yemen, but only about a dozen of them were ex-SAS. The operation ran on for almost five years, but such were the difficulties in communication that many of the teams were left largely to their own devices. Much of the weaponry was supplied by the Saudis who had originally obtained it from the Americans, so it was paradoxical that the American government was highly suspicious of the British and French presence in the Yemen, which to them smacked of the dreaded neo-colonialism. American policy remained one of *rapprochement* with the Egyptians. Jim Johnson turned to buying arms on the open market, often of East European origin. It was later alleged that he tapped the Israelis, who had a vested interest in tying down Egyptian troops in Yemen. The web that was being woven started to become extremely tangled indeed, especially as one of Cooper's jobs on his return was to organize airdrops of supplies.

Equipped with a powerful transmitter and sacks of gold coins to pay the tribesmen, Abdullah bin Nassar, as he was known, arrived back at royalist headquarters where he met up with the two remaining French members of his team who were military intelligence agents. They set up the radio and started broadcasting back to bases that had been established in Aden and Saudi Arabia, but it seems that Egyptian locating devices detected their position. Early one morning when Cooper had gone down the valley for a walk leaving the Frenchmen near the radio, two Egyptian transport aircraft flew over and dumped canisters of poison gas. One of the Frenchmen as well as dozens of the tribesmen were blinded, and little could be done for them with the facilities available. Cooper's two comrades were evacuated and for the following nine months he was left on his own at Prince Abdullah's headquarters. He spent his time gathering intelligence, training the irregulars and organizing a medical clinic, using supplies sent in by a relief committee that had been set up in London by Lady Birdwood. On the active front he led regular patrols which mined the main tracks used by Egyptian armour and supply convoys, creating as much alarm and despondency as possible.

A further team in the area that did useful work was led by Bernard Mills who had served with B Squadron in the Malaya campaign. On the French side, the veteran Congo mercenary leader Bob Denard became closely involved, delighting in setting regular ambushes to keep his loyal band of tribesmen happy. Certainly the training paid off as the royalists gradually gained the initiative, pinning the Egyptians more and more behind the fortified perimeters of their bases. Cooper began to receive regular airdrops which were initially flown in a variety of chartered aircraft provided by an obscure Rhodesian airline. Later on, it has been alleged, the Israelis took on the job, flying straight down the Red Sea. It was an irony that the good Muslim tribes may have been supplied clandestinely by the supposed arch-fiend, who was doing so largely out of self-interest. Johnny Cooper said that even the shavings used to pack equipment in the crates were imported from Cyprus, and all serial numbers were carefully filed off.

In February 1964 Cooper received reinforcements; a signaller from the 21 SAS territorial regiment and a young ex-National Service officer who had volunteered. Four months later, Cooper was pulled out for a spell of leave and to submit a report. His weight was down to about eight and a half stone: he had been surviving on a diet which consisted mainly of unleavened bread and Lyle's Golden Syrup which was freely obtainable because the local people would not eat it. Unknown to himself at the time, he had contracted tuberculosis, a disease prevalent among the tribespeople that spread through the sharing of eating utensils. He was thoroughly debriefed by the intelligence agencies and after a haircut was flown home, where an unwelcome surprise awaited him as he found himself the focus of media attention.

On 5 July the *Sunday Times* published copies of letters addressed to Johnny Cooper, dating from January and February of that year, including one using the address of Stirling's business premises. It appears that they had been intercepted or purchased when in transit through Yemen, by Egyptian intelligence agents. These letters were the first public sign of the presence of a mercenary force in the area, and naturally the news caused a furore. Other papers picked up the fag-ends from the article and besieged Cooper's house in Essex. He was smuggled out by Jim Johnson's secretary and quickly flown back to the Yemen, where he got on with the job of organizing the airdrops. He stayed in the area until early 1966 when he was withdrawn and returned to the service of the Sultan of Oman.

The whole Yemen operation remains shrouded in mystery. It certainly soured relations between Britain and the USA. One positive effect was that the royalists succeeded in tying down nearly 70,000 Egyptian troops and numerous aircraft, so they were not available to fight the Israelis at the time of the Six Day War in August 1967. The British decision to withdraw from Aden, however, largely negated the goodwill that had been built up by the teams in their relationship with the tribal leaders. The affair blew up from time to time in the media, which retained a strong interest in allegations of mercenary activity. Tony

Geraghty refers to an article in the *People* in August 1967 in which Richard Pirie, who was adjutant of 21 SAS, stated that his office had been used as a recruiting base for mercenaries for Yemen. What is surprising is that he went on to claim that they had been paid by the British government, which of course was vehemently denied. Yet the government certainly knew about the operation, gave it tacit consent and profited from the intelligence gathered, including evidence of Egyptian use of poison gas.

David Stirling, who had been involved only on the fringe of the Yemen operation, had begun to see the need for a trained force to intervene in countries friendly towards Britain whose rulers might be faced by a *coup d'état*. He felt that the withdrawal from Aden coupled with Nasser's obvious ambitions in the area represented a real threat to the Saudi government and eventually the various Gulf sheikhdoms. He had been talking about the potential of the SAS Regiment to John Woodhouse, and when the latter left the Army in January 1965 he became involved with Stirling, who set up a Jersey-registered company called Watchguard International. Woodhouse's first assignment was to go to the Yemen to report on the state of the royalist forces when a cease-fire was declared. At the same time, Stirling was cultivating his contacts in the Iranian government and exploring the chances of obtaining work in Africa.

It is clear from documents reproduced in Alan Hoe's recent biography of Stirling that he intended to command an eventual mercenary force in Yemen. In fact, the proposals never really took off, which was probably just as well. David Stirling leading jeep raids on Egyptian airfields would have caused uproar both in sensitive Arab countries and in Whitehall. The company did operate in Zambia and in Sierra Leone, providing training teams and advising on security matters, but its founder's maverick ways of doing business caused its eventual downfall. Stirling himself was intensely patriotic and quite happy to turn over lucrative contracts to the British government, which in effect meant employment for the SAS. An example was the sending of an SAS team to Kenya to advise on security for Jomo Kenyatta.

But Stirling was quite incapable of keeping a low profile and had little notion of secrecy. Rumours about the company abounded, which made co-operation with Whitehall difficult. Woodhouse resigned as Director of Operations after a series of disagreements and Stirling himself ceased taking an active part in 1972. Before that, Watchguard's dirty linen was extensively washed in the columns of the newspapers, notably the *Sunday Times*, whose 'Insight' team published an article on 18 January 1970 which essentially accused the company of acting against British interests in Africa. That was followed two weeks later by a proposal to publish a further article concerning the Yemen operation which would openly allege the Israeli connection. In self-defence, Stirling put up Jim Johnson to give a series of interviews to Ian Colvin of the *Daily Telegraph* in an effort to 'spoil' the impact of the *Sunday Times* story. On 9 February Stirling wrote to Lord Thomson of Fleet, the proprietor of the *Sunday Times*:

> The story of the British participation in the Yemen which all concerned would have far preferred to remain under wraps, had to be paraded in three articles in the Daily Telegraph in order to avoid the infinitely worse evil of allowing your Insight team to make its claim of Arab-Israeli collusion.

One could argue that if Watchguard had been placed discreetly at the disposal of the British government and had its founder been a less flamboyant character, it might have done well. As it was, its potential was never properly developed, but the idea led to the establishment in the 1970s of a number of similar firms employing ex-SAS men in various aspects of 'private security'. Their activities will be discussed in a later chapter.

The other mercenary groups which hit the headlines during that period had little to do with the SAS. Stirling was involved on the fringes of a plot to spring 150 anti-Gaddafi prisoners from gaol in Tripoli in Libya and thus foment an uprising. The operatives included some French and Belgian ex-SAS personnel, but Stirling's contribution, according to Alan Hoe, consisted of little more than providing names and contacts. In the end, the operation, which became known as the Hilton Assignment after the nickname of the prison concerned, fizzled out when Italian secret service men seized one of the plotters' boats at Trieste.

In 1975 a certain John Banks, who had served briefly with the Parachute Regiment, made the headlines when he openly placed advertisements for mercenaries in a number of British newspapers. The initial brief was to mount sabotage raids from Zambia into Rhodesia and those recruited found themselves in Angola the following year. Only one of them was ex-SAS. He had nothing to do with the activities of the self-styled Colonel Callan, the commander of the group, or the massacre of newly arrived mercenaries.

The SAS disapproves of its members becoming involved in such activities, as does the government. The regiment has, from time to time, conducted operations for and on behalf of Whitehall which cannot be mentioned and it is official policy to deny the deployment of SAS units on such undercover missions. The Yemen operation was of a mercenary nature but received at least a measure of official approval. Some men who have served in the regiment have, upon leaving, hired themselves out for service abroad, often in a training or advisory capacity, but there has never been a huge pool of the 'Dogs of War' hanging around the pubs in Hereford waiting for the telephone to ring – in spite of what certain sections of the media and left-wing politicians wish to believe.

8

Firqats, Adoo and Dhofar

Following the withdrawal from Aden and the winding down of the Borneo campaign, 22 SAS Regiment was without a combat situation, but not idle. John Slim took over command from Mike Wingate-Gray, and under his leadership training continued for any role the squadrons might be called upon to perform anywhere in the world. In 1967 the Guards Independent Parachute Company returned to Britain and after passing selection, many of its members were formally incorporated into the SAS as G Squadron. That brought the regiment back up to its full strength of four 'Sabre' squadrons, as they are known, and provided valuable extra manpower to face future commitments. The empire had practically ceased to exist but a new threat was hovering just over the horizon – international terrorism. Essentially though, the SAS man of the late 1960s was still a specialist infantry soldier with no real training in counter-revolutionary warfare (CRW) techniques although some experience of such work had been gained by those involved in the keeni-meeni squads in the back-streets of Aden. Chapter 9 will discuss the development of the regiment's strategic and tactical thinking during that crucial evolutionary period between fighting classic low-intensity campaigns on the fringes of the empire and becoming the world's élite anti-terrorist force. In the meanwhile, however, there were still threats to Britain's vital interests in the South Arabian Peninsula, which would embroil the regiment in six years of undeclared but nevertheless vicious warfare in Oman. The Oman conflict is of interest in that for the first time a senior SAS participant, Colonel Tony Jeapes, wrote a book about it which was published as early as 1980.

The British withdrawal from Aden had led to the creation of a Marxist-oriented People's Republic in South Yemen which abutted on to the southern province of the Sultanate of Oman, Dhofar. Sultan Sa'id who ruled his territory as a personal fiefdom was seen by many of his subjects as a despot, kept in place by expatriates who ran more or less everything in the country. The Sultan's Armed Forces (SAF) were led entirely by British officers on contract, men like Johnny Cooper who had returned to service in Oman after his escapades in Yemen. As a result there was a state of almost constant rebellion somewhere in the territory, inspired both by tribal feuds and by outside interference. For Britain, and the West in general, the whole Gulf area was a vital source of oil, although at that time the regime of the Shah kept the peace in Iran. Revolutionary Iraq, however, was also in the business of creating trouble among the Gulf states by training and arming guerrilla groups.

It was one such that was the cause of the first deployment of SAS troops in the area since the Jebel Akhdhar campaign. Intelligence reports produced disquieting news that guerrillas infiltrated from Iraq were stirring up trouble among the tribes in the Musandam Peninsula, arguably one of the most strategically sensitive areas in the world. The peninsula is a sharp tongue of land that sticks out between Oman and the United Arab Emirates where the Gulf narrows to form the Straits of Hormuz. In those days the Shah was firmly in control of the other side of the narrows through which the West's oil tankers must pass, but today control is in the unstable hands of the Iranian fundamentalist government. One SAS squadron was sent out from Britain in 1969, accompanied by a troop from the Royal Marines Special Boat Squadron. In what was almost certainly the first operational high-level free-fall parachute drop carried out by the SAS, a reconnaissance troop was inserted from 10,000 feet into mountainous territory. One man was killed when his canopy failed to deploy properly. The remainder of the squadron was landed by the SBS using inflatable Geminis, to patrol the area.

That short and sharp assignment concentrated the minds of senior figures in the regiment on the general situation in the Oman. The Labour government of Harold Wilson, as part of its general defence policy, had announced the intention that Britain would withdraw from the Persian Gulf, which was guaranteed to create further instability in an already volatile area. The election of a Conservative government in the summer of 1970, however, changed the equation in that there was a greater realization of the strategic importance of the area to British interests. If the planned withdrawal was to go ahead, the situation in the Oman had to be radically altered. In July, a palace coup, partly engineered by senior British officers on the spot, ousted the old Sultan and replaced him with his son, Qaboos, a young, intelligent and British-educated man who had passed through Sandhurst. Sultan Sa'id was flown by RAF VIP transport aircraft to comfortable exile in London, where he died two years later.

At the time John Watts was in command of 22 SAS Regiment, and even before the coup he had been working on a plan for deployment of the SAS in the area. In the intelligence and planning cell at Hereford, known as the 'Kremlin', such exercises are carried out all the time, to cover any eventual deployment. Planning at that level requires sound political antennae and an ability to forecast developments. Based on the wisdom garnered from previous campaigns and a realistic view of the political limitations likely to be imposed, Watts and his planners came up with a five-point scheme.

He naturally proposed a military solution, based, however, on the use of a minimum amount of force to avoid alienation of the local population. That was fair enough, as order had to be restored, but it was the rest of the plan that demonstrated the breadth of vision at Hereford. First there was to be a medical deployment into the Dhofar mountains, on the lines of the successful campaigns in Malaya and Borneo that had been waged by SAS medics. This was to be coupled with a practical aid programme encompassing the drilling of waterholes, road-building, sanitation and the assistance of vets to improve farming methods. On the psychological front, efforts were to be concentrated on persuading the rebels to change sides and support the government. Finally there would be an intensive intelligence-gathering operation to provide in-depth knowledge of the opposition.

Straight after the coup, Watts flew out to the capital, Salalah, accompanied by his operations officer and a troop under the command of Captain Tony Shaw. The immediate task was to provide a reliable interim bodyguard for the new Sultan and to make an assessment of the military situation and the needs of the population as a whole. The Sultan's Armed Forces then consisted of a brigade of Arab soldiers led by British officers who were either seconded from the Army or employed on contract. In command of the force was Brigadier John Graham. The air force numbered a few transport aircraft and six Strikemaster jets.

Opposition was centred on the southern province of Dhofar, a mountainous plateau that had become virtually a no-go area for the SAF, which at the time was a defeated force suffering from low morale. The enemy, however, was also in difficulties, a situation which the tactics of John Watts were designed to exploit. The Dhofari tribesmen, who regarded themselves as separate from the rest of Oman, may have had no love for the old Sultan, but they were staunch Muslims. They had established a political party as a backing for their rebellion, known as the Dhofar Liberation Front (DLF). At the same time, over the border in Yemen, another movement was born, the Popular Front for the Liberation of Oman (PFLO), which was essentially Marxist and strongly backed by the Soviet bloc. At first the tribal elders were seduced by the money and arms promised to them in exchange for an alliance with the PFLO, but soon discovered that they were no match for the highly motivated young revolutionaries who were determined to smash the feudal tribal structure. They forbade ritual prayers and in a series of vicious actions executed a number of local leaders who were lukewarm in their support.

The installation of Sultan Qaboos in July 1970 came just at the right time, as he was prepared to offer modernization to the Dhofaris. A steady trickle of men came down from the mountains willing to defect, and one of the first activities of the SAS team was to accelerate that impetus. An intelligence cell was set up and embryo civil aid teams were formed from Tony Shaw's troop and attached specialists. As the emphasis had to be on enabling the Omanis to settle the affairs of their own country, the military specialists became the British Army Training Teams (BATT), who got down to training the local forces. The psychological warfare group produced leaflets offering amnesty to the rebels, or *adoo* as they were known, and these were dropped on to the Dhofar jebel.

John Watts flew back to London after two weeks, armed with an extensive shopping list of urgent non-military supplies such as well-drilling equipment, pedigree bulls and even prize cockerels. The government was eager to help and Taylor Woodrow was contracted by the Sultan to set up a construction team to build a hospital, schools and roads. At the end of 1970 a full squadron of SAS was authorized to deploy to the Oman in secrecy; initially it was to be restricted to training, and forbidden to engage rebel forces head-on. A Squadron, commanded by Major Tony Jeapes, was selected for the tour and finally deployed in mid-February. Jeapes already had some knowledge of the country, where he had won his MC on the Jebel Akhdhar twelve years earlier. He arrived in Oman in January 1971 and found BATTs stationed at the small coastal towns of Mirbat and Taqa. Others were busy with the extensive 'hearts and minds' campaign, organizing medical clinics and the supply of reliable information to the rebels, from an SAS base camp near Salalah.

One of Jeapes's first actions was to form groups of irregular fighters from the ranks of Dhofari tribesmen who had defected to the cause of the Sultan. These were known as firqats, or 'furks' to the SAS men who trained them and grew to respect them as individuals and warriors. Often unreliable, frequently mutinous, they became the backbone of a low-intensity campaign that in the end was to prove victorious. Many regular officers in the SAF, however, mistrusted them and disdained to work with what they regarded as little better than bands of brigands. The first such firqat, which took the name of Salahadin, after the Saracen warrior who fought the Crusaders, was led by a charismatic man from the jebel, Salim Mubarak, for whom Jeapes had great respect. He put Captain Ian Cheshire's boat troop in charge of training the firqat, which was to carry out its first operation towards the end of February. In the meantime, two other bands were in the course of formation. Jeapes well understood the philosophy that it was cheaper to induce a man to join you than to spend money fighting him.

The decision was made to mount an amphibious raid on the small coastal town of Sudh which was a known *adoo* base, as a reasonably soft target to 'blood' the firqat. Two troops of the squadron were involved, Cheshire's and Peter Farran's. They were embarked with the irregulars in a local boat for the night trip along the coast. In a classic example of such an attack they landed while it was still dark and marched overland to lying-up positions overlooking the town, which when dawn broke proved to be empty of the opposition. The firqat moved in and set up a perimeter guard, while their commander assembled the local male population and harangued them for half an hour about the benefits of the new régime. The Omani flag was hoisted over the Beau Geste white-walled fort, and by midday a company of the SAF had arrived to take over control. Jeapes left behind a civil action team and a BATT to complete the garrison of Sudh, which had been captured without a shot being fired.

The job of squadron commander was a busy one which called for a high degree of diplomacy, reasonable fluency in Arabic and endless patience. Besides the responsibility for running his headquarters and supervising the work of four troops, a comparatively young major had to engage in endless parleys over cups of coffee with firqat leaders and local officials, always being careful not to wound any individual's sensibilities. He also had to deal with the brigadier commanding the SAF and local regimental commanders in the field, wheedle flying time from the Sultan's air force and beg weapons for his firqats. There was a chronic shortage of modern self-loading FN rifles and many had to make do with old Lee Enfield 303s. As an example of the comparatively lowly rank of all concerned, the intelligence cell was run by a warrant officer and the man responsible for psychological warfare was a corporal. The troop commanders were officers in their early twenties who not only had to cope with their men, who usually had considerably more military experience, but also deal, in Arabic, with the firqats.

By the beginning of March Tony Jeapes knew he had to carry the war into the enemy's camp by establishing a toehold on the jebel which was where the conflict would be decided. To stay there would require a strong force and a lot of preparation, but he felt that a demonstration of force would help to persuade more of the tribesmen to defect to the Sultan. In an operation reminiscent of the Jebel Akhdhar battle, he chose an area of the escarpment 3,000 feet high leading up from the plain that had no actual pathway. It would entail a night climb by the same two troops and the Firqat Salahadin, who would have to arrive at the top by dawn and eliminate any *adoo* pickets they found there. As a preliminary recce, he sent Peter Farran with a patrol from his mountain troop and six men from the firqat, to discover a practical route to the top. After an exhausting climb in the dark they found themselves just below the summit when the sun rose and were forced to lie up on a ledge for the whole day without talking, cooking or smoking. Farran took out a book and spent the time quietly reading in the blistering heat, as each man tried to find what shade he could without being able to move about. When dusk came they were able to scramble up to the top, where they discovered a suitable position to establish the main force, although there was no source of water.

The main operation was mounted on the night of 13 March with the two troops, and sixty firqat under a new leader, as Salim Mubarak had died. The entire force reached the plateau unmolested and in the morning the squadron commander flew in by helicopter bringing jerry cans full of water as the firqat men had drunk all of theirs during the long climb. The natural SAS habit of water conservation was totally unknown to the tribesmen, who simply assumed that Allah would provide. The force stayed in place for three days with no sign of the enemy, and Ian Cheshire, who was in overall command, decided to move. They ambushed three *adoo* and then rapidly sought cover to wait for the reaction, which came quite quickly. Cheshire had an 81mm. mortar helicoptered in, but the opposition also had one and began a regular bombardment of the position. The problem was lack of water at the site and after several days dehydration took its toll. Airlifting in water would have risked the loss of an aircraft, and although a further group of firqat was sent up, Jeapes decided that his men were too exhausted to carry on and resolved to withdraw the entire force on the twelfth day. They had managed to kill nine *adoo* without loss to themselves and the firqat had demonstrated their ability to fight, which was one of the main objects of the exercise.

Tony Jeapes returned to fighting his other battle for stores and equipment for the increasing number of irregulars who were starting to pour in as a result of the various methods of persuasion that were beginning to work most effectively. He realized that the task was becoming too great for a single squadron of SAS and that it would be necessary to turn over much of the administration of the irregulars to the SAF – thus putting them on a more regular basis. His available force had inevitably become subdivided into various BATT teams attached to individual firqats as well as the civil action teams who were busily running effective medical clinics. It was also clear to him that in order to establish regular bases up on the jebel occupied by permanent forces, he would have to persuade the SAF regulars to co-operate with the firqat, and vice versa. The key to success was to persuade the mountain tribes that their future lay with Sultan Qaboos rather than the insurgents, although the latter were still a force to be reckoned with.

A specific problem was that the coastal town of Taqa was being regularly bombarded by an artillery piece fired by rebel forces from a position somewhere in the mountains, which was proving impossible to locate. Regular strafing runs with rockets, flown by the pilots of the Sultan of Oman's Air Force, were having no effect, and the townspeople were taking casualties. The estimated position of the enemy weapon was on a hill feature known as the Jebel Aram and it was too large an objective for the two SAS troops and two firqats that were available. Accordingly it was agreed to bring in an SAF battalion and to mount a full-scale assault. Commanded in person by Jeapes, the SAS and their irregulars made the usual night climb up the side of the mountain; just before dawn they were right under the summit, exactly where they wanted to be. As the light strengthened, however, they were fired upon by an *adoo* patrol and had to take cover. From then on the operation developed into a running firefight across the rocky plateau. The *adoo* were driven off and the SAF battalion arrived promptly, although it had taken a number of casualties. In such conditions the advantage lay firmly with the *adoo*, who were fighting on their own territory and usually had the advantage of the commanding heights. During the fighting it became obvious that the gun had been withdrawn and eventually its position was found empty. The battle on the jebel continued for three days, and considerable numbers of the enemy were accounted for. One useful lesson learnt was how to operate together: it became clear that the regular SAF were ideal for taking a piece of ground and holding it, while the SAS and firqat men excelled at loose patrolling around the defended perimeters.

The Jebel Aram was the last major operation to be mounted by A Squadron and at the end of May 1971 they started to pack for home while the advance party of B Squadron moved in. Jeapes and his men, the first full SAS deployment of the campaign, together with their support elements, had achieved results out of all proportion to their relatively small numbers. When they had arrived, the Sultan's troops were on the defensive and the civil aid programme existed mainly on paper. Tony Jeapes put his regimental commander's five-point plan into action and in addition had started to raise the firqats as part of the policy to get the Omanis themselves into action. By the time he left, it was the *adoo* who were increasingly on the defensive and suffering from low morale, while the SAF had overcome their fear of the jebel. With two of his four troops spread out in small training and civil aid packets, his remaining thirty-two combat men and their irregular friends had waged war up on the jebel to start the long process of regaining that territory for the new Sultan. In spite of all they had achieved, officially they had not even been there, the Ministry of Defence neither confirming nor denying reports that the SAS had been seen in the area.

Initially, B Squadron busied itself with training the firqats during the summer monsoon season, but planning for the permanent occupation of a base on the Dhofari jebel was well underway, with G Squadron scheduled to join them. The starting date was October, once the rains were over, but as Ramadan was due to start on the 20th, a dispensation was given by the religious leaders to permit the troops to fight on through what was regarded as a holy war against atheistic Communism. Together with five firqats and SAF troops, nearly a thousand men were concentrated, to be led by John Watts, who was coming to the end of his tour as regimental commander. The aim of Operation Jaguar was to capture and hold an old airstrip known as Lympne, and a series of deceptions was mounted to disguise the real target area.

B Squadron, commanded by Major 'Duke' Pirie, was airlifted to a disused oil exploration camp known as Midway and from there a further fifty miles by truck to the base of the jebel, from where the men would have to march to a lying-up area at the Mahazair Pools where there was a plentiful supply of water. Pirie was to lose his life the following year in a traffic accident during an exercise in France. One of his men was Soldier 'I' who formed part of a team operating the GPMG. On the basis, 'All you need is bullets and water', he was carrying 400 rounds of link ammunition draped around his body, a further 600 rounds in his Bergen, four SLR magazines on his belt and three full water bottles plus his own SLR rifle. That was not all, however, as he was also responsible for the tripod mount for the machine gun which he heaved on to his shoulders with the front legs trailing over his chest. He reckoned that the total weight of his load must have been around 130 lbs.

The assault team set off through the night of 1–2 October to seize the strip in what was to become a veritable endurance march. Carrying full Bergens and the necessary weaponry, the men moved in and out of boulder-strewn wadis on a hot sultry night as they ploughed their way uphill. The more lightly loaded firqat men began to flag and many discarded their rations along the track. Several of the participants considered it a far worse march than anything they had encountered during their selection period, especially when they began to run short of water. One man collapsed from exhaustion while carrying no less than three radio sets, and his load had to be distributed among the others. They made it, just as dawn broke, and breaking into skirmishing order fanned out across the barren plateau – which to their surprise was devoid of the enemy. They later discovered that a diversionary raid carried out by Captain Branson's BATT and a strong group of firqat to the south had occupied the *adoo* in the area, causing them to evacuate Lympne. Soldier 'I' wrote of the march, which had lasted twelve hours: 'Each man's thread of life had been frayed through until all that remained were the flimsiest of fibres, held together by the extremes of endurance.'

Safe arrival, however, brought no respite. Major Pirie and the colonel were on the scene directing the building of *sangars* when the first stage of a comprehensive airlift began, using helicopters and light transport aircraft known as Skyvans. They brought in mortars, light artillery, more men and a plentiful supply of water which was desperately needed, but had the effect of breaking up the airstrip. The day proved free of interference from the opposition except for a short, sharp outburst of firing in the afternoon. The following day, John Watts decided to move his force to Jibjat which had a firmer airstrip and was also an *adoo* base. They managed the move quite safely except for another brief firefight and by midday on 4 October were well dug in around the landing ground. The *adoo* were still preoccupied with Captain Branson's force, which they perceived as a far greater threat. They viewed the occupation of Jibjat as just another two-day-up and two-day-down government operation.

But Jibjat was the key to Watt's strategy; stores, ammunition and water were airlifted in during the following two days to consolidate his hold on the position. Jibjat was to act as the base for a two-pronged attack outwards into enemy-held territory on either side of the Wadi Dharbat. Both East Group and West Group encountered heavy fighting over the following five days as they slowly consolidated their hold on the area above the wadi that the *adoo* had reluctantly ceded, withdrawing into the ravine itself. A new base was secured at a place nicknamed White City and was put in a state of all-round defence covered by solidly constructed *sangars*, from which aggressive patrolling by small groups of SAS and firqat was conducted. SAS headquarters moved up to White

City; from here Watts could organize the building up of a fortified position known as the Leopard Line which was designed to cut off *adoo* supply routes inward from the Yemen. The line itself consisted of three strongpoints garrisoned by SAF, from which BATT and firqat patrols could operate. It was not totally impenetrable but it did succeed in sharply reducing the supplies reaching the *adoo*, and the idea of linear defence caught on, as will be seen later in this account of the campaign.

The immediate priority was to establish a civil aid and official government presence up on the jebel, to prove that they meant to stay there. Even though White City was still subject to occasional mortar attack, work was started on the erection of permanent buildings. The Dhofaris themselves began to congregate there with their goats and cattle, and demanded that the government buy them. Soon the bases began to resemble a set from a Western film. Faced by threatened firqat mutiny, Watts had to be seen to do something, so he conceived Operation Taurus. On 28 November several hundred head of cattle were driven across the plateau and down into Taqa on the coast, supported by fighter aircraft and artillery shelling, while the firqat men and SAS fought running battles with *adoo* detachments on the high ground.

At the end of the year, John Watts was due to hand over command of the regiment to Peter de la Billière. He left behind him a vastly improved state of affairs. Jeapes states that Watts felt he had been let down by two of the firqats who had refused to carry on fighting through Ramadan, thus robbing him of an even more complete victory on the plateau. Yet as the architect of the original five-point plan he had laid a solid foundation stone, had fought a careful but successful campaign with minimum casualties and was entitled to the plaudits he ultimately received. A Squadron returned to replace B and G which were exhausted by their month of solid fighting and glad to return for a spell of leave in England.

A Squadron's tour was spent patrolling out of Jibjat and White City, keeping control of the surrounding jebel and watching the Leopard Line, coupled with the ongoing responsibility for running the firqats and the civil aid programme on the jebel. In the spring of 1972 the SAF mounted a major operation along the coast and established a base hard up on the Yemen border at a place named Simba. That marked the start of a far more aggressive attitude on the part of the Sultan's forces which gradually took on more and more responsibility for running the campaign. During the same year the advance party arrived of what was to become the Imperial Iranian Battle Group, later joined by a Jordanian special forces detachment. The Omanis themselves could see the battle turning in their favour, as well as the tangible results of the modernization programme instituted by Sultan Qaboos. This does not mean, however, that Oman had become a sideshow for the SAS, which as we shall see in the next chapter was becoming increasingly preoccupied with the terrorist threat nearer to home. One-quarter of the regimental strength remained committed to the Oman, where further casualties would be suffered.

Life in the Oman was not exactly a picnic for the SAS. Soldier 'I' described the base camp at Um al Gwarif as 'a sandblown dump in the middle of nowhere'. They did their best, however, in spite of the patrol bases up on the jebel being 'dry'. David Arkless, who served with them as an air dispatcher, was impressed with the cuisine:

> The regiment certainly knew how to choose their cooks, because each meal I had at Um al Gwarif was excellent, and each of them cooked by a No. 1 petrol burner and a field oven. On some occasions, when Scouse laid on a curry, he would bring along an Indian cook to make fresh chapattis to add a local flavour. He would wheel and deal with the locals, exchanging some compo rations for fresh food such as the large crayfish he would serve with a salad.

Up at White City and Jibjat, the highlight of the week was resupply day when a Skyvan brought in mail and fresh food, a welcome change from compo stewed up in a mess-tin or the occasional goat shared with the firqat. With typical ingenuity, the *sangars* in which the men lived were fitted out with as many creature comforts as possible. One man who served there told me that he actually sold his *sangar* to a local when his troop pulled out, as it was far more comfortable than the usual Omani roundhouse. Payment was offered in the form of a camel, but they finally settled for a few silver Maria Theresa dollars.

Whichever squadron was on tour, medical work remained one of the most vital contributions to winning the 'hearts and minds' campaign. Pills were dispensed, injections given, basic hygiene was taught, and such complications as botched circumcisions were dealt with. It took a long time for the tribesmen to accept a male medical orderly examining their womenfolk. Tony Geraghty recounts the story of the young girl suffering from a stomach ailment, brought by her mother to one of the clinics. When the medical staff asked whether she had missed a period, her mother replied,

'she has not been with any man'. It was clear to one of the more experienced SAS 'bush doctors' that the girl was pregnant (as she was later proved to be). He reacted by walking to the window, opening it and looking out for a long time. His companion asked, 'Why are you looking out of the window?' 'Well,' came the reply, 'it's a long time since anything like this has happened. In fact, the last time, three wise men came from the east, following a star.'

B Squadron returned in the spring for what should have been a quiet time during the monsoon period. Major Pirie divided up his force, which as usual had to be spread thinly on the ground. Apart from the strongholds up on the jebel there were BATTs to be provided for the coastal towns and support personnel to man the squadron headquarters and the base. A young troop commander, 23-year-old Mike Kealey, was sent with seven men to take charge of the base at Mirbat, a small town on the beach to the east of Salalah. Just outside the town and separated from it by a shallow wadi stood an old stone fort which was garrisoned by a group of Dhofar Gendarmerie, together with the BATT house and the house of the *wali*, the local headman. The whole area was surrounded by a wire fence and at the fort there was a 25-pounder gun, while the SAS team was equipped only with a mortar, .5 Browning heavy machine gun and GPMGs.

They had had a relatively uneventful tour training the local firqat and on 19 July 1972 were starting to pack up for the return trip to Hereford. They had all complained of boredom during their stint at Mirbat; there was little to do but eat, sleep and fight off the flies. Yet unknown to them, a force that has been estimated at 250 *adoo* had been quietly assembling at the edge of the jebel, only two miles away, well supported by mortars and recoilless artillery. Their intention was to secure a propaganda coup by capturing the town, executing the *wali* and then retreating back into the mountains. The PFLO leadership badly needed such a victory as their support was being constantly eroded by defections among the tribes on the jebel. The pitifully small garrison at Mirbat was regarded as a pushover, and mutilated bodies of white soldiers displayed to the tribesmen would reinforce the *adoo*'s waning power. During the night they crept into positions surrounding the small town, with low scudding monsoon clouds obscuring the moon. Just to the north was a small hill, the Jebel Ali, where there was a Gendarmerie outpost. The *adoo* crept up on the unfortunate men and knifed several of them silently, although one managed to fire off a single rifle shot to give the alarm.

The first ranging shots from the mortars woke the men in the BATT house at 0500 hours. The immediate reaction was that it was just the usual long-distance morning stonk which had regularly disturbed their rest, but as the fire increased they ran to their stand-to positions. Soldier 'I' raced up on to the flat roof where the Browning was housed in a *sangar* and fed a belt on to the feed tray, staring in disbelief at the scene in front of his sleep-drugged eyes. 'Two thousand metres away, in the dark foothills of the Jebel Massif, I could clearly see the vivid flashes of six mortar tubes leaping into the night, dramatically illuminating their concealed baseplate positions. Nearer, from the Jebel Ali, the muzzle flashes of incoming machine-gun and rifle fire sparked white-hot holes in the gloom.' The battle that was about to unfold would equal the heroism of Rorke's Drift in the Zulu War, as a handful of SAS men fought for their lives for nearly twelve hours.

Mike Kealey, still wearing his flip-flops, and his corporal, Bob Bradshaw, also raced up on to the roof, while the BATT mortar opened up. Tak, one of the two Fijians, manned the radio, while Labalaba, the other, ran across the open ground to the the gun-pit which housed the 25-pounder. Crouched behind their sandbag parapet the men could hardly hear each other speak over the crescendo of noise that had erupted all around. This was obviously no hit-and-run affair but an all-out assault on the base. Kealey discovered that most of the available firquat had gone outside the perimeter on patrol, and realized that the Gendarmerie who were only armed with old Lee Enfields would not be of much use. The radio crackled and they learnt that Labalaba had been wounded in the chin; grabbing a medical pack, Tak ran from the building and across the open ground towards the fort. A brilliant rugby player, he was going for the greatest try of his life as he dodged and weaved to avoid the fusillade that was poured in his direction. One of the others then got through to Um al Gwarif and, ignoring the complicated coding procedure, sent out the alarm in clear Morse.

Labalaba and Tak fired the 25-pounder at point-blank range towards the wire while the men on the roof held their fire as they watched the mass of *adoo* running across the plain. As they reached the wire, the machine guns opened up and scythed many of them down. Bradshaw and another man, serving the mortar, desperately needed to elevate it further than the mounting permitted, so they took it off and while one hugged it to his chest, the other stuffed bombs down the tube. Kealey radioed for a helicopter to evacuate the wounded Labalaba and for an air strike to break up the enemy concentrations, but he was not optimistic on account of the low cloud ceiling.

Back at Um al Gwarif the cavalry was being assembled. By sheer coincidence, the relieving unit, G Squadron, had been flown in, and although the troop commanders and their advance parties had already been airlifted up to the bases on the jebel, a sizeable rear party was available. When the alarm from Mirbat was raised they were about to move out into the desert to zero their weapons. Instead the trucks were diverted to the airfield and the stores personnel, who had been thinking about a quiet breakfast, ran to the armoury for spare ammunition – 20,000 rounds, which cleaned the place out. Major Alistair Morrison, the squadron commander, took personal command of the rescue party that was liberally equipped with GPMGs, grenade launchers and rifles, as they piled into two Huey helicopters for the dash along the coast.

The helicopter sent to evacuate the wounded had approached the position and one of the SAS ran down to the beach to receive it. He threw a green smoke grenade, but as the pilot came down to the hover, every *adoo* gun seemed to be firing at it. There was nothing for it but to abort, and the man flung a red flare to warn the pilot off, risking his life by standing in the open as bullets whistled around him. Enemy fire then concentrated on the fort; it was bombarded with anti-tank rockets and mortar bombs, as the Fijians fired round after round, the spent cases filling the pit around the body of a severely wounded Omani gendarme. Throughout the heat of battle, Bob Bradshaw continued serving the mortar, giving fire control orders as if on the ranges at Hereford and popping off at the odd target with his rifle.

After about an hour of intense fighting there seemed to be a lull in the enemy fire, as they paused to regroup and recharge their magazines.

Kealey had become worried that that he could no longer get through to the fort or the gun position and that the 25-pounder's rate of fire had slowed down. There followed a tense discussion among the remaining men in the BATT house as all volunteered to go to see what had happened, but in the end Kealey decided that he would make the attempt himself, accompanied by Trooper Tobin, his medical orderly. They had 400 yards of more or less open ground to cover, and as the two figures detached themselves from the building, the lull ended. Weaving and ducking, they ran for their lives and both made it safely, slithering down into the shelter of the gun-pit, where a horrific scene met their eyes. Tak, badly wounded in the back and head, had propped himself against the parapet and was firing away with his rifle. Labalaba, his chin bandaged with a bloodstained field dressing, was firing the gun alone, his giant frame heaving open the ammunition boxes, shoving in the rounds and banging the breech shut. Tobin got to work on the wounded Omani gunner while Kealey, who had discovered another terrified gendarme in the pit, set him to work refilling rifle magazines.

Labalaba probably never felt the Kalashnikov round that killed him instantly, and as he fell back into the pit, Tobin reached over to attend to him. He in turn was caught by another round that smashed his jaw. Kealey and Tak, alone, faced an enemy force that was determined to overrun the fort and capture the gun. With the barrels of their SLRs almost red hot, they coolly fired into the packed ranks of assailants, who responded with grenades – which miraculously failed to explode. Then – just as in a tense film – with the gun-pit about to be overrun, down from the clouds screamed two Strikemasters, fanning out at zero feet and firing their machine guns and rockets. The *adoo* fired at the jets but were soon diving into cover, which took the heat off the fort area momentarily. One aircraft was slightly damaged and limped away, but the enemy had taken a severe beating from which they never fully recovered. That morning at dawn, Mike Kealey had been a young inexperienced officer, but still in the gun-pit he calmly gave orders over a hand radio, directing covering fire from the mortar at the BATT house, while blazing away with his rifle.

As the jets departed, the men on the roof of the house heard firing coming from a new direction, behind them in the town, and assumed that they were totally surrounded. But they were wrong. The two Hueys carrying Alistair Morrison and twenty-three well-armed men had arrived and were methodically clearing the area, helped by the remaining firqat. Two more Strikemasters roared in and, directed from the ground by Bradshaw, loosed off a bomb and rocketed the enemy mortar positions on the Jebel Ali position. More helicopters with G Squadron men and a medical team dropped in, as Morrison's men fanned out to harry the retreating *adoo*. The men on the roof of the BATT house had a bird's-eye view of the enemy streaming back across the plain towards the distant jebel, totally defeated, and below them in the compound, the sad debris of battle. A helicopter landed to take out the dead and wounded, and refusing all help, Tak walked to the open door of the helicopter that would whisk him away to hospital. The body of the great Labalaba, mourned by his friends, was taken away, together with that of Tobin. The stunned survivors could not take it all in, as Morrison and his men set about restoring order.

The defence of Mirbat was honoured by a number of awards, although they were not gazetted until 1976, when the conflict was over. Kealey, who received the DSO for his outstanding bravery and leadership, was to lose his life from exposure in the Brecon Beacons in 1979. Tak received the non-commissioned equivalent, the Distinguished Conduct Medal, and Bradshaw, the Military Medal. Labalaba was awarded only a posthumous mention in dispatches, when surely he merited a far higher decoration. But the SAS has always eschewed what it calls gong-hunting. Although only a small action in a small-scale war, the successful defence of Mirbat broke the back of *adoo* resistance: they were never able to put together such a large force again. In a part of the world where 'face' is all-important, the rebels had been decisively beaten, a fact that was not lost on the tribesmen in the hills. The war as a whole was destined to linger on, and before its conclusion the regiment would lose further lives.

One grave problem caused by the monsoon that summer was that the positions along the Leopard Line could no longer be supplied, and it had to be abandoned. The loss of the line enabled *adoo* patrols to sneak up close to Salalah and fire rockets into the town and the airfield, to prove that they were still there. The essential difficulty remained that of cutting off the enemy supply routes that ran over the border from Yemen, and the Simba position that the SAF had established down the coast at Sarfait on the border had only limited success in achieving this. The *adoo* hated it and regularly shelled it, but it was overlooked by a series of hills, behind which supply convoys could move in dead ground. To hinder shelling of the capital itself, the SAF established blocks across the wadi mouths down which the *adoo* moved from the mountains; these were known as the Diana positions. The success of the Leopard Line, however, led to the construction of the Hornbeam Line which ran forty miles inland from the coast at Mugsayl. This consisted of a continuous stretch of wire backed by defensive positions every 2,000 metres. It was not totally *adoo* proof but only small determined groups on foot and without heavy weapons could get through at night.

During 1973 the squadrons continued to rotate into Oman, training the firqats and manning the old positions up on the jebel, gradually extending their hold over the surrounding areas by establishing new posts, each with a resident BATT and firqat team. The Iranians built up their forces and by the end of that year the SAF had doubled in size, with the Dhofar area becoming a command for a brigadier. In early 1974 Peter de la Billière moved on, having been awarded the DSO for his period in command of the regiment. He handed over to Tony Jeapes, another officer of the home-grown variety destined for higher rank in the future. Much of that year was taken up with searching wadis for arms dumps and keeping the small *adoo* units on the move. One young troop commander, Captain Simon Garthwaite, was killed in an attempt to rescue some of his firqat who had been pinned down by an enemy ambush.

Towards the end of 1974 another new broom arrived, in the person of Brigadier John Akehurst who took over command of the Dhofar area and was the architect of the final victorious campaign. His strategy was to press the enemy slowly but surely back towards the Yemen border. He re-established the old Leopard Line, renamed the Hammer Line, and moved the bulk of the Iranians into an old desert airstrip known as Manston. Their units were keen to fight but tended to operate as a mass, backed up by massive firepower, which was not really suitable for operations against small groups of guerrillas. In December 1974 they started a large offensive south from Manston towards Rakyut on the coast, aiming to seize a large *adoo* stores complex in the caves at Shershitti. The enemy, however, were waiting for them and from well-concealed positions on high ground they pinned down the cumbersome Iranian formations and forced them to retreat.

The caves were a prime target, so it was decided to make a further attempt using SAF troops. The position was difficult to assault as it lay at the top of a long wadi and was dominated by high ground which was easily defended. As none of the local units was available, a battalion was brought down from the north and given a crash course in mountain warfare to prepare them for the terrain they would encounter, in an attack that would be supported by BATT teams and forty firqat. As far as the SAS was concerned this would be a squadron operation led by the commander of B Squadron, Major Arish Turle. They started off on 4 January 1975 and seized a suitable airstrip on the high ground at Defa, but the flying in of stores and additional troops was poorly organized. A further complication was that the firqat showed no real appetite for the fight, but as usual the SAS pressed on regardless. They were advancing through trees that reduced visibility to a minimum and gave a decided advantage to the defender.

The attack on the following day called for one company of the SAF to guard the base while the other three dominated the high ground above the wadi. When that had been achieved, the SAS and the firqat would move into the wadi and take out the caves. That was fine in theory, but in practice it all went terribly wrong. The capture of the airstrip and the heavy preliminary bombardment demanded – according to Tony Jeapes by the firqat leaders – destroyed all element of surprise. The *adoo*, well dug in, were waiting, and when one inexperienced infantry company commander came upon a stretch of open ground, the ambush was sprung. The company was literally cut to pieces; thirteen men were killed and twenty-two wounded. The BATT component with the company then swung into action, led by a lance-corporal, and rallied the dazed survivors, persuading them to start firing back. Turle, back at battalion headquarters, sent his second-in-command, a Fijian sergeant, to co-ordinate the battle from the front, and finally, under a hail of mortar and artillery fire, the *adoo* attack slackened off. The wounded were recovered and the survivors retreated to their starting point to rethink their tactics. No further attempt was made to capture the caves frontally, as a junior SAS trooper came up with the bright idea of bringing up artillery and shooting the enemy out of the position. That was carried out, initially with recoilless guns borrowed from the Iranians, and after a track had been bulldozed, a Saracen armoured car lumbered up to take over. For the rest of the war the *adoo* were denied the use of the caves and system of tracks in the area.

Although the assault on the caves had been a defeat, it had attracted such large numbers of the enemy that the Iranians were able to capture Rakyut, from where a new defensive line was built to cut off *adoo* infiltration along the coastal plain. Gradually the enemy was being prevented from penetrating into the interior and squeezed back against the Yemen border. In a major attack carried out at the end of 1975, the remaining *adoo* forces were pushed back over the border and their supply bases captured, which virtually ended the war, although roving pockets of the enemy still remained a nuisance. The SAS stayed on in Oman until September 1976, carrying on their work with the firqats and running civil aid programmes. The price that had to be paid was not too grievous: during the six years of the conflict, the regiment lost twelve men killed in action and several more permanently disabled. Officially not even there, the impact of the small groups of SAS men had been out of all proportion to their numbers. Without the foresight of John Watts right at the beginning, the coup that brought the new Sultan to power might have been strangled at birth, and an *adoo* victory would have meant a Communist régime astride the West's oil supplies. Even today, the Oman is still a haven for ex-SAS officers and men, many of whom elect to serve in the SAF on contract after retiring from the British Army.

1. Members of the 2 SAS War Crimes Investigation Team in the Vosges Mountains in 1945. Dubbed the 'Secret Hunters' they tracked down those responsible for the murder of uniformed SAS men during the War.

2. A pre-war photograph of Moussey in north-eastern France. Behind the church can be found the official war graves of ten men whose fate was uncovered by the Secret Hunters.

3. Second from right, Lt.-Col. Brian Franks, the founder of the post-war SAS family of regiments. This photograph was taken at a parade in Norway in the early summer of 1945.

4. A trooper of 22 SAS Regiment in full fighting order for service in Malaya in 1957. In the foreground is a typical pack layout weighing 70lbs and sufficient for jungle survival for 14 days.

5.   A typical army base in the Sarawak jungle, accessible only by helicopter. From such centres the SAS patrols along the frontier could be supplied.

6.   Local tribesmen in Sarawak watch as a patrol receives supplies from a helicopter. The SAS ability to befriend the indigenous people where they operate has paid dividends in many campaigns.

7.   Selection in 1975. Lonely figures on a bleak hillside in the Brecon Beacons set out on an endurance march, as they still would today.

8.   Helicopters fly over the barren rocky terrain of the Radfan Mountains, where men of the SAS found conditions among the worst ever encountered.

9.   Morning ablutions for men of A Squadron before setting out on patrol in Oman.

10.   An SAS 'bush doctor' at work in Oman, treating a tribesman with an eye infection. Winning hearts and minds made a significant contribution to ending the rebellion there.

11.   One of the most famous photographs ever taken of the SAS in action. Two hooded figures prepare to blast open a window from the balcony of the Iranian Embassy in London in 1980.

12.   The remains of the van used in the terrorist attack on the police station at Loughall in Northern Ireland in May 1987. The van was ambushed by the SAS.

13. The whaling station at Grytviken on South Georgia, with the wreck of the Argentine submarine *Santa Fe* in the foreground. A mixed force of SAS and Royal Marines recaptured the island in the first victory of the Falklands War.

14. Two wrecked helicopters on the Fortuna Glacier on South Georgia. Only the superb flying of the Royal Navy pilot of the third machine saved an entire troop from death in the blizzard.

15. A WS70 Westland Blackhawk hovers with an LSV. This was a typical method of insertion of light vehicles behind enemy lines in the Gulf War.

16. The epitome of an SAS soldier, General Sir Peter de la Billière, who commanded British forces in the Gulf War, and served in the Regiment successively as troop, squadron and regimental commander and then as Director of the SAS Group.

9
Into the Future

During the 1960s and early 1970s, 22 SAS Regiment and the two territorial units became firmly established and took on more or less the form in which they exist today, having finally evaded the clutches of the Parachute Regiment and occasional threats of disbandment. The SAS also developed its own identity, ethos and set of tribal customs during that period when it remained an élite infantry unit, confounding the Queen's enemies in Borneo and Aden, and, in the case of Oman, confounding the enemies of one of the Queen's friends. It was the rise in international terrorism and the campaign of violence in Ulster that was to change role of the regular regiment, and ultimately to propel it into the public limelight for the first time. Until that time the SAS was not a secret organization, although naturally it shunned publicity and at times it was in the government's interest to play down the regiment's activities, as in Oman. The beige beret was openly worn in public when the occasion warranted it; every year, for instance, members of 21 SAS in full uniform mounted guard in the forecourt of Burlington House in Piccadilly for the opening of the Royal Academy summer exhibition – a tradition that maintained the link with their original identity as the Artists Rifles. I can well remember when driving along the A27 to the north of Portsmouth that the drill hall of the detached squadron at Cosham had a large sign stating that it was the headquarters of an SAS TA unit.

In a previous chapter I described the birth pangs of the post-war regiment and the difficulty it faced in becoming accepted by the military establishment. In the early 1960s a permanent headquarters entity was established as a directorate to oversee all three regiments. Initially an appointment for a full colonel, this was later changed to a brigadier, with the title Director SAS Group, based in London. One of the earlier incumbents was Colonel John Waddy whose original mind contributed a great deal in developing new roles for the SAS at the end of the era of colonial wars. The prime role of all three regiments in the 1960s, however, was to prepare for the third world war scenario in Europe, so much of the training for the TA was concentrated in Germany, Denmark and Norway, with occasional exercises elsewhere. The director represented the regiment at senior level and co-ordinated policy within the Ministry of Defence.

After its brief sojourn in Malvern, 22 SAS moved to Bradbury Lines in Hereford in 1960, which was then a wartime hutted camp without any particular security precautions. It was not until 1979 that work started on the construction of permanent buildings. In those early days the selection centre was based at Dering Lines in Brecon, run by a captain and three NCOs. We have seen how the remaining two squadrons became three with the reforming of B during the Borneo confrontation and the addition of G in 1967. C Squadron, although still considered part of the SAS 'family', ceased official relations with Hereford when Rhodesia declared independence in November 1965. Within the squadrons themselves, troop specialization became the norm, with a mobility, free-fall, mountain and boat troop in each. The troops were split into four four-man patrols, a basic structure that is still applied today. Each patrol included a specialist signaller, a medical orderly, a demolitions expert, and often a linguist. Another basic principle that became enshrined was cross-training, with each individual being able to take on the job of everyone else, and each troop studying the specialities of the others.

A brilliant succession of commanding officers built up the regiment during the 1960s, starting with John Woodhouse, the 'founder' of the post-war SAS, which no longer had to look outside for its leaders. The officer problem was essentially at junior level as it was difficult to find sufficient subalterns prepared to take time out from the promotion chains of their parent regiments to accept the inherent risk involved in passing selection. The high failure rate, on average 70 per cent, deterred many from applying. For those who passed there was the reward of early promotion to captain and a three-year tour as a troop commander, but for many young officers it was a difficult transition to make. The newly badged captain found himself in charge of a group of men, many of whom were older than himself and certainly far more experienced. Among the 'other ranks' in the SAS there has always been a traditional suspicion of the officer class, who tend to be referred to as 'clowns' or 'Ruperts' – until they have proved themselves. Rank does not confer status in the regiment; only ability, and hence acceptance by those an officer is called upon to lead. The ultimate accolade is when the 'sir' is dropped and the term 'boss' used instead. There are no batmen, and on active service no comfortable mess into which to retire. Officers and men drink from the same tin mugs, perform their bodily functions in close proximity and share the same damp, soggy holes.

Many of those who made the grade as troop commanders, however, left after three years, bitten by the SAS bug and with the ambition to return as a major commanding a squadron – and perhaps even aspiring to command of a regiment. It has been said that an SAS career can be a bar to promotion for an officer, yet several have reached high rank, notably Peter de la Billière. He commanded successively a troop, a squadron, the regular regiment and SAS Group, before his appointment in the Gulf War which made him a household name and a full general. Both John Watts and Tony Jeapes reached the rank of major-general, having started off as troop commanders. The system of officers doing tours of service with the regiment, rather than becoming permanent fixtures, ensures a constant influx of new ideas and prevents the sort of mental stagnation that can sometimes infect an infantry or armoured battalion. Shortage of officer and other-rank recruits together with the high wastage rate during selection has from time to time led to calls for a lowering of standards, which the SAS has stoutly resisted. It was regarded as preferable to have a troop commanded by a senior NCO rather than an unsuitable officer.

As the SAS matured during the early 1960s, a basic pattern of other ranks also became established. Volunteers for selection came from within the ranks of the Army and were normally in their mid-twenties. If accepted for service in the regiment they had to drop down to trooper, regardless of rank in the parent unit. Initially they served a three-year tour and, if still acceptable, could stay on as permanent cadre, thus ensuring an element of continuity.

The previous chapters have concentrated on the campaign history of 22 SAS, but although on average only one sabre squadron at a time was committed, the others were not idle. The regiment has always emphasized training: most of its members are continuously engaged in polishing old skills and learning new ones. So how did an SAS man spend his time? During the period in question there was always a significant number of men detached for duty as permanent staff instructors with the two TA units, which meant a tour of one or two years away from Hereford. There was a call from various friendly countries for specialist expertise, which meant frequent trips abroad training presidential bodyguards or foreign army units. Others were sent as either instructors or pupils to specialist warfare schools in Germany, or were assigned to exchange postings with the American special forces or overseas SAS units. A man could also find himself on innumerable courses both within and extra to his own speciality. There were exotic languages to be learnt and specialist medical skills to be practised, new methods of advanced signalling to be acquired and new weaponry to study.

In addition to individual and patrol training there were frequent squadron tours and exercises. As mentioned above, the prime wartime role was in support of NATO forces and thus the regiment participated in the regular major manoeuvres in northern Europe. At first mobility troops took their Land Rovers to Libya, but when the kingdom there was overthrown by Colonel Gaddafi, Sharjah in the United Arab Emirates, and Jordan, became favourite venues. Boat troops often trained with the Royal Marines Special Boat Squadron. Detachments went to Kenya and Belize for jungle warfare training while others climbed mountains in Norway.

The territorial regiments benefited from the formation of a group directorate: they grew more professional in their approach, and their selection and training systems became integrated. During the 1960s and 1970s, however, there was a certain amount of friction between them and the regular regiment, the members of which tended to look down on the territorials as amateur soldiers. Men from 22 SAS disliked being attached to them as instructors, and were regarded at times by the TA as overbearing and condescending. Yet TA soldiers consistently did extremely well in NATO competitions, beating the regulars on many occasions. Some of the more hide-bound regulars even resented the fact that TA men wore the same insignia, badge, beret and wings as they did; they viewed the part-timers as a form of second-class SAS – which was quite untrue. Those who elected to serve as volunteers went through an equally rigorous selection process and further training, all of which had to be done in their spare time. Many sacrificed holidays to attend courses and participate in exercises abroad.

21 SAS, although firmly based in London, extended its recruiting area by forming detached units in Hertfordshire and Hampshire. 23 SAS expanded its range from Birmingham by establishing formations in Yorkshire and Scotland. In 1967 there was a wholesale reconstruction of the Territorial Army which did not seriously affect the SAS volunteers, but it did mean that a number of units disappeared or were reduced in size. From among the various signals units that were to be disbanded, volunteers were sought to form 63 SAS Signal Squadron (V), whose role was to provide a forward and rear base communications facility for the two regiments.

The essential change of emphasis for 22 SAS occurred during the late 1960s in the quiet period between the campaigns in Aden and Oman. The commanding officers of that period were faced with the need to 'sell' their services, just as David Stirling had done in the Middle East in 1941, and their thoughts turned to the world situation in general. The late 1960s had witnessed the start of international terrorism on a large scale and the spectre of governments giving in to terrorists' demands, powerless in the face of threats. In Britain the police were neither trained nor even entitled to undertake paramilitary-style operations on the mainland, and the various intelligence-gathering organizations had no comparable military arm. A hesitant start was made when a close quarter battle (CQB) training facility was initiated at Hereford, the syllabus of which owed much to experience gained in Aden with the keeni-meeni patrols. The purpose was to train body-guards, mainly for foreign potentates, although from time to time the regiment did provide marksmen for duty in British embassies in particularly threatened locations. CQB-trained teams from Hereford roamed all over the world imparting their skills, which had been taught in a specially constructed house where they had learnt to shoot in a confined space.

Minds became even more concentrated as a result of the murder of Israeli athletes at Munich during the Olympic Games in 1972. Eight members of a Palestinian organization known as Black September broke into the Olympic village, shot two athletes and took nine hostage. They demanded the release of various prisoners and an aircraft to take them to Cairo. The German government was taken totally by surprise and after lengthy negotiations appeared to accede to the demands. The terrorists were taken to a military airfield together with their hostages in two helicopters. When the helicopters landed and in poor visibility, police marksmen opened fire from too great a range. The whole operation was bungled and the terrorists blew up both the helicopters and the hostages.

Perceiving the need for a trained team to deal with such a situation in future in Britain, the government authorized the establishment at Hereford of the Counter-Revolutionary Warfare (CRW) Wing, which was based on the CQB facility. Initially consisting of one officer and four instructors, it was tasked to train a team of twenty men drawn on a rota basis from all four squadrons. At the same time, an intelligence database was compiled of all available information on terrorist organizations, and an intense study was made of new weapons for the embryo unit. Later chapters will deal with the development and deployment of the CRW teams and discuss how their tactics were refined in the face of the ever-increasing sophistication of the potential threat.

Apart from purely military activities, members of the regiment made names for themselves as a result of various feats of endurance. The Devizes to Westminster canoe race was a popular event in which teams from 22 SAS and the TA regularly competed. Free-fall parachuting in this country was largely developed by the regiment, and in 1965 a team set a new British altitude record. Many SAS soldiers do not in fact enjoy parachuting, regarding it purely and simply as one of a number of ways of getting to where they have to go. Others helped introduce free-fall techniques as a civilian sport in their spare time. One such was Sergeant Michael Reeves, who in 1967 was spending a weekend at the Staffordshire airfield known as Halfpenny Green, supervising a group of novices who were making their first jumps with a normal static line attached to the aircraft. As one man left the aircraft something malfunctioned and he was left dangling below on the end of the line which had failed to open his canopy. Reeves had to do some very quick thinking – it was quite impossible for a landing to be made with the pupil hanging underneath. Attaching his own free-fall chute he climbed down the man's line and clasped him firmly with his legs, as the pilot circled over the drop zone gaining height. Reeves then hacked through the line with his knife and as the two of them fell free, he pulled the release handle of the pupil's reserve canopy. It snapped open. Although this could have carried the weight of both men it would have entailed a very heavy landing. Reeves let go of his charge and floated away in free fall to gain space before opening his parachute at the very last minute. He was awarded the George Medal for that act of bravery.

Another SAS soldier, Corporal David Smith, was awarded the British Empire Medal in 1969 for an extremely hazardous mountain rescue. He was with a group of climbers of mixed ability in the Italian Alps, commanded by a young Royal Engineer officer, Lieutenant Elliott, when a rock fall badly injured one man. The following passage is quoted from the citation in the *London Gazette*:

> Cpl. Smith with Lt. Elliott evacuated the injured man, under the most arduous circumstances, to the summit. This climb of 200 feet took two and a half hours to accomplish. With Lt. Elliott, he then descended for help down a strange route across ice and snow slopes, which he well knew to be in a most dangerous state. He acted throughout the events after the accident with a steadiness and coolness of judgement far beyond that expected of his rank.

The two most famous SAS mountaineers are 'Brummie' Stokes and 'Bronco' Lane, who were members of a joint British and Nepalese Armies expedition to Everest in 1976. They formed the final party for the assault on the south summit of the mountain, which they managed to reach. On the way down they realized that they were not going to reach the safety of their tent and had to bivouac in the snow. Both men nearly died of exposure that night; only their indomitable wills and incredible fitness kept them from slipping into a coma. A relief party found them in the morning. Both were suffering from frostbite, and Stokes had the additional affliction of snow blindness. It took four days to help them down to the base camp, where a helicopter rushed them to hospital. They truly had dared and won.

No less incredible are the feats of several men who have braved the oceans. The fashion was started by John Ridgeway and Chay Blythe, who were the first to row the Atlantic in 92 days. In 1969 Trooper

McLean made a solo crossing on a diet of sardines and curry in 72 days, and in 1982 he sailed the world's smallest vessel, only 9 feet and 9 inches long, across the same ocean. Lance-Corporal Hornby even attempted to row the Pacific single-handed from Japan to Vancouver. Over the intervening years, Chay Blythe's name has become synonymous with long-distance ocean yacht racing, both solo and with full crews.

The late 1960s and early 1970s may have been a period of transition for the regiment, but the new interest in counter-terrorist activity did not mean that general military standards were allowed to drop. It is a fact nevertheless that the end of the disengagement from overseas territories meant that British forces were no longer required to fight a series of brush-fire wars in Third World countries. An exception was the Falklands War, but that was a one-off affair that nobody expected to happen – and the fall of the Soviet bloc was equally unexpected. The remaining chapters bring the story of the regiment, as far as it can be told, up to date, as it became sucked into the fog of Northern Ireland and learnt to cope with the ever present threat of terrorism. Inevitably, public perceptions of the SAS were to change, reflecting to a large extent the polarization of views within British society. Previously, very few people had even heard of the SAS, and to those who had, it was a small élite army unit. But as a result of 'coming to the aid of the civil power' in the British Isles, members of the regiment became far more subject to the scrutiny of journalists, many of whom were distinctly unsympathetic. Epithets in the left-wing press, such as 'Maggie's Butchers', were one side of the coin, counterbalanced by jingoistic headlines in some of the tabloids every time the SAS allegedly went into action. In previous years nobody had worried if a few terrorists, freedom fighters, insurgents or guerrillas had been gunned down in some distant land. The shooting of people in Belfast or Gibraltar became somehow different, depending upon which side of the political divide one stood. The more anonymous the regiment tried to be – and this was forced on it by the need to protect its members and their families – the more the public appetite for information was whetted.

10

The Ulster Commitment

This chapter cannot pretend to be a definitive history of the conflict in Northern Ireland, nor of the involvement of the SAS there. For obvious reasons, notably the personal security of those concerned as well as restrictions imposed by the lack of solid information, the full story will only be told by a later generation of historians. I will not be breaking any confidences, however, by recounting in general terms what is known of SAS activity in the province, in an effort to set the record straight. In the Republican media, the SAS has been held responsible for just about every crime committed, and blamed for all sorts of unaccounted-for bodies that have been found. In *The SAS in Ireland*, Raymond Murray writes, 'The history of the SAS in Ireland since 1969 is not merely one of intelligence-gathering. It is a history of torture, kidnapping, unjustifiable killing and murder.' This is pretty strong stuff, so I feel justified in examining that and similar claims.

During the 1960s there was a strong civil rights campaign in Northern Ireland, where for many years the dominant Protestant community had manipulated the election system to the detriment of the Catholic minority. Those protests by and large were supported by the majority of people in mainland Britain, and as the situation deteriorated into a state of imminent civil war between the two communities – the protestors on the one hand and the Protestant-dominated police force on the other – a reluctant decision was taken in 1969 to send troops to the province. There they were openly hailed as saviours by the Catholics, who gave them cups of tea as they patrolled the streets and bleak housing estates of Belfast and Londonderry. In August 1969, the uniformed D Squadron of 22 SAS were sent quite openly to Ulster, and were based at Bessbrook in South Armagh. They paraded at the grave in Newtownards of the legendary wartime commander of 1 SAS Regiment, Lieutenant-Colonel Paddy Mayne, DSO and three bars, and otherwise patrolled the countryside looking for evidence of Protestant gun-running; they found none. A number of photographs from that sortie show the men wearing their berets and driving in their standard long-wheel base Land Rovers. Soon involved in the war in Oman, the regiment found itself unable to spare time for Northern Ireland, and it was only when that conflict ended that SAS troops returned there at the behest of the government.

The whole story of the conflict in Ulster has been dogged by controversy, culminating in the Stalker inquiry into an alleged 'shoot to kill' policy, which was only indirectly concerned with the SAS. Successive British governments and secretaries of state have wrestled with a seemingly insoluble problem – that while a small number of determined terrorists can totally stymie all attempts to impose law and order, the intransigence of the local politicians makes an equitable settlement appear impossible. Ulster is not some distant Third World country struggling out from under a colonial yoke; it is an integral part of the European Community in which a form of civil war is being waged over issues that are to a large extent left-overs from the seventeenth century and even earlier. On the ground, the theory is that security is a matter for the local police force, the Royal Ulster Constabulary (RUC), yet a force of some 15,000 British troops is constantly deployed in the province, fighting what would appear to be an undeclared war against a hard core of about 200 paramilitary terrorists – who naturally regard themselves as freedom fighters.

When the conflict escalated during the early 1970s, the main problem faced by the security authorities was lack of hard evidence about the main enemy – the Provisional IRA (PIRA, in army jargon). At that time the various Protestant paramilitary bands were seen as less of a threat as they tended not to attack the security forces. A number of agencies became involved, and one of the more distressing aspects of the whole Ulster story has been the constant bickering between them. There was a migration of intelligence experts to the province, which inevitably resulted in overlapping competencies and rivalries. The Army naturally needed its own sources of information, so set up an extensive intelligence-gathering operation, while at the same time, MI5 arrived on the scene. Affairs in the Irish Republic were monitored by the Secret Intelligence Service (SIS or MI6) which, generally speaking, did not communicate easily with anyone else. Not to be outdone, the RUC greatly expanded its own Special Branch. They had the advantage of years of experience on the ground, but the web of family and religious ties in Ulster led to mistrust on the part of the Army – which has never truly understood the tribal structure of the local society.

Much of the confusion that has led to the SAS being accused of covert activities in the province, long before members of the regiment arrived there as part of the general order of battle, seems to stem from the Army's efforts to involve itself in clandestine operations. Desperate to penetrate the inner reaches of the PIRA, the Army 'turned' a number of Republican prisoners by persuading them to work for the British as undercover agents in plain clothes. Known as the Military Reconnaissance Force (MRF), and locally as the 'Freds', they were run from Holywood Barracks in Belfast. Their job was to identify their erstwhile comrades while driving around in unmarked cars; few survived long enough to enjoy a comfortable old age. The job of running the ex-IRA men was given to soldiers who volunteered for plain-clothes work and were put through an intensive course in covert operations. Part of that training was carried out by the SAS, but the pupils remained separate, and after their tour of duty returned to their original regiments. IRA paranoia, however, preferred to imagine the hand of Hereford in everything to do with the MRF, and it continued to wage a dirty war of increasing ferocity between 1972 and 1974. A further reason for the confusion that clouds this period may well be the status of SAS officers, which the IRA has never properly understood. A man may well have served a tour as a troop commander with the regiment and then, in the normal course of his career, have been posted to intelligence duties in Northern Ireland. That does not make him a member of the SAS although he may remain tarred with that brush. The fact is that in the early 1970s there were simply not enough officers or men in the regiment available for such plain-clothes duties.

A further weapon in the Army's undercover armoury was the deployment in 1974 of 14th Int. (Intelligence Company), a volunteer force designed to gather intelligence about the enemy. Operating in plain clothes they were also partly trained by experts from Hereford. Together with the MRF 14th Int. was the creation of Frank Kitson, the leading low-intensity warfare expert, who was then commanding 39 Brigade based in Belfast. The IRA tendency has always been to blame the SAS for the activities of 14th Int. squads and individuals, which certainly testifies to the power of legend and mystique. It is not clear how the myth of the omnipotence of the SAS was planted in IRA minds, as in 1969 the unit had received virtually no training in counter-terrorist warfare and in the following years was mainly deployed overseas. During the early 1970s the regiment was certainly developing new skills, but these were hardly being publicized.

There is some evidence that an SAS detachment was deployed for a short period in 1974 to cope with an upsurge in IRA violence coupled with a lack of skilled volunteers for service with the Army's clandestine units. According to Tony Geraghty, the men involved were nominally 'returned to unit' and posted to the province for plain-clothes duties, while at the same time officers with experience in the regiment were employed on intelligence tasks. This is a particularly opaque period in the history of the conflict as both sides escalated the dirty war. In August 1974 a certain Patrick McElhone, who was not known to have had any terrorist connections, was shot dead in a field in County Tyrone by a patrol from the Royal Regiment of Wales. He had been arrested and was reportedly killed 'while attempting to run away'. The soldier responsible was tried for murder and acquitted, which prompted the IRA to claim that McElhone had been executed by a member of the SAS secretly attached to the unit.

On 7 January 1976 a statement from 10 Downing Street announced that elements of the SAS Regiment were to be based in South Armagh for 'patrolling and surveillance tasks', and it was emphasized that they would wear uniform and carry normal-issue weapons. During the following days there was intense speculation in the press about their role, and opinion was coloured, both in parliament and outside it, by the right versus left conflict. In Ulster itself the Army generally welcomed the new initiative but the RUC certainly did not: they felt it was both a slight on their own efficiency and a further attempt by the mainland to take control of the war against the terrorists.

The decision to send in the SAS was essentially a political one, which dictated the publicity surrounding the deployment. Public opinion had gained the impression that the IRA could kill British soldiers with impunity in the border area of South Armagh, and there had also been a spate of gruesome sectarian murders during the latter part of 1975. The government of Harold Wilson was under pressure to be seen to be doing something, yet many of those involved in the conflict felt that their job was to win over the hearts and minds of the local population rather than let loose a bunch of trigger-happy hoodlums. Certainly, the initial use of the regiment was plagued by the lack of understanding of their capabilities on the part of senior army commanders, who insisted on sending them out in patrols of eight to ten men.

The first party to leave Hereford consisted of only a dozen men, one of whom was Soldier 'I', who in his remarkably frank memoirs summed up the essence of the 'other ranks' attitude to service in Ulster:

Belfast. The home of barricades, bombs and marching bands. The graveyard of the professional soldier's ambitions, the career charnel house of the military intelligence officer. We were heading into the gutters and backstreets, bowed under the weight of bergens loaded to overflowing with Whitehall edicts and the ten commandment Rules of Engagement. We were to face an opposition unfettered by constitutional laws and diplomatic niceties. It seemed we were completely pinioned, like men buried to the neck in sand, watching the rising tide of political confusion, intelligence confusion, military confusion and legal confusion. Belfast! A nervous breakdown just waiting to happen.

Although Soldier 'I' initially seems to have spent some time in Belfast, the detachment was sent to Bessbrook to form the advance party for the rest of the squadron some weeks later. The numbers finally involved were about sixty operatives plus support – nowhere near the 150 claimed by the IRA. When properly established the unit reverted to its normal pattern of four-man teams and instituted a programme of covert observation throughout the South Armagh area. Even the chain of command was unclear in those early days as the squadron was at first placed under the lieutenant-colonel commanding the battalion on the spot, who probably had little knowledge of their abilities. One of the few pieces of evidence concerning this period is to be found in an interview which the journalist Simon Winchester carried out with a senior SAS officer whom he met on a train journey. This was published in the *Guardian* on 11 December 1976. The officer stated that the SAS had been in and out of the province between 1972 and 1975 on quick jobs, and commented that in the 1976 deployment they had stopped patrolling with the resident battalion because of low morale.

The first blow was struck on 12 March when a certain Sean McKenna, who had already been interned for three years and was known to army intelligence as a leading IRA operative, was kidnapped allegedly from his home just south of the border in the Republic: grabbed by two men from his bed, made to dress, then hustled back over the border where he was handed over to an army patrol. He was subsequently tried for a string of terrorist offences and sentenced to twenty-five years in prison. At the trial it was stated that a patrol had found him stumbling around apparently drunk, north of the border, rather than that he had been lifted in the Republic, but wherever he was caught the fact is that he was arrested, when an SAS unit could as easily have killed him and left the body in a hedge.

About a month later the first fatal shooting of a suspect occurred. This was to set the pattern for a series of similar incidents in which neither side was prepared to tell the whole truth – for obvious reasons. Peter Cleary was admitted by the IRA to have been a staff officer in the first battalion of their South Armagh Brigade and the security forces wished to question him about a number of terrorist incidents. As a result of an intelligence tip-off the Army learnt that he was to visit the home of his fiancée, just north of the border. At the subsequent inquest the SAS troop commander stated that he had been ordered by his commanding officer to arrest Cleary, so the house had been placed under covert observation. When the suspect crossed the border and was seen to enter the house, he was arrested. It was also said that when he was taken outside while the patrol waited for a helicopter to lift them out, he lunged at one of the soldiers, who shot him. The IRA of course claimed that Cleary had been murdered by the SAS.

The next incident severely dented the image of the SAS Regiment and to reinforce the view prevalent among many senior officers in Northern Ireland that the Prime Minister had saddled them with a gang of cowboys. It also caused severe embarrassment to Her Majesty's government. Late in the evening of 5 May 1976 two men in civilian clothes driving a locally registered car were arrested at a police checkpoint some 600 yards inside the border of the Republic. They claimed that they had made a map-reading error and assumed that they would be released, since in many places the border is not clearly defined. In the meanwhile, two more cars containing members of the SAS, who had set out to find their friends, ran into the same checkpoint. The Gardai now had eight members of the British Army, three vehicles and an impressive collection of weapons in their custody. They took their haul to the police station in Dundalk and then to Dublin, where the men had to appear in court charged with firearms offences. Released into army custody on bail, the eight, one of whom was a Fijian, were formally tried a year later under false names. Acquitted of possession of firearms with intent to endanger life, each was fined £100 for having unlicensed weapons.

The affair received widespread publicity and helped to boost IRA claims that the SAS in the border area was a law unto itself. In a history of the regiment it is impossible to go into detail about the legality of operations in Northern Ireland, about which a number of useful books have been written. However, it is worth considering some of the restraints governing the activities of the special forces, which in theory are there 'to aid the civil power'. Killing the wrong person, especially an unarmed civilian, provoked an unfortunate political backlash.

Both soldiers and police in Ulster are bound by the same laws as civilians, especially concerning the use of force. The onus is placed on the man who actually pulls the trigger rather than the person who issues the order to fire. The fact that a German soldier on trial for war crimes claimed that he was 'only obeying orders' did not save him from being found guilty. This has naturally caused resentment among SAS men who have found themselves in the dock, who believe that they have been placed in an impossible situation by the 'powers that be'. They are highly trained soldiers, specialists in the rapid elimination of their enemies, yet they are sent into a conflict with one hand tied behind their back. For its part, the Army knows full well that if soldiers are prosecuted for their actions there will be a severe crisis of morale in the ranks, and so it does its best to confuse the issues before the courts or coroners' inquests. Yet the authorities desperately need to ensure that justice is seen to be done in order to claim the moral high ground: that they operate within the rule of law – while the IRA does not.

The rules of engagement in Ulster are laid down on the so-called

Yellow Card which is issued to all soldiers serving there and which stresses that firearms should only be used as a last resort. In theory it is established that a suspect must first be challenged unless an engagement has already started, and that opening fire is justified only if a suspect is committing or about to commit an offence likely to endanger life. Experience has shown that it is often difficult to convict members of the IRA simply by arresting them, unless irrefutable evidence of intent can be produced. They have to be caught with their fingers in the till, which means being armed and on their way to mount an operation. It is very easy for the liberal-minded to imagine that all a soldier has to do, in the middle of the night on a lonely road, is to jump out of the hedge and shout, 'Hands up!' But it is extremely unlikely that the suspect will instantly freeze and raise his hands slowly. He will probably react with surprise, making some sort of movement which will indicate to the soldier that he may be going for a concealed weapon. The soldier will be aware that his challenge will have alerted the suspect's companions, so to eliminate the danger to himself he will open fire. A further myth is that soldiers should shoot to disable an opponent, which is exceedingly difficult. In a close encounter in darkness it is next to impossible to aim for fast-moving limbs. If the soldier is convinced that his own life is in danger he will pump as many bullets into the body of the suspect as possible and worry about the consequences later. He may well be cold, wet and hungry after several days hidden in a hole in the ground; he will be afraid and the adrenalin will be pumping. Considering these circumstances, it is difficult to apportion blame in the sterile atmosphere of a court of law under hostile cross-examination.

A typical illustration of the dilemma facing soldiers is an incident that happened in January 1977 in which the army authorities openly admitted that the SAS was involved. One version is that a suspect car was seen parked on a road near Crossmaglen and a four-man patrol of the SAS was sent to stake out the position. According to the IRA version, the SAS had parked the car there themselves to act as a decoy. What is not in dispute is that a man, Seamus Harvey, approached the vehicle, dressed in a combat jacket, boots and wearing a black face mask. He had a bandolier of ammunition and was carrying a sawn-off shotgun. When one member of the patrol rose to challenge him he raised the gun as if to open fire. The SAS trooper opened up, and as he did so came under fire from other IRA men hidden in a hedgerow. As he dived for cover the remaining members of the patrol aimed at the muzzle flashes of the IRA guns. Harvey was well and truly dead. Two of the bullets found in his body had come from his own friends and he was quite clearly involved in a terrorist crime. It was not disputed that a genuine attempt had been made to challenge and arrest him.

Shortly after this shooting, in May 1977, Captain Robert Nairac was caught by the IRA while visiting a bar in County Armagh in plain clothes without any form of back-up. He was taken away, tortured and then shot, becoming in the process a popular hero and being awarded posthumously the George Cross. It has always been alleged that he was a member of the SAS, which is untrue: he was serving with 14th Int. He would have had dealings with members of the regiment as the two units worked closely together, but he was an officer in the Guards.

During 1977 the SAS squadron was no longer concentrated in South Armagh, but was divided up into its component troops and spread throughout the province. One was left at Bessbrook in 3 Brigade area, one was based in Londonderry with 8 Brigade and a third went to 39 Brigade at Belfast. The fourth troop was held as a reserve under the direct orders of the Commander Land Forces (CLF). It is quite clear that at the time the SAS was seen as a possible answer to the IRA and it was official policy to use them offensively whenever there was a possibility of confrontation. The fact that terrorist shootings had diminished in South Armagh 'bandit country' was cited as evidence, yet there were to be two incidents in 1978 that caused the authorities to reconsider SAS deployment and tactics.

In June 1978 four unarmed IRA members hijacked a car and set out to firebomb a post office depot in the Ballysillan area of Belfast. Lying in wait for them was a mixed force of SAS and members of the RUC's Special Patrol Group acting on a tip-off from an informer. As the terrorists walked towards their intended target three of them were killed by soldiers, who afterwards stated that they had shouted a challenge. The fourth member of the party fled, and in the confusion a certain William Hanna, who was walking home from the pub with a friend, was shot dead. Immediately afterwards, the army press authorities put out a number of contradictory statements designed to sow confusion, claiming that the IRA men had opened fire first. It was even claimed that Hanna had simply been caught in crossfire instead of having been summarily shot.

Far worse was the killing of 16-year-old John Boyle, son of a farmer in Dunloy, County Antrim. The lad had accidentally discovered an IRA arms cache under a fallen headstone in the local cemetery, and by doing so set off an unfortunate chain of events. He told his father, who telephoned the police. As a result, a four-man SAS team was sent covertly to the scene to set up an observation post. They split into two pairs, concealed themselves and settled down to wait for someone to arrive to claim the weapons. The following day, 11 July, young John, presumably consumed with curiosity, left his father and went to the scene of his find. Apparently he stooped, picked up an Armalite rifle and was then shot dead. His father and elder brother, hearing the shots, ran to the scene and were hurled to the ground by SAS men, who were then removed by helicopter.

The result was a public relations disaster for the Army and led to the first and so far only trial of SAS personnel for murder in a Northern Ireland court. The PR people at Army Headquarters, Lisburn, initially claimed that Boyle had pointed a loaded rifle at the patrol, which proved to have been incorrect. They also stated that a warning had been shouted. The RUC were furious and even went so far as to hint to journalists that the Army was lying. Corporal Bohan and Trooper Temperly were formally charged with murder as it was they who had fired the fatal rounds. During the trial there was much disputed post-mortem evidence as to the direction from which the shots had entered the boy's body. If they had come from behind then he would have been shot while bending down to pick up the rifle; if the opposite, he would have been pointing it in the direction of the two soldiers. The two men were acquitted, as the prosecution was unable to prove that the men had gone there with the intention of killing whoever entered the cemetery, but the judge did remark that Corporal Bohan was not a reliable witness.

The IRA scored a propaganda triumph, which they exploited with exquisite cynicism. The case also strengthened the hand of the RUC, whose Chief Constable was worried about the extent of the Army's undercover activities. Yet it is difficult to see how the soldiers concerned could have reacted differently, as they were convinced that they had opened fire on an armed terrorist. Sadly, it emerged at the trial that the RUC had telephoned the Boyles after they had left for work to warn them not to go near the graveyard – when it was too late.

In June 1978 the regiment suffered its first casualty, when Staff-Sergeant David Naden was killed in a road accident. In March, Lance-Corporal David Jones was killed in a shoot-out in which a well-known IRA figure, Francis Hughes, was wounded and captured. It has often been assumed that Jones was a member of the SAS, yet it would appear from research carried out by Mark Urban for his book *Big Boys' Rules* that he was serving with 3 Para.

In September there was a tragic own goal when a man out hunting with some friends was killed. James Taylor, a Protestant, was simply in the wrong place at the wrong time, exercising his legal right to hunt, but armed with a shotgun. An undercover patrol in the area stumbled upon the hunting party's broken-down car; inevitably, two different versions of events emerged at the inquest. In November an IRA member, Patrick Duffy, was shot dead, again in controversial circumstances. An SAS team was hidden in a house in Londonderry in which a quantity of arms had been discovered. Duffy arrived at the house, unarmed, entered it and went to the hiding place in a wardrobe. One of the soldiers involved stated at the inquest that he had shouted a warning before the team opened fire. The usual conflicting evidence was heard concerning the direction that the bullets had been fired from, and as usual in such cases there was no way in which the actual sequence of events could be pieced together.

By the end of 1978, after the first two years of a regular SAS presence in the province, ten people had been killed, three of whom had had nothing whatsoever to do with a terrorist organization. An effective stop was placed to offensive ambushing and for five years the SAS Regiment killed nobody in Northern Ireland. Instead the RUC expanded its own Special Branch undercover squads and assumed a far greater responsibility for the clandestine conflict in town and countryside. The SAS was not removed from the province, but its tasks became more and more directed towards covert observation and intelligence-gathering. The aim was to collect evidence upon which successful prosecutions could be based, and to arrest terrorists caught in the act. Towards the end of 1980 a new group structure was evolved with the creation of the Intelligence and Security Group (Northern Ireland), commonly referred to as Int and Sy Group, which combined 14th Int. and the SAS under one commanding officer. At the same time, the SAS element was reduced to form an enlarged troop of some twenty men who went to Ulster on a one-year posting, which established an element of continuity. In case of need, reinforcements could be flown in from Hereford at short notice.

Before the new system was laid down a most bizarre incident made headlines in the press, and the SAS unfortunately became linked with it. During the late 1970s allegations had been made about the torture of detainees at the Castlereagh interrogation centre in Belfast. The Bennett Report, published in March 1979, found that there had been ill-treatment. Its findings were partly based on the testimony of a police surgeon, who was interviewed for *Weekend World*, an investigative programme screened by the Independent Television network in Britain, which the government did their level best, unsuccessfully, to suppress. The upshot was that the *Daily Telegraph* published an article on 16 March 1979, alleging that in 1976 this surgeon's wife had been raped by an SAS NCO. Ostensibly this was based on a leak from the security forces designed to discredit the worthy doctor by making him seem anti-RUC because they had failed to bring the culprit to justice. The surgeon himself stated in the article that the authorities had whisked the culprit out of the country and were determined to discredit him in view of the serious allegations he made in the Bennett Report. In the end the story seemed to die a natural death, but not before the CO of 22 SAS was stung into the rare step of issuing a public statement denying that any of his men were involved, in a letter to the *Daily Telegraph* on 19 March. In the June edition of the regimental journal, *Mars and Minerva*, an editorial appeared, quoting a statement by the colonel commandant of the SAS, Colonel Brian Franks.

I believe the time has come to rebut the ever-growing, ill-informed comment in the press and elsewhere about my Regiment. In particular, of course, I refer to the spurious reports suggesting an SAS soldier was involved in the rape [. . .] in Belfast in 1976. At that time, no SAS soldier is known to have been in Belfast. Evidence is quite conclusive on this point and the whereabouts of every man in the Regiment serving in NI at that time has been checked and accounted for.

Some newspapers have suggested that the culprit was 'Spirited Out' of NI. So far as the SAS is concerned I am satisfied that there is no vestige of truth in this allegation.

I am disturbed at the increasing tendency to report on the SAS as if it were some secret undercover organisation. In fact, it is a Corps of the British Army subject to both military and civil law in exactly the same way as any other Corps listed in the Army List.

During the early 1980s SAS operations were far less spectacular, as those involved learnt the bitter lessons of undercover warfare in the province, which was worlds apart from the steaming jungles of Borneo and the open spaces of the Omani desert. A considerable band of journalists, not necessarily friendly, covered every event, and the soldiers had to appreciate that every dead terrorist might well land them in the dock. In addition, the unit on the spot remained caught up in internal power struggles between the various secret services, the RUC and the Army hierarchy.

Successful SAS operations depend to a large extent upon flawless intelligence garnered in advance. If a unit is sent into action on the basis of misleading information, the best training in the world may not be able to bale the men out, as was the case on the afternoon of 2 May 1980. An eight-man team in plain clothes travelling in two civilian cars were on patrol in Belfast, commanded by Captain Herbert Westmacott. Headquarters received information about a possible cache of weapons in a house on the Antrim Road, Number 369, and the men were ordered to search the premises. No effort was made to cordon off the area or to ascertain if the place was occupied. On arrival, one car with four of the team went to the rear of the house, while the patrol commander's car pulled up outside the front door. As they got out, they came under fire from an upstairs window which they believed to be that of the house they were about to search.

Three men charged in, heavily armed, and carried out a classic house search operation, moving from room to room, only to find that it was unoccupied. In fact, the gunmen were in the neighbouring house and when the SAS men went back outside they found Captain Westmacott lying dead on the pavement: he had been killed instantly as he left the cover provided by the car. The gunfire had alerted the Army and the RUC, who moved in to surround the area, and the gunmen subsequently surrendered. Westmacott, a young captain from the Grenadier Guards and a troop commander in G Squadron, was the first member of the regiment to be killed in action in Northern Ireland. He was awarded a posthumous Military Cross. Three days later a group of his erstwhile colleagues stormed the Iranian Embassy in London to the plaudits of the press.

That SAS teams were perfectly capable of carrying out arrests was amply demonstrated during the early 1980s. In September 1980 two known IRA men were apprehended when they arrived to collect a sniper rifle that had been concealed in a hen coop. The following year, in March, the SAS surrounded a lonely farmhouse in County Fermanagh which was occupied by four IRA terrorists led by the later notorious Seamus McElwaine, who were known to be well armed. Rather than face a shoot-out with the security forces, they surrendered. These two cases have often been cited in defence of the SAS when they have been criticized for being too keen to shoot people in cold blood.

During that same period IRA members were still being gunned down, but those responsible were RUC undercover squads which had been set up to reinforce police claims that they were taking greater responsibility for security in Northern Ireland. For much of 1982 the SAS was deeply committed to the Falklands War in which at least two entire squadrons took part and where the regiment suffered considerable casualties. Towards the end of the following year, however, there was a return to the policy of mounting active ambushes. In December, a tip-off from an informer indicated a cache of weapons near Coalisland in County Tyrone, and a search of the area revealed the presence of a rifle, a shotgun and other items. Int and Sy Group was alerted and a six-man SAS squad was sent to stake out the scene.

The watchers split up into three groups of two and concealed themselves around the field where the weapons were hidden in a hedgerow. Working in pairs in a hide meant that while one man slept, the other kept constant watch. Bearing in mind the time of the year, it would have been a lonely, wet and cold vigil without the chance of cooking a hot meal. They lay in wait for two days, until in the middle of an afternoon in daylight, a car drew up containing three men. While one of them stayed behind with the vehicle, the other two got out and went straight to the hiding place of the weapons. Colm McGirr pulled out an Armalite rifle and handed it to Brian Campbell, who moved off towards the car. According to evidence given at the inquest, one of the soldiers shouted a challenge, upon which McGirr swivelled round with the shotgun in his hands. One of the soldiers opened fire and, hearing the shots, Campbell who was running towards the car, hesitated. He was hit by two rounds and fell, mortally wounded. The driver of the car, realizing that it was a trap, leapt in and drove off past two of the soldiers who were hidden in a ditch beside the road. They pumped several rounds into the vehicle which was later found abandoned and blood-stained, but minus the driver.

What orders were issued to the men we will probably never know. The detachment commander, Soldier A, stated at the inquest that he briefed the men that their mission was to apprehend anybody attempting to move items from the cache. The IRA version disputed the fact that a warning had been shouted and even tried to claim that the two men had been shot before they reached the hiding place. There was the usual outcry that they were unarmed, although how the soldiers were meant to know that is unclear, and it was further claimed that the SAS team should have unloaded the hidden weapons first, to ensure that their lives would not be threatened. It is unfair, however, simply to blame the soldiers involved, who fully realize that they are dealing with an extremely dangerous enemy.

During the early 1980s there was quite a galaxy of SAS talent in the province. Mike Rose who had led the regiment in the Falklands took command of 39 Brigade in November 1983, and in 1985 Major-General Tony Jeapes was appointed CLF.

In July 1984 there was a classic SAS ambush based on sound intelligence that an IRA active service unit was intending to mount an attack on a factory which made kitchens in Ardboe, County Tyrone. The operation was an interesting one in that the SAS quite clearly intended to make arrests, thus disproving the claim that a blanket 'shoot to kill' policy existed. A team of eight SAS took up positions in the late evening around the factory. After only a short wait, two men were seen walking along by a hedge. They were challenged and one of the soldiers opened fire, wounding William Price. He ran off with his companion; realizing that the game was up, two more members of the IRA unit rushed out of a field on to a road where two soldiers were waiting. They issued a challenge. Raymond O'Neill stopped and put his hands up, but Thomas McQuillan ran on. Two shots were fired at him; they missed, but he fell to the ground and was arrested. A search for Price and the other man was made and the former was found hiding in a field. According to the soldier responsible he made a threatening movement and was killed with a shot to the head. A number of weapons were recovered from the area as well as the ingredients for making petrol bombs, and two men would later face trial.

The next known operation in which SAS members were said to have been involved was a complete disaster. Intelligence had discovered that a part-time member of the Ulster Defence Regiment was the intended victim of an assassination by the IRA. A team was inserted into an area where the intelligence people believed that the terrorists could be engaged, at a road junction which the victim passed regularly on his way to work in the morning. The Provisionals duly arrived in a hijacked van and the soldiers opened fire – just as a civilian, Frederick Jackson, drove out of a haulage contractor's yard opposite. He was hit in the chest by a single round and died; the terrorists made their escape.

Most of the operations discussed so far were of the pre-planned ambush variety based upon intelligence information gathered well before the event. In December 1984, however, an operation had to be mounted 'on the move' which was to result in the death in action of a second SAS member in the province. The aim of the IRA was to plant a large bomb in a culvert in the road near a well-known country restaurant, the Drumrush Lodge in Fermanagh. They would then telephone the police to say that there were firebombs at the Lodge, in the hope of blowing up the security forces as they arrived. A total of seven SAS men were sent to the area in two civilian cars, ordered to look for a 'blue van of foreign make', which was in fact a Toyota that had been stolen just over the border in the Republic. 'In it were four members of the PIRA, two of whom had been involved in the mass escape from the Maze prison in September 1983, and several milk churns full of explosives.

That night was bitterly cold with thick, freezing fog blanketing the area, and the subsequent chain of events is extremely confused. The SAS patrol sighted a suspicious van parked on a country road and positioned their two cars to block off both ends. Apparently, one of the cars stopped near where three of the IRA party were preparing the detonation point for their bomb. Two SAS men, armed, got out to approach the van, while the third stayed behind to man the radio set. On that occasion the boot was on the other foot – the IRA popped out from behind the hedge and opened fire at point-blank range, killing Lance-Corporal Alistair Slater of B Squadron. There is a number of versions of what happened next. It appears that flares were fired by the soldiers and that the IRA men ran from the scene. One of them, Tony MacBride, was shot dead. In statements laid before the coroner, the soldiers stated that they had first captured him but that when he attempted to escape they fired at him. The PIRA claimed that he had been caught, beaten and then shot, before Slater had been killed. Two of the bombers succeeded in crossing into the Republic, where they hijacked a car and were arrested after a chase by the Gardai. The fourth man was found several days later drowned in a local river, probably dragged under by the weight of his clothing.

One man's terrorist is another's freedom fighter. Most members of the Loyalist community in Northern Ireland greet the news of the death of a member of the Provisionals at the hands of the security forces with glee – and call for more. The Republicans mourn yet another true son of Ireland who has been shot while fighting for the cause. Both sides do their best to distort the facts of a fatal incident, and 'justice' tends to get swept aside. Republicans remain convinced that there is an officially condoned 'shoot to kill' policy, conveniently forgetting that 'their boys' have been doing just that for years. Usually caught in the middle of the lethal struggle, the SAS cannot win. One side hails them as heroes and the other regards them with bitter hatred as instruments of British oppression. Yet one can argue that, as soldiers, they should not be employed to do the police's work for them and that blame for their activities should be accepted by those who have ordered them into Northern Ireland in the first place. The issue is further muddied by the political divide in Britain itself where left-wing politicians and journalists regularly do the Provisionals' work for them by criticizing the security forces, and where right-wing tabloids hail every successful ambush as a resounding victory.

Only a few days after the death of Tony MacBride, the security forces obtained information of an IRA plan to murder a part-time UDR member who worked at the Gransha Hospital just outside Londonderry. I use the term 'murder', but in the terrorists' terms they were going to execute their intended victim. A large detachment of Int and Sy Group was deployed in civilian cars, with orders to apprehend the terrorists, according to the later testimony of the officer who briefed them. Daniel Doherty and William Fleming, each armed with a handgun, set off on a stolen motorbike, with the former at the controls. Both were hardened members of the IRA and Fleming was the cousin of the man who was drowned after the operation referred to above. It was not disputed that they were armed and in the hospital grounds for an illegal purpose.

What was disputed at the inquest was the necessity of killing them, and it appeared that the RUC had not been informed of the operation in advance. One of the soldiers, who was in a car, stated that Fleming had had a pistol in his hand, and the soldier believed his life to be in danger. He rammed the motorbike and Fleming fell off. The soldier jumped out of the car and opened fire with his Browning 9mm. pistol. He stated that he fired three rounds and saw the gunman attempt to rise. He fired three more, and another of the soldiers present joined in. While this was going on, Doherty was gunned down as he tried to escape on the motorbike. Solicitors for the families of the two men attempted to claim that capital punishment had been carried out and questions were asked in the House of Commons. Whether or not the two men could or should have been arrested is a moot point, depending on the actual orders issued as opposed to those quoted in statements to the coroner. It would also depend upon the conditions prevailing at the scene and the split-second decisions that had to be made by the soldiers – which no outsider can judge. It is, however, specious for the IRA publicity machine, which claims that the IRA is fighting a war against the British government, to complain when two of its 'soldiers' on 'active service', as they like to call it, are gunned down.

Even more contentious was a shoot-out in Strabane in 1985. A local PIRA cell was tasked to grenade an RUC vehicle and to shoot any occupants who emerged. On the night of 22–23 February a five-man IRA team had been out in search of their prey but no suitable target had appeared. Two of the team handed their weapons to the other three whose job it was to hide them in a prearranged cache. That same night a small team of presumed members of the SAS was in the area, this time with the knowledge of the local RUC. As there were only six of them, three of whom remained at the police station as part of the back-up force, it seems unlikely that a major ambush had been planned. It is far more probable that they had had a tip-off about a possible weapons cache and were on an observation mission. The other three took up position in a hedge at the top of a steep bank, overlooking a field with, behind them, a road and a line of houses forming part of a council estate. The three IRA men, carrying their weapons, walked into the field and were gunned down. A total of 117 rounds were fired from Heckler and Koch automatic rifles at close range and all three terrorists were killed. The police later raided a house and captured a fourth member of the IRA group, Declan Crossan. There was a fifth member, but he was never apprehended.

The three men who were killed were all locals, Charles Breslin and the brothers Michael and David Devine. Several residents from the estate said that they had seen fire from a machine gun coming from a cemetery overlooking the area, but this was denied by the Army and no forensic evidence was produced. Claims were also made that at least one of the men was heard pleading for mercy and that all three were finally dispatched with a *coup de grâce* to the back of the head. On the other hand, all three were armed with automatic rifles and wearing black balaclavas. In the dark the SAS men could not tell whether or not the rifles were loaded so would have had to assume that they presented a definite threat. Whatever the facts, the inquest failed to uncover them and the families of the dead men claimed that it had been a whitewash. As a postscript, an article in the *Sun* claimed that Captain Simon Hayward, the Household Cavalry officer jailed in Sweden for drug-smuggling in August 1987, had been responsible for setting up the operation. He certainly had served in Northern Ireland in one of the various clandestine units, although he was not a member of the SAS Regiment.

After Strabane there was a sharp decline in shooting incidents in which the Army was involved for a couple of years, but whether this reflected official policy or lack of suitable targets to engage is impossible to determine. In February 1986 an IRA weapons cache in a farmyard at Toomebridge, County Londonderry, was placed under covert observation. A car was heard to draw up and two men entered the yard, one of whom was a local man by the name of Francis Bradley, who it was later discovered had no known connections with any terrorist organization. He was, however, wearing gloves and was probably moving the weapons for the IRA. He was shot dead with eight rounds when he made as if to recover a rifle from the hiding place. The soldier responsible stated that he had called out 'Halt' and the man had turned towards him, whereupon he opened fire. Yet the reaction might have been a normal one in the circumstances. Although Bradley was not engaged in innocent pursuits, his death did cause considerable embarrassment to the authorities.

Far more straightforward was an operation in April which resulted in the death of the Seamus McElwaine we met in County Fermanagh. He was one of the Maze prison escapers and a hardened member of the PIRA captured by the SAS in 1981. His companion, whose name was Sean Lynch, was wounded and captured. A member of a routine army patrol had seen what appeared to be the command wire set to detonate a culvert bomb placed under the road and a covert investigation was mounted. According to a Republican account, the bomb had previously malfunctioned and the two men had decided to take command themselves. What is certain is that a group of soldiers, assumed to have been from the SAS, lay in wait near the detonation point. The two IRA men, both armed with rifles, approached the scene and the soldiers opened fire, killing McElwaine outright. Lynch managed to crawl away and was discovered by a search party some hours later. What is interesting is that he later stated that he thought the soldiers had deliberately aimed low so as to disable him and McElwaine. In the same account, quoted by the Roman Catholic priest, Raymond Murray, in his book *The SAS in Ireland*, he also said that he thought that the soldiers had questioned McElwaine for some time before finishing him off with three shots.

The next fourteen months were a relatively quiet period for the security forces although their covert observation activities did not diminish. In the spring of 1987, indications gleaned from an informer led the security forces to believe that a big operation by the IRA was in the pipeline, and they soon had a pretty good idea of who would be responsible. In the meanwhile, however, the IRA had scored a notable propaganda success: on 25 April they killed Lord Justice Sir Maurice Gibson and his wife as they returned across the border on their way back from a holiday in England.

In May two noted IRA activists, Patrick Kelly and Jim Lynagh who commanded active service units in the East Tyrone Brigade, joined forces for an attack on a small, lightly manned police station in the village of Loughgall in North Armagh. In a carbon copy of a similar attack on a police post known as the Beeches a year earlier, the idea was to mount a massive bomb in the bucket of a stolen JCB excavator and to ram that into the perimeter fence before detonating it. In a vast surveillance operation a close watch was kept on the plotters while the SAS presence was increased by a group sent over from Hereford. The code name was Operation Judy, and press reports later speculated that the location of the explosives and weapons the IRA intended to use had been under surveillance for a week or more in advance.

The indicators all came together in the late afternoon and early evening of Friday 8 May, when the Loughgall police station had ostensibly shut down for the weekend. Masked IRA men stole a Toyota van in Dungannon, and shortly afterwards a JCB was taken from a farmyard in the area. At least two terrorists remained to guard the family of its owner, indicating that more were involved than those who actually entered the village. In the meanwhile, the security forces were moving into position after a full briefing, and a comparatively large force had been assembled. One party of SAS was actually inside the police station, which was at a certain amount of risk from the blast of the bomb; they may have been placed there so that the Army could afterwards claim that, under the rules of engagement, there had been imminent danger to service personnel. The main group was secreted in a line of trees and bushes opposite the police station, with a football field behind them. According to some accounts they had, in addition to their automatic rifles, two general-purpose machine guns. Other small groups were said to be in various locations in the village, keeping watch on the entry roads. The inhabitants had not been informed of the operation and no attempt had been made to evacuate anyone, as this could have compromised secrecy.

From the various accounts it is possible to get a reasonable idea of the flow of events. The Toyota van, with five men in it, entered the village at 7.15 p.m. and made at least one pass in front of the intended target before being followed back by the JCB, with its bomb hidden under a load of rubble. Riding on it were three men, Declan Arthurs who was driving, Michael Gormley and Gerald O'Callaghan. The van came to a halt just past the police station and the back doors flew open. Three men apparently jumped out, including Patrick Kelly, and opened fire at the station, as the JCB rumbled into position and rammed the gate. The ambush party opened up with a hail of automatic fire which riddled the van and killed the driver, Seamus Donnelly. Either Gormley or O'Callaghan lit the fuse of the bomb with a cigarette lighter. Both men ran for their lives and were cut down by the hail of bullets. Arthurs, the driver, and Eugene Kelly were killed as they tried to shelter by the van. Patrick Kelly lay dead on the ground and the two other men were found dead inside. It had been a clean kill, almost.

The mounting of such a large-scale covert ambush always carries the risk that an innocent person will stumble on the scene, as had already happened on a number of occasions. Just before the explosion two brothers, Oliver and Anthony Hughes, drove into the village past the church. As they had been repairing a truck, they were wearing blue overalls, similar to those worn by the terrorists. The two men decided to reverse away from the scene and as they did so, soldiers opened fire on them, killing Anthony and severely wounding his brother. It is clear that they were mistaken for terrorists, and certainly no challenge was issued. Several other cars also appeared but no further injuries were sustained by passers-by. As the fire died away a hush descended on the village as the inhabitants cautiously raised their heads to see what had happened. Their police station was largely wrecked, the JCB had disintegrated and several bodies lay in the road. Later the IRA was to claim that the men had been finished off, apparently because they had sustained head wounds. There was also the accusation that they had been shot in the back, but as fire was being directed at them from both sides of the road and they were in the middle, that would hardly be surprising.

As far as the authorities were concerned, Loughgall had been a satisfactory operation that had wiped out a hardened bunch of terrorists. It was marred only by the shooting of the Hughes brothers – who had nothing to do with any paramilitary organization. As they had arrived just before the bomb blew up, it is difficult to see how a cordon could have been placed around the village to stop cars entering without alerting the bombers, who had to be let through. The government paid compensation to the widow of Anthony Hughes and to Oliver for the injuries he sustained. The usual requests for a public inquiry were, as always, refused. In the flood of journalistic comment the usual claims were made that the men should have been arrested.

The year 1987 had been a disastrous one for the IRA as a whole. Electoral support for Sinn Fein, the political wing of the movement, had dwindled alarmingly, Loughgall had considerably reduced the strength of those available for offensive operations, and at the end of October French customs seized a shipment of arms from Libya. Yet instead of lying low and licking their wounds, the IRA perpetrated its worst and most stupid atrocity when a bomb placed in Enniskillen was detonated at a Remembrance Day ceremony in the town. Eleven were killed and more than sixty injured. Among the dead was a young trainee nurse, Marie Wilson, who was standing beside her father, Gordon. The tragic loss of his daughter propelled Gordon Wilson into the international limelight with his sincere appeals for common sense to prevail.

The following March, perhaps as revenge for Loughgall, the IRA set out to plant a bomb in Gibraltar and three terrorists were shot by the SAS. That particular incident, which became a *cause célèbre*, is dealt with in another chapter. The SAS, however, is still engaged in Northern Ireland and likely to be so for the foreseeable future as the senseless war of attrition rumbles on. They still mount ambushes, kill terrorists from time to time and get blamed for deaths with which they had no connection. In January 1990 three men were shot while attempting to rob a bookmaker's premises in Belfast, but that was the responsibility of 14th Int. and not the SAS, despite Republican claims to the contrary. In 1992 several terrorists were shot by the SAS while setting up a mortar attack at Coalisland.

This chapter has attempted to give a brief summary of SAS operations in Northern Ireland and to explain some of the constraints of the type of warfare in which members of the regiment find themselves caught in political crossfire. It is up to readers to judge the legitimacy of such operations. Some people naturally feel that the best terrorist is a dead one and there are repeated claims that if the SAS were to be let loose the IRA problem would miraculously disappear. It is generally stated that the senior members of that organization, the so-called 'Godfathers', are known to the security forces and that they could be 'taken out' were a government prepared to suffer the inevitable political fall-out that such a programme of assassination would generate. Whether or not that would actually solve the deep-rooted problems of Northern Ireland is another matter, as to achieve this one would also have to disarm the Loyalist paramilitary groups.

II

Counter-Revolutionary Warfare

The same strictures apply to this chapter as to the previous one: any assessment of recent SAS activity must be confined to matters which have already attracted some publicity or which will not in any way compromise the privacy of those members of the regiment involved. What follows is a broad-brush treatment of the subject, which in time scale largely corresponds to the period of the regiment's engagement in Ulster. The two chapters complement each other to a large extent, as the basic skills used by counter-revolutionary warfare teams at home and abroad are similar to those needed by the men fighting the lonely war in Ulster.

At the end of the 1960s when the regiment was busily seeking a new role in the world of post-colonial warfare, it started close quarter battle (CQB) training to provide a pool of expert marksmen to act as bodyguards. There was a great demand for their services, both as guards and as trainers for the forces of friendly powers. Individuals and small teams travelled all over the world for a number of years, but the commitment to the war in the Oman reduced the manpower available for such missions, although the training cadre at Hereford was maintained. A Counter Revolutionary Warfare Wing was authorized with an establishment for one officer, to monitor developments worldwide; this was essentially an intelligence-gathering post.

The humiliation suffered by the German authorities in the bloody aftermath of the hostage crisis at the 1972 Olympic Games concentrated minds on the new threat of organized terrorism. Palestinian guerrillas from a splinter group known as 'Black September', in an attack on the Israeli team quarters, killed two athletes and took nine hostages. An attempted rescue at a military airfield outside Munich failed, resulting in the death of all the hostages.

No European government had forces available to counter such a situation, and as a result governments often caved in to terrorists' demands. The British government tasked the SAS with preparing a force capable of dealing with situations in which hostages had been taken, and authorized the expansion of the CRW wing at Hereford. The Germans responded with the foundation of a special unit known as GSG9 which draws its personnel from the paramilitary frontier police, and the French formed a unit of the Gendarmerie Nationale, the GIGN.

Terrorism in the early 1970s came in a bewildering variety of forms, often characterized by strident names. Much of the problem stemmed from the internal struggles in the Middle East, which spawned a variety of Palestinian groups opposed to Israel. These groups saw any Western governments which supported Israel as legitimate targets. They were also prepared to attack Israeli installations overseas and were not above carrying out their own internal feuding in Europe. Iraqis fought Iraqis, and after the fall of the Shah, Iran played a prominent role in the terrorist stakes by exporting militant Islam. In addition to the Middle Eastern groupings, there was home-grown terrorism of the European variety, from Maoist urban guerrillas to Italian neo-Fascists and ethnic freedom campaigners. Inter-police co-operation was vastly expanded to co-ordinate intelligence-gathering, and that information became available to units such as the SAS, which was also briefed by the British Secret Intelligence Service and MI5.

The following illustrates SAS versatility at the time. Staff-Sergeant Clifford Oliver was one of a four-man team that parachuted into the Atlantic on 18 May 1972 in response to a bomb scare on board the liner *Queen Elizabeth II*. The team leader was an army bomb disposal expert, Captain Williams, and the other two members were from the Royal Marines. It transpired during the flight that Williams had had little experience of parachuting, the weather was appalling and the men had to drop with heavy loads through cloud. On the fourth pass over the ship, the drop was made and the men were picked up, although their search of the ship revealed no explosive device.

As in Ulster, the rule of law was still paramount in mainland Britain, where the containment of a terrorist 'incident' was initially a matter for the police, and a military solution only a final option. Studies were made of the psychology of terrorism and the subtle techniques of patient negotiation became a powerful weapon in the police armoury. If the military option had to be invoked, to save the lives of hostages, the rule was that minimum force should be applied. Those same parameters still apply today. The paramount aim is to save the lives of the hostages and to ensure that if a gun battle breaks out, innocent civilians do not become caught in the crossfire, which in an urban environment is always a danger. The definition of 'minimum force', however, remains a matter of interpretation and, as in Ulster, potentially a minefield. The soldier who is tasked to carry out an operation that may have been sanctioned by politicians, and which the police can no longer handle, can still find himself in the dock afterwards.

The SAS was not exactly unprepared to take on the role of developing techniques to counter terrorism as they already had a vast amount of experience in training marksmen for close protection work, which mainly involved highly accurate pistol shooting. To assist their training a facility that has since become known as 'the killing house' was constructed. In its early days this was simply a room in which paper targets representing a VIP and potential attackers were placed. The aim was to teach men to sort out who was who and to eliminate would-be assassins or kidnappers. For the new scenario, the parameters to be considered became more complicated. A group of terrorists could take hostages and hold them in an aircraft, a train, a building or even on a ship. Such a situation could be created by British nationals either as a criminal enterprise or for political ends; or by foreigners applying pressure on the British government or a foreign power. Finally, the situation could take place in the British Isles or abroad – on British territory or in a foreign country.

The main new technique to be studied was how to gain entry to a space where hostages were being held, which necessitated a lot of experimentation. Initially the basic close-quarter weapon used was the standard British sub-machine gun, the Sterling, but this was replaced by the American-made Ingrams. For opening doors, the Remington shotgun firing a heavy ball to blow off hinges and locks was adopted. In addition, each man carried his own Browning 9mm. pistol as a back-up weapon. Immediately entry had been achieved it was necessary to disorientate the opposition, which led to the development of the stun grenade, which is filled with fulminate of mercury and magnesium; the SAS tend to refer to them as 'flash-bangs', an accurate description. The loud explosion and blinding flash can disorientate someone for up to 45 seconds, giving the assault team time to pick their targets and shoot them. Because of fumes in a confined space and the potential use of CS gas grenades, assault team members wore respirators and a plain zip-front overall. It took several years of patient experimentation to arrive at the present-day high-technology outfit worn by anti-terrorist squads worldwide.

In those early days the Special Project Team numbered twenty men drawn from all four squadrons, who were trained at the CRW wing by an officer and four instructors. Their first known deployment was in January 1975 when a civilian airliner was hijacked at Manchester Airport by an Iranian student armed with a pistol. He demanded to be flown to Paris and the pilot agreed to comply. The Special Project Team had been alerted, and it headed for Stansted Airport to set up a reception committee. The hijacker genuinely believed that he had arrived at Paris, and when the SAS stormed the aircraft the man gave himself up. His weapon turned out to be a replica.

In December of that year the fact that there was an SAS anti-siege unit was announced by the BBC at the instigation of the government. The police had cornered a four-man Provisional IRA team who had entered a flat in Balcombe Street in London after a car chase and a gun battle and were holding a Mr and Mrs Matthews hostage. With the use of high-technology surveillance equipment the police were able to eavesdrop on what was happening inside the flat and patient negotiation was carried out by telephone. The SAS had arrived on the scene and the police asked the BBC to insert into a news bulletin the information that they were considering handing over conduct of the operation to the military. The terrorists, who were known to be listening regularly to the radio, promptly decided to give themselves up. This happened before the first full deployment of the regiment in Ulster, and illustrates the fear that the initials SAS inspired in the ranks of the Provisionals.

During those early years when squadrons were being rotated to the Oman and training had to be maintained for the European war threat, the small CRW capability had little real opportunity to practise its skills, other than to relentlessly rehearse for any eventuality. Contacts, both formal and informal, were maintained with overseas anti-terrorist units, new weapons were tried out and intelligence about potential enemies was collected. Many of the skills learnt were put to good use when the commitment to Ulster began in 1976. It is obvious that the Entebbe raid carried out by Israeli commandos in June 1976 was extensively studied despite the fact that the regiment has no any official links with that country. A group from the Popular Front for the Liberation of Palestine hijacked an aircraft and forced the pilot to fly to Entebbe in Uganda where they released 100 passengers but kept a further 106, who were mostly Jewish, hostage. The terrorists were actively supported by the régime of Idi Amin, and the Israelis resolved upon a desperate venture. They flew 2,200 miles in three Hercules, landed at the airport in an extremely daring and well-planned raid, freed the hostages from the terminal building and destroyed Amin's MIG fighters on the runway. That operation may well have been the prototype for some of the proposed raids during the Falklands War which are discussed in the next chapter.

In the Netherlands the authorities were grappling with the problem of terrorist outrages committed by South Moluccan exiles, and the SAS was called upon for advice and technical assistance. In Germany, the so-called Red Army Faction was waging a bitter guerrilla war against the authorities although many of the leaders, including Andreas Baader, had been arrested in 1973. It was this group that indirectly led to the involvement of SAS CRW specialists in a German operation.

On 13 October 1977 a Lufthansa Boeing 737 *en route* from Palma to Frankfurt with eighty-six passengers on board, was hijacked by four terrorists, who demanded a ransom of £9 million and the release of members of the Red Army Faction from prison in Germany. A request was made to the British government for SAS assistance for GSG9. This was granted, and two men were selected – Major Alistair Morrison, who had led G Squadron to the relief of Mirbat, and Sergeant Barry Davies. They set off for Dubai where the airliner had landed, taking with them a supply of stun grenades, which the Germans did not have.

On arrival, Morrison and Davies met up with the commanding officer of the German unit, Otto Wegener, and two of his men. The rest of his team were in another aircraft which was still in Turkey, where it had followed the terrorists, with the ransom money actually on board. Outside the terminal in searing heat stood the 737 with its frightened passengers, as Wegener and Morrison struggled to set up an operation to free them. Before they could make an attempt, the Lufthansa jet took off and headed for Aden, where a distinctly unfriendly Marxist government was in place. The Wegener–Morrison team was refused permission to land but followed the migration of the terrorists to Mogadishu in Somalia, where they met up with the remainder of the GSG9 team. Matters were precipitated when the body of the captain of the hijacked aircraft, who had in fact been murdered in Aden, was thrown out on to the tarmac.

Proof of the fact that a hostage has been killed generally triggers an end to the negotiating process and the resort to the military option, as there can be no going back. What Morrison and Davies had practised time and again now had to be put into action, and an attack was approved by the Somali authorities. The job of the SAS team was to effect an entry while the terrorists' attention was diverted by a fire which had been lit on the runway. The assault team climbed silently with rubber-coated ladders on to the wings of the jet and simultaneously blew in the emergency doors on both sides. In went the stun grenades followed by the Germans, who opened fire – above the heads of the hostages who were strapped in their seats. In spite of the duty-free alcohol and aviation spirit which had been spread in the fuselage, there was no fire, and two grenades rolled along the floor by the terrorists exploded harmlessly under the well padded seats. The battle is said to have lasted eight minutes, but it resulted in the death of three hijackers, and the wounding of the fourth, a woman. Also injured were one German attacker and a hostage.

Discreet awards that reflected the government's satisfaction were made to the two SAS men in the birthday honours list in 1978 – an OBE for Morrison and a BEM for Davies. The successful outcome of the operation did not stop the hijacking of aircraft but it did at least prove that well-trained and determined assault teams could manage the job without wholesale carnage. In such situations governments were often in a cleft stick. While they could not be seen to be giving in to terrorist demands with the subsequent accusations of cowardice in the face of blackmail, neither could they afford a botched release attempt. An aircraft full of dead hostages was an equally grave political impediment and a gift for those journalists who persistently afforded comfort to terrorist organizations.

As a direct result of the Mogadishu operation, the government ordered an expansion of the CRW role and a full squadron was deployed at Hereford in rotation between tours in Ireland and other training commitments abroad. More money was made available for the purchase of the best equipment on the market, especially in the field of communications. From their German colleagues the SAS adopted the Heckler and Koch MP5 sub-machine gun, which is still very much in use today, as their standard close-quarter weapon. One-piece flame-retardant suits and body armour were adopted, as well as new helmets and respirators with reliable built-in microphones that enabled each member of a team to speak to the others.

Obsessive dedication to continuous training is the main hallmark of the SAS, yet there is the danger of boredom setting in if there is no prospect of action, as was the case from 1977 until 1980. By 1980 the 'killing house' consisted of six rooms, with terrorists and hostages being represented by standard NATO paper targets of a charging Russian soldier. There was also a mock-up of the interior of an airliner, and several old aircraft had been assembled on one of the training areas in Wales. The men who were on duty as the instant-readiness team were equipped with bleepers and had to keep their holdall containing assault gear handy at all times. Regular exercises were held, which aimed to be as realistic as possible and to cover different situations.

When the call eventually came, it was very sudden. On 30 April 1980, 6 Troop of B Squadron was in the killing house practising standard routines. Splitting into teams of four, they kicked open doors, burst into rooms, fired at targets and afterwards pasted squares of paper over the holes. At 11.48 the bleepers went, gear was hastily packed and the men ran off to be briefed. The reason for the alert was that a telephone call had been received at the 'Kremlin', the SAS operations centre at Hereford, informing the duty officer that a group of terrorists had taken over the Iranian Embassy in Prince's Gate, London. The caller was a certain Dusty Gray, an ex-NCO from the regiment who was working as a dog-handler for the Metropolitan Police, and who happened by chance to be outside the Embassy. Most accounts state that the SAS team left Hereford and travelled to London on their own initiative, before clearance had been given by the Ministry of Defence. Driving in their unmarked Range Rovers up the motorway, they arrived in the early evening and established a holding area inside Regent's Park Barracks.

The background to the 'incident' and its ultimate resolution is well known, mainly because it was acted out in the full glare of the television cameras. In spite of the distaste felt by the SAS for publicity, one could conjecture that the government was not exactly displeased. The success had demonstrated to other would-be hostage-takers that Great Britain was an unhealthy area for such activities, and it increased overseas demand for SAS know-how. The offer of the latter could heighten Britain's political influence all over the world and the know-how could even be sold, at a price.

The bare facts of the matter are as follows. A group of six men, who had been in Britain for several weeks beforehand, had pushed their way into the Iranian Embassy, pulled out weapons and claimed to be members of an organization dedicated to independence for Arabistan, an area in the south of Iran inhabited by ethnic Arabs. They took the twenty-six people in the building hostage, who included two sound technicians from the BBC, a policeman from the diplomatic protection squad and the embassy chauffeur. The remainder were Iranian members of staff.

At that time, the Director SAS was Brigadier de la Billière. He had a seat on an organization known as the Joint Operations Centre (JOC) of the Ministry of Defence, which also included representatives of the Foreign and Home Offices as well as the intelligence services. The JOC is responsible for activating the SAS, but in the case of a terrorist incident with political connotations the final say rests with a group known as COBRA – Cabinet Office Briefing Room – which is chaired by the Home Secretary and reports directly to the Prime Minister.

Initially, however, the incident was a matter for the police, who brought in their experienced team of negotiators and ringed the building with marksmen. They set up headquarters a few doors down, in the premises of the Royal School of Needlework. Oan, the leader of the terrorists, demanded an aircraft to take his group, the hostages and an Arab ambassador to an unnamed country. A delicate cat and mouse game then developed, and five hostages were gradually released in exchange for food and an agreement to broadcast Oan's demands on the BBC.

For the team planning the eventual assault the building was unknown territory, but luckily the British caretaker proved to be a mine of information. In addition, Chris Cramer, one of the BBC men taken hostage, was released on account of illness and could be carefully debriefed. A plywood model was constructed. One thing that was discovered was that the ground-floor and first-floor windows were armour plated and could not simply be smashed through with sledge-hammers; explosive charges would be needed.

The following evening the assault team members were moved out from the barracks in hired vans and established themselves in a new holding area in a side street near the target building. For them the waiting began, as negotiations continued. On the night of 2 May a reconnaissance was made across the rooftops of Prince's Gate to reach number 16, where it was discovered that a skylight could be opened. From then on, however, it was a question of waiting – for the negotiated release of the hostages, or for the terrorists to decide to kill someone. By the morning of Monday 5 May the atmosphere in the holding area was becoming claustrophobic, the only relief being a chance to jog in Hyde Park. But at 1.45 p.m. the situation suddenly altered when three shots (in some accounts, two) were heard coming from inside the Embassy. Oan, the terrorists' leader, had carried out his threat: he had killed a hostage. Final proof came at seven o'clock that evening when the body of the Iranian press attaché was dumped outside the front door, and from then on matters had to be resolved. At 1907 hours precisely, the senior policeman signed a handwritten sheet of paper and handed it to Lieutenant-Colonel Mike Rose, the commanding officer of 22 SAS.

Although the negotiator continued to talk to Oan on the telephone about arrangements for a coach to take them to the airport, the command of the operation was in the hands of the military. Ever since the shots had been heard the assault team had been on full alert and had moved into number 14, the premises of the Royal College of Physicians next door to the Embassy. All the equipment had been prepared, weapons were loaded and the final briefing had been carried out. The aim was to create a diversion at the front while entry was effected at the rear, with teams entering the ground floor via the garden and others abseiling down on to the first-floor balcony. At 7.23 p.m. demolition charges went off at the front and CS gas was pumped into the building through the broken windows. As the ground-floor assault team ran into position with shaped charges to smash the windows they saw above them the inert form of one of their comrades, a Fijian, who was caught up in his abseil harness. If they used explosives they would kill him, and he was in danger of being roasted alive in the flames that were licking through the window. He was cut down and, despite his injuries, rushed inside with his team. The men below used a sledgehammer to break open the door and they too charged in, with Soldier 'I' in the lead:

> The adrenalin was making me feel confident, elated. My mind was crystal clear as we swept on through the library and headed for our first objective. I reached the head of the cellar stairs first, and was quickly joined by Sek and two of the call signs. The entry to the stairs was blocked by two sets of step-ladders. I searched desperately with my eyes for any signs of booby-traps. There wasn't time for a thorough check. We had to risk it. We braced ourselves and wrenched the ladders away.

The team on the first floor rushed up the stairs to the second where the hostages were being held, while the ground-floor men systematically cleared the lower part of the building. There was total confusion: bursts of firing from the sub-machine guns, women screaming, smoke billowing, the roar of stun grenades and clouds of tear gas. The assault teams, encumbered with heavy body armour and their respirators misting up from perspiration, moved automatically, assessing and reacting. Oan was on the first-floor landing; before he could shoot, the policeman, Trevor Lock, wrestled him to the floor. An SAS man shouted at him to move away and dispatched the terrorist with a burst from his Heckler and Koch. Elsewhere, terrorists had started to shoot wildly, killing one hostage and wounding two or three others before the rescuers burst in. The terrorists threw away their weapons and tried to mingle with the hostages as the SAS yelled for them to be pointed out. Two were instantly killed and another was dispatched by the team on the ground floor.

In eleven very long minutes, the action was over. A line of SAS formed on the stairs and bundled the hostages, none too gently, down to the back lawn where they were thrown to the ground, tied up and held at gunpoint. Suddenly there was a shout as one of the people coming down the stairs was identified as a terrorist. Soldier 'I' saw him – and the fact that he had a fragmentation grenade clutched in his fist. He could not fire, as his mates at the bottom of the stairs were in his line of sight:

> I've got to immobilise the bastard. I've got to do something. Instinctively, I raised the MP 5 above my head and in one swift, sharp movement brought the stock of the weapon down on the back of his neck. I hit him as hard as I could. His head snapped backwards and for one fleeting second I caught sight of his tortured hate-filled face. He collapsed forward and rolled down the remaining few stairs, hitting the carpet in the hallway, a sagging, crumpled heap. The sound of two magazines being emptied into him was deafening.

In fact the pin was still in the grenade. Then the order came crackling though the men's headphones to abandon the building as it was on fire. Back in number 14 they stripped off their assault kit as the adrenalin rush ebbed away. A few minutes later they were outside, bundling themselves into the hired vans, having handed over their weapons to the police for forensic examination. They were driven back to Regent's Park Barracks where there was time for justifiable self-congratulation and the task of emptying cans of beer that had been thoughtfully provided. The celebrations were interrupted by the arrival of the Prime Minister, Margaret Thatcher, accompanied by her husband. She was obviously delighted and took the time to move around the room speaking to everyone. The men sat down to watch the events on television, then it was off back to Hereford. The Fijian abseiler had been taken to a hospital in Fulham, but that night he was abstracted by the SAS and flown back to base in a helicopter. In spite of being quite badly burnt, he made a full recovery. Of the terrorists, only one had survived; he had been discovered wounded among the hostages when they were sorted out on the lawn.

James Adams, who was defence correspondent of the *Sunday Times*, states quite unequivocally in his book *Secret Armies* that on this occasion, it was made quite clear to the SAS that they were to take no prisoners. Governments had long since come to realize that putting terrorists in prison could often lead to further hostage-taking by members of their group endeavouring to exert pressure for their release. It is unlikely that we will ever know if such orders were actually given as the authorities would not admit to flouting the so-called rule of law. The press generally welcomed the outcome, although there was some comment on the fact that several of the hostages stated that the SAS had killed the terrorists after they had surrendered. The job of the assault team was to rescue hostages and remove them from the premises as quickly as possible; there is no time for niceties such as requesting people to surrender. It was known in advance that the enemy were armed and they had proved that they were prepared to kill if their demands were not met. They had also stated that they had explosives in the building and would blow it up if attacked. It is obvious that they had to be killed before they had a chance to do further mischief, and this is what such SAS teams are taught to do in the 'killing house'. Some months later four of those concerned had to give evidence at an inquest, which turned into a game of cat and mouse with the media as they tried frantically to get photographs. The soldiers gave their evidence identified only by letters, and in due course a verdict of justified killing was pronounced by the jury.

As far as the regiment was concerned, it wished to sink back into obscurity and get on with the round of tours in Northern Ireland and with training for the next 'incident'. As a spin-off from the media coverage, a record number of would-be volunteers applied to join TA units, and speculation about the role of the regiment refused to die away.

The call came just over a year later, while the country was celebrating the marriage of the Prince of Wales. One of the guests was the President of the Gambia, a small ex-British colony in West Africa. Some Marxist-oriented rebels used his absence to stage a coup, seizing vital installations in Banjul, the capital, including the airport. Although small, the country was a successful democracy, had no standing army and remained in the British sphere of influence. News of events reached the Foreign Office on 30 July 1981 and urgent consultations were held with Washington and Paris, since both the United States and France also had an interest in the region. As a result, Hereford was alerted, where Major Ian Crooke was on duty in the absence of Colonel Rose.

According to accounts published at the time, Crooke was ordered to take whatever he needed and to get to the scene. For some reason, never explained, the duty Special Projects Team was not employed and the RAF was not ordered to provide a Hercules. Crooke gathered up two other men, and with holdalls packed with weapons, explosives and a portable satellite telephone, they flew to Paris. There, they boarded a routine Air France flight to Banjul, the problem of their luggage having been solved discreetly by an employee of the British Embassy who arranged diplomatic passage through the security checks. In Banjul itself, a squad of French-trained troops had arrived from neighbouring Senegal and had retaken the airport, where they had been joined by the President who had flown in from London – which raises the question of why Crooke and his team had not travelled with him. On arrival, Crooke discovered that the hostages were being held seven miles outside the town, but other than that, nobody seemed to be taking any form of initiative.

Now comes the fantastic bit. The three SAS men, fully armed, made their way through the lines of rebel troops surrounding the airport and into town, where they knocked on the door of the British Embassy. There they found the ambassador, who was having to evade sporadic gunfire; and discovered that one of the President's wives together with her four children had been taken to a hospital in the town. They moved on to the spot and while Crooke, posing as an unarmed bystander, engaged the guards on the gate in conversation, his two colleagues crept up and overpowered them. They released the prisoners, delivered them to the safety of the Embassy and then discovered that the Senegalese, poorly led, had attempted to break out from the airfield and had been beaten back. Undeterred, Crooke led his small team back, gathered a group of Senegalese and staged a counterattack. In four days he and his men broke the back of the resistance and captured the leadership.

Meanwhile the Americans, smelling a Libyan plot, had alerted their Delta Force who had flown into Dakar, the capital of Senegal. The State Department then got cold feet and left them there. The British Foreign Office also panicked, but Hereford, with Nelsonian blindness, stated that they had lost contact with Crooke's team, which was quite untrue as they had a satellite phone. In the end there was quiet satisfaction with the outcome, discreet awards were no doubt made, and Britain retained a staunch friend in a volatile region. One can but wonder whether, if the Americans had telephoned Hereford rather than invading Grenada with vast forces to dislodge a few Cubans, they might have saved themselves a lot of money and casualties. The Gambia mission was a classic example of a few men, inserted into the right place and with initiative and determination, being able to master a fluid situation.

From time to time the SAS has been asked by the Home Office to test the security of prisons by attempting to break in; they carry out similar exercises at such establishments as nuclear power stations. On 3 October 1987, however, they had to do it for real, at the top-security Victorian Peterhead prison in Aberdeen. Four days previously a group of three inmates, one of them a convicted murderer, had taken a prison officer hostage, and from time to time had paraded him on the roof, threatening him with a hammer. The authorities had instigated a patient negotiating process which was getting nowhere. Presumably they felt that sending in a riot squad of police or prison personnel could lead to the hostage being injured or even killed. In the pitch darkness of early morning witnesses heard a shouted 'Let's go!' from inside the compound. One group of SAS men threw stun grenades and tear gas into the wing as an assault team abseiled down from the roof and entered through a window. Five explosions were heard and smoke billowed out through a hole in the roof that had been made by prisoners. It was all over in seconds and the hostage was released unharmed. Had the prisoners had firearms, the outcome would probably have been different, but the Peterhead operation does prove that an SAS attack need not necessarily be lethal.

The final operation to be discussed in this chapter certainly was lethal, and what started out as the simple termination of three known IRA terrorists in Gibraltar in the spring of 1988 was to end up with the British government and their executive arm, the SAS, in the international dock. The matter was extensively aired at the time and much has since been written about it. By its ineptitude the government handed the IRA a propaganda victory and once again reopened the whole question of a 'shoot to kill' policy. The affair is still, at the time of writing, being aired in the European Court, as the relatives of the deceased try to claim compensation. As a sub-plot to the main drama there was trial by television; and when some of the evidence presented was found to be flawed, there was a trial of television reporting itself. An increasingly paranoid government attempted to gag the press, which only made matters worse.

The facts of the case were relatively simple. A well-known IRA man and suspected bomb-maker, Sean Savage, had been located in Spain in the autumn of 1987, as had Daniel McCann, by trade a butcher and accomplished terrorist. An extensive intelligence-gathering operation then got underway and at the beginning of 1988 an MI5 team was sent to Gibraltar. By that time, the experts were fairly certain that the target was to be the resident military band which performed the ceremony of changing the guard outside the Governor's residence in the colony. There was also disquiet about the fact that the IRA had perfected a remote-controlled detonating device that could be activated by pushing a button in a coat pocket. On 4 March, Savage and McCann arrived at Malaga Airport where they were joined by a woman, Mairead Farrell, who had a long record of terrorist offences. It was a star team that the IRA had assembled, in revenge for Loughgall perhaps, and nobody could pretend that they were there for a holiday in the sun.

The Spanish police had been initiated into what was thought to be afoot, yet through ineptitude they lost trace of the bombers as they left the airport. Their men were still doing the rounds of hotels showing pictures of the suspects a couple of days after all three were dead. Two days earlier, intelligence indicated that the operation was imminent, as a fourth member of the team, a woman, had made several trips to the Rock to scout the area where the band performed. The JOC in London assessed the situation and authorized the deployment of a troop-sized (sixteen-man) SAS team, which included an explosives expert. They flew out on 3 March. In charge on the spot was Joseph Canepa, the Gibraltar police commissioner, and from all the evidence there has never been anything to suggest that his orders were anything other than to apprehend the terrorists.

The operation was given the code name Favius. In a thorough briefing to all concerned, Canepa stated that the object was to arrest the terrorists, disarm them and make the bomb safe. The assumption was that a car bomb would be used, parked in the small square where the bandsmen assembled before the performance, and that it would be detonated by remote control. All the SAS men involved stated that it was stressed to them most emphatically that it would be a push-button detonator. It was also assumed, quite naturally, that the terrorists would be armed.

So far, all seemed relatively straightforward. With hindsight we know that the three were unarmed, that the bomb was still in a car park in Marbella and that they intended to use a timing device to detonate it. Had that information been available, the local police could have handled the affair and all three would be behind bars, still alive.

On the afternoon of Sunday 6 March watchers were deployed around the town. Among them were four members of the SAS team, working in pairs. Each man was wearing denims and a lightweight jacket with a Browning 9mm. pistol tucked into the waistband of his trousers. Small radios with microphones hidden in the lapels of the jackets ensured adequate communications. The reception committee was in place and waiting. Savage was seen to approach a white Renault 5 parked in the square where the band would assemble, open the door and 'fiddle with something inside' – which effectively signed the death warrants. As he loitered near the car, Farrell and McCann were picked up walking into the town from the Spanish border post.

Soldier G, the explosives expert, was sent out from the operations room to examine the car, but would have been well aware of the probability that it was booby-trapped. There were no outward signs of uneven springs denoting a heavy weight inside, but although it was a relatively new vehicle, it was fitted with a rusty aerial, which might have indicated that it had been tampered with. On that basis it was felt that the car could contain a remote control bomb, and at 3.40 p.m. Canepa signed the authorization for the military to take responsibility for the operation. At that time all three terrorists were walking together northwards towards the Spanish border, followed by the four soldiers. Then, for some reason, Savage separated and started to walk back in the direction of the town, which caused those shadowing the trio to split. Soldiers A and B continued behind McCann and Farrell while C and D stuck with Savage.

Just before 4 p.m. a local police inspector, who was not aware of the operation, was called back to base as his car was required – ironically, to take the arrested terrorists to prison. Owing to the heavy traffic he switched on his siren, which seems to have alarmed the trio, who became noticeably jumpy. McCann turned his head and made eye contact with Soldier A, who was about ten metres behind him. In evidence, the soldier said that he was about to issue a challenge as he pulled out his pistol, when McCann moved his hand across his body. Assuming that the man was going for the button, Soldier A fired one round into McCann's back and then, seeing Farrell make a movement towards her bag, he shot her too with a single round. As he fired again at McCann, Soldier B fired at Farrell and then also at McCann. Hearing the shots, Savage spun round and Soldier C shouted 'Stop!' As he did so, he noticed his target make a movement towards his pocket. Both soldiers opened fire. At 4.06 p.m. Soldier F, the SAS officer in charge of the team, relinquished military control.

Initially it all seemed quite simple. An active service unit consisting of three ruthless IRA members, caught in the act of planting a bomb which could have killed hundreds of innocent bystanders, had been eliminated. The tone of Monday's newspaper headlines was one of jubilation, but that afternoon in the House of Commons the then Foreign Secretary, Sir Geoffrey Howe, made a statement concerning the affair on behalf of the government. He laid out the facts as known but said that the white Renault did not actually contain a bomb and that the three dead IRA members were unarmed at the time. The bomb was not discovered until the following day in a car in a car park in Marbella.

The government found itself on the defensive, forced to explain the apparent cold-blooded killing of the terrorists, and once again the SAS was accused of being Thatcher's assassins with an 007-type 'licence to kill'. The press went on the rampage, attempting to dig up every possible detail of the shootings, and printed the Spanish police version of their side of the operation. They flatly denied that they had lost the terrorists at Malaga Airport and claimed they had shadowed them all the way to the Gibraltar border. What had originally been a disaster for the IRA was turned into a triumph: they had three new martyrs to mourn, and every movement of the soldiers concerned was analysed second by second. Allegations by witnesses and supposed witnesses were printed which stated that the SAS pumped shots into their victims when they were already on the ground. Raymond Murray gives a detailed analysis of the general press coverage in his book, *The SAS in Ireland*, since much of what was written at the time was favourable to the Republican cause. He states:

> Having shot the three IRA members dead in the head and back from a close range in cold blood, the British prepared their defence. First by misinforming the media, tabloid and quality alike. Secondly by delaying the inquest to September on a flimsy excuse, to cool the atmosphere, to give more time for misinformation, to nobble [or attempt to intimidate] key witnesses.

Father Murray, who celebrated the funeral mass for Mairead Farrell, went on to state that the alleged worry about a press-button detonator for the bomb was a 'classic *post-hoc* invention'.

The present book is a history of the SAS Regiment and not a critique of British government policy. The rules of engagement for the operation, which were furnished to the coroner and are thus in the public domain, are probably similar to those for similar missions in Ulster and on the UK mainland. They authorize the operatives to 'open fire against a person if you ... have reasonable grounds for believing he/she is currently committing, or is about to commit, an action which is likely to endanger your or their lives, or the life of any person, and if there is no way to prevent this'.

If the suspicion about a 'button job' was not a complete government invention after the event, which seems unlikely, then it was the job of the SAS to eliminate the threat by killing the terrorists once they became alarmed. Otherwise, why were they sent there in the first place? If it was simply a government plot to kill the terrorists, why do so using four unmasked men in plain clothes, in broad daylight on a busy thoroughfare? They could simply have been arrested, taken to the military base and 'shot while attempting to escape'.

The two-week inquest ended on 30 September 1988 and, by a majority of nine to two, the jury brought in a verdict of lawful killing, which satisfied the government as well as a large section of British public opinion which had been annoyed by the efforts of the lawyer representing the families of the dead trio to blacken the SAS men. They had to endure a lengthy grilling in the witness box simply for carrying out their duty. If any 'secret' orders had been given, then surely those responsible for them should have been called, rather than the soldiers? But, however much the regiment may deplore the harsh glare of publicity, the fact remains that they are subject to the rule of law and there is little the government can do to protect them. Other countries use specially trained police units for counter-terrorist work, but Britain has chosen a military option, which places soldiers in a difficult position. They are essentially trained to wage war rather than to do police work and if the government sends members of the SAS fully armed on to the street, it should shoulder the responsibility.

Gibraltar is probably not the last time that the CRW team has gone into action, and they are still there, training, and training yet again. From its post-war origins as a specialist infantry unit employed in fighting brush-fire wars abroad, the SAS has become the world's élite anti-terrorist unit. Although regarded by some sections of the community as bogeymen, the fact that they are there ensures a high level of deterrence to any would-be terrorists who might decide to operate on British soil.

12

A Corporate Operation

Operation Corporate, the war fought by Britain to regain the Falkland Islands from their Argentine occupiers in 1982, was in many ways a reversion to old-style colonial conflicts, a form of high-tech gunboat diplomacy. To one who observed events closely from a journalistic point of view, it seemed to bring out both the best and some of the worst aspects of the British national character. The famous headline 'Gotcha' which celebrated the sinking of the cruiser *General Belgrano* by a British submarine was a prime example of the latter, as was the tendency in much of the media to regard the contest as a form of lethal football match. On the other hand, it gave a dispirited Britain, seemingly relegated to the status of a third-class power, something to celebrate for a change. A popular hero was created, in the person of Colonel 'H' Jones, killed in action at Goose Green and posthumously awarded the Victoria Cross. And who can forget the vast wave of emotion and national pride generated as the rust-streaked *Canberra* glided up Southampton Water past the packed crowds there to welcome their 'boys' back home?

A large contingent of special forces was involved in the war – two squadrons from the SAS, from the Royal Marines, the Special Boat Squadron and the Mountain and Arctic Warfare Cadre, and from the Royal Artillery teams of naval gunfire observers. The SAS suffered severe casualties, mostly as the result of an accident; owing to the close proximity of a keen pack of journalists, who could not be avoided in the confines of the ships, they found their activities subject to scrutiny.

Anonymity to a certain extent went by the board, as the name of the commanding officer was published, as were the names of several other officers, but no great secrets were breached. The regiment found itself fighting an old-fashioned sort of war dating back to the 1960s and 1970s as it reverted at times to being a superior form of raiding force. Several operations were reminiscent of ones carried out during the Second World War, while at the same time small parties were engaged in their more modern speciality of covert intelligence-gathering. The conduct of some of the regiment's activities was later to be severely criticized by Major-General Jeremy Moore, the task force commander.

On 2 April 1982 the military junta of Argentina invaded the Falkland Islands, catching Britain's defence planners completely by surprise. Commanding officer of 22 SAS Regiment at the time was Lieutenant-Colonel Mike Rose, who apparently heard about the invasion from the BBC news and, following in the footsteps of several of his predecessors, promptly set out to get his men involved. While his operations and intelligence cell in the so-called 'Kremlin' at Hereford scoured around for maps and any available information about the distant islands, D Squadron commanded by Major Cedric Delves was put on immediate alert for a move south. That meant pulling men back from leave, from courses and even from foreign assignments. Rose offered the squadron's services to Brigadier Julian Thompson of 3 Commando Brigade, whom he flew to see on 3 April, and two days after the invasion an advance party flew out to Ascension Island off the west coast of Africa. The following day, the rest of the squadron together with their kit left for Ascension, which says a lot for the quality of the regiment's quartermasters and storemen.

On 6 April, Colonel Rose, a small staff from Regimental Headquarters and the members of G Squadron embarked on HMS *Fearless*, a commando landing ship which was Brigadier Thompson's floating command post. The colonel formed part of a small team of tactical planners known as R (for reconnaissance) Group, who dreamed up a whole variety of dastardly schemes to discomfit the enemy, and worked in a Portacabin lashed on to the deck.

Initially the two squadrons were deployed separately and were controlled directly by their own commanding officers, while their colonel remained on board *Fearless* at Ascension. D Squadron, after only a short pause on Ascension, embarked on board the Royal Fleet

Auxiliary *Fort Austin*, to form part of a force detached to recapture the island of South Georgia. That particular operation was essentially a political one as the government was under pressure to instigate some form of action. G Squadron's mission was reconnaissance, and on arrival at Ascension it was re-embarked on the RFA *Resource* which sailed south with the main carrier battle group.

The South Georgia mission was known as Operation Paraquet, which soon became corrupted to Paraquat after a well-known brand of weedkiller. The original plan called for one troop of D Squadron to join the task force, but Cedric Delves decided to take everyone as they all wanted to have a go at the enemy. Besides D Squadron, 2 Section of the SBS and M Company of 42 Royal Marine Commando, known as the 'Mighty Munch', were to be deployed. Initially there was some confusion over the command structure. Major Guy Sheridan of M Company was extremely surprised, as was the Navy, when instead of the expected SAS troop, a whole squadron commanded by another major transhipped from *Fort Austin*. In the event, Sheridan was given command and the plans were approved by Brigade HQ. The whole process had been complicated by an almost total lack of intelligence about the island and the size of the Argentine presence.

On 13 April the small naval task force rendezvoused with HMS *Endeavour*, the ice patrol ship whose threatened withdrawal and scrapping had to a certain extent prompted the Argentine invasion. The warships then replenished their fuel and stores, and the troops involved were cross-decked by helicopter to their battle stations. 17 and 19 Troops together with Squadron HQ were on board the flagship, *Antrim*, 16 Troop was in *Endeavour* and 18 Troop on board *Plymouth*.

On 21 April the small force was in sight of the island, a bleak, mountainous wilderness with only two small whaling stations, Leith and Grytviken. In appalling weather, with gale-force winds, the mountain troop, No. 19, was inserted on to the Fortuna glacier by helicopter with the mission of gathering intelligence on the whereabouts of the Argentine troops. Once there, they found that the combination of the weather and the difficult terrain made movement impossible. The troop had to spend a night out on the glacier in the worst possible conditions with totally inadequate tents, and the following morning the troop commander, Captain John Hamilton, radioed to *Antrim* for the force to be taken off. Three Wessex helicopters managed to land on the glacier and embarked the men, but then disaster struck. Shortly after take-off one of the helicopters crashed after the pilot suffered a total whiteout which caused him to lose his horizon. All the men on board managed to scramble out while the other two machines succeeded in landing and picking up the survivors. Once again they took off, and a second Wessex crashed in similar conditions. The pilot of the third, Lieutenant Commander Ian Stanley, made it back to *Antrim* to report.

Thirteen men were stranded out on the glacier with two wrecked helicopters and in no condition to spend a further night in the open. Again Ian Stanley took off in the remaining machine, an act of almost foolhardy bravery, located the survivors and piled the whole lot on board; with the crew that made a total of sixteen instead of the normal complement of nine. Dangerously overloaded, the helicopter got them back to the ship, where it had to crash-land on the heaving deck as it was unable to hover. One of the most richly deserved decorations awarded for the Falklands War was the DSO for Ian Stanley.

For the planners, it was back to the drawing board. Catastrophe had been averted, but only just, as the task force's airlift capability had been reduced by two-thirds. That night, 22–23 April, *Antrim* slipped into Stromness harbour and launched the SAS boat troop, No. 17 in five Gemini inflatables. Two suffered engine failure but three crews did manage to get ashore and establish themselves in a position to observe the enemy. The indefatigable Ian Stanley located and winched up one of the missing crews as they were being steadily blown out into the South Atlantic. The fifth crew had scrambled ashore at the last minute and hid up for three days before announcing their presence by activating a search beacon.

Plans to recapture the island had been badly hampered by the delays in gathering intelligence, and Delves and Sheridan were beginning to consider direct action when they were informed on the evening of 24 April by Fleet Headquarters at Northwood in England that an Argentine submarine was in the area. This was the aged *Santa Fe* but it was nevertheless a threat as it was armed with torpedoes. The decision was made to send *Endurance* and the RFA *Tidespring* out of the way, but as they had the bulk of M Company on board, the potential assault force was severely reduced.

The following morning, Ian Stanley in the remaining Wessex was flying back from inserting an SBS patrol ashore when he spotted a submarine cruising on the surface some five miles out of Grytviken. He dropped a pair of depth charges and that was followed up by missile and gunfire attacks by the small helicopters from the other warships. The *Santa Fe*, badly damaged, limped back into Grytviken, and Sheridan decided that the initiative had to be seized. He had some seventy men available in all – a few marines, two troops of SAS and an SBS section, scattered around various ships – against 130 of the enemy. As a forward artillery observer laid down a barrage from the warships' guns against the settlement, the motley force was flown in by helicopter to a point about two miles away from the settlement. John Hamilton's mountain troop led the way and as they moved over the ridge they saw that the buildings were displaying white sheets. Sheridan moved forward to take the official surrender of the demoralized garrison, while Sergeant-Major Gallagher of D Squadron hauled down the Argentine flag and replaced it with a Union Flag which he happened to have upon his person.

A day later two troops were flown into Leith, where the garrison also surrendered without bloodshed. In Britain, the news of the bloodless victory was greeted with enthusiasm and with calls for the task force to get on with liberating the Falklands themselves. On 28 April D Squadron transferred to the destroyer HMS *Brilliant* and set off to rejoin the main task force as it prepared to insert the first reconnaissance patrols from G Squadron. Starting on 1 May, over a period of three days, eight four-man patrols were inserted by Sea King helicopters from the aircraft carrier HMS *Hermes*. The earlier intention to parachute into position was abandoned as being too risky. Each team was landed up to twenty miles from its ultimate lying-up position and had to carry everything needed for an indefinite stay. Cumbersome morse transmitters, personal weapons, rations, spare clothing, sleeping bags and a plentiful supply of ammunition had to be carried in the darkness from the landing site, with the men fully realizing that by daylight they would have to burrow underground into total invisibility.

The positioning of such observation posts was somewhat of a hit-and-miss affair as the maps available were inadequate and quarters on the various ships often extremely cramped. On HMS *Antrim*, the special forces planning was carried out in the admiral's day cabin, reserved for use when she was being used as a flagship. Captain Hugh McManners of the Royal Artillery described the scene in his book,

Falklands Commando, the only first-hand account of the war written by a member of special forces.

> The carpets were still down and the magnificent oak table was covered with army blankets and bore maps, half-filled Armalite magazines, notebooks and pencils, sellotape and scissors and bits of signals pads.... Around the walls were piled Bergen rucksacks, painted with black, green and brown paint and open with contents spread out over the surrounding area of deep-pile Wilton. There were 9mm pistols, several sorts of Armalite, rocket and grenade launchers, camouflage nets, shaggy camouflage suits, tent-poles, bags of tinned food, bars of chocolate, many half eaten and lying on the tables and chairs (everybody stocking up on food while they could), boots, plimsolls and waterproof suits; in fact such confusion that one wondered if anyone would ever sort out who owned what.

Once a covert OP had been established a grim routine set in with the men forbidden to engage the enemy, no matter how tempting the target, unless under attack themselves. Each position was different, depending on the nature of the terrain, but common to all was the ceaseless bitter cold and perpetual dampness. Most of the Falklands is a lump of rock covered by a peat bog – putting in a spade one encounters either granite or water. Some men had to live in shallow scrapes roofed over with ponchos and nets covered with turf. One man was constantly on watch, the radio had to be manned and the others tried to cook on their hexamine stoves without making any smoke, and grab what rest they could – in wet, freezing clothes in wet sleeping bags. Plain words cannot do justice to the conditions endured, and as darkness fell, men crept out to attend to bodily functions, carefully brushing the grass upright behind them as they returned to their hides. One patrol commanded by Captain Alvin Wight endured twenty-six days up on Beagle Ridge above Port Stanley.

Danger was ever present, as well as uncertainty. One mistake in the camouflage could alert an enemy patrol, and as the Argentines were equipped with radio direction-finding equipment, transmission times had to be kept to a bare minimum. In the Falklands the individual patrols were not equipped with radios capable of sending burst-transmissions – lengthy messages encoded into a special machine and then sent out in a matter of seconds. The squadrons, as well as Regimental Headquarters, however, had the latest satellite telephones which enabled them to communicate easily with each other and back to base at Hereford.

At that period of the conflict, the nearest friendly troops were still 3,500 miles away at Ascension and there was no certainty that an amphibious landing would be made. Thus there was no back-up force to call in if a patrol was under attack and the men had no idea when they would be relieved. A lot of their equipment proved unsatisfactory, especially the boots, and trench foot became a problem. The diet was monotonous; the only relief was the chewing of chocolate and occasional brews of tea. In such a situation you get to know your companions really well, regardless of rank or social background, as just about the only form of amusement was to hold whispered conversations about what one would do when one got home, and which pubs would be visited.

Simultaneously with the G Squadron observation patrols, small SBS teams were paddling ashore to check out all possible landing sites for the task force. Using the same techniques as the SAS, they established themselves in hides to observe their assigned area as well as scouting suitable beaches with deep water and easy exits.

D Squadron rejoined the main carrier force and were transferred on board HMS *Hermes* to plan their next mission. Apparently Major Delves had had the idea of mounting a raid on Pebble Island, off the coast to the north of West Falkland, where a small enemy garrison was thought to be. Initially the overall task force commander, Admiral Woodward, was not enthusiastic about the idea as he would have to risk his ships by moving them in close enough for helicopters to insert the raiding force. The sinking of HMS *Sheffield* on 4 May had made everyone painfully aware of the threat from Exocet missiles, and the loss of one of the carriers might well have caused the government to call off the attempt to recapture the islands. In fact, on 8 May the decision had been taken to send the landing force south from Ascension and nothing was to be allowed to interfere.

The Navy remained lukewarm about the planned raid until indications were received that there might be a radar transmitter on the island which could have detected the movement of ships. Overflights failed to detect it and it was reluctantly agreed to put D Squadron ashore. After a twenty-four-hour postponement, two four-man patrols from the boat troop, equipped with folding kayaks, were inserted on to West Falkland opposite Pebble Island on 11 May with orders to set up an OP. If there was no sign of the opposition, they were to paddle across the island and carry out a reconnaissance of the airstrip at the settlement.

The two patrols reached the island successfully, and while one stayed to guard the canoes the other four men made their way to a point overlooking the settlement – where, to their surprise, they observed eleven assorted enemy aircraft. That information was radioed back to *Hermes* and immediate plans were made to insert a full raiding party, to destroy the aircraft and eliminate the garrison. The only problem was the chronic lack of helicopters, but on the night of 14 April three Sea Kings flew in the rest of the squadron and Captain Chris Brown's naval gunfire support team. But the time of insertion was delayed and it would only be possible to wreck the aircraft.

The original boat troop marked the landing zone and, when the men were ashore, provided guides to the settlement which was six kilometres away. John Hamilton's mountain troop was ordered to deal with the enemy aircraft while the rest of the squadron contained the garrison. As the warships opened fire on the area, Hamilton's men hammered away with small arms and rockets at the mixture of Pucara ground attack machines and trainers, setting them alight, and it was only when the raiding party was leaving that the enemy began to react in a sporadic way. One man was slightly wounded by shrapnel and another was injured when the garrison set off a remote-controlled mine. Otherwise everyone got off safely and returned to *Hermes*. In an operation reminiscent of David Stirling's raids in the Western Desert during the Second World War, a serious threat to the safety of the task force had been inexpensively eliminated.

On 18 May the assault force arrived from Ascension to rendezvous with the carrier group, and Colonel Rose was reunited with his two squadron commanders. Most of G Squadron was still out in the field in their holes watching and waiting, and the landing was planned to take place on 21 May. To tie down the enemy garrison which the SAS had located around Darwin and Goose Green, it was intended to insert D Squadron who would make as much noise as possible, simulating an attack by a much larger force. For this mission they had to transfer with all their gear from *Hermes* to the commando landing ship *Intrepid*, sister to *Fearless*. The move took place on 19 May and was purely routine, with just a five-minute flight between the two ships. Several trips were necessary and finally, in the late evening, there was only one more load left – a mixture of men from 19 Troop including the two wounded on Pebble Island, a few G Squadron members and several attached specialists including an RAF flight lieutenant. Nobody on board bothered with a cumbersome immersion suit as the Sea King took off, flying over the cold heaving sea at around 400 feet altitude. The helicopter had to make a second pass as another one was still on the flight deck of *Intrepid*, and it was then that disaster struck. Those who survived reported hearing a loud bang from the engine like a heavy blow and then they were in the water. A large bird had impacted with the air intake, probably an albatross or storm petrel, and the pilot had insufficient height to recover control.

The ten survivors managed to cling on to a dinghy and had to spend nearly half an hour in the dark, freezing water. When rescued they were all suffering from hypothermia and in a few more minutes would have been dead. Twenty men from the regiment and its support formations died, including two squadron sergeant-majors and six sergeants. It was a terrible blow for such a small unit to lose so many irreplaceable senior NCOs at one stroke, and in any lesser formation morale might have crumbled. But the SAS mourned its dead then simply got on with the job. In fact, replacements were at hand, on Ascension Island, where a detachment from B Squadron had arrived, fully kitted up for a mission that had originated in the regimental commander's planning cell. The idea was to crash-land two C130 Hercules aircraft straight on to the runway in Port Stanley, from which the desperadoes of B Squadron would rush out to cause alarm and despondency among the Argentine defenders. Not being privy to the details of the planned mission, it is difficult for me to make an objective analysis of the idea. It is known that the whole area of the town was ringed with modern anti-aircraft defences which would probably have managed to shoot down two large slow-moving aircraft – yet, if they had landed and been let loose? According to Soldier 'I' they were all ready to go and had actually arrived on the airfield when the mission was cancelled.

The following night, D Squadron had to get back into action as the Darwin/Goose Green raid was to go ahead as planned. There was a G Squadron OP in the area which had been in place for nearly three weeks, so there was sufficient intelligence available about the position of the Argentine troops on the ground. The mission was to simulate a battalion attack which meant using as much heavy weaponry as possible, all of which had to be carried on a twenty-hour approach march, in fighting order, from the landing place: 81mm. mortars, bombs, machine guns and Milan anti-tank missiles were distributed among the men, who in addition had their own personal weapons and full load of ammunition. On arrival, the troops spread out and poured in a devastating hail of fire upon the 1,200 enemy lodged in the area. At the same time, the SBS mounted a similar raid on Fanning Head where they had to eliminate an Argentine outpost which could fire on ships approaching the site of the main landings the following morning.

Both raids achieved their aim and the Commando landing on the morning of 21 May was not interrupted by enemy ground forces. The majority of the brigade was successfully established ashore before the first of the devastating Argentine air raids on the ships of the task force in the exposed San Carlos anchorage. Early that same morning, two Hercules lifted off from Ascension carrying 6 Troop and 8 Troop of B Squadron, who instead of crash-landing in Port Stanley were to parachute into the sea off the Falklands as replacements for the men lost in the helicopter crash, and be picked up by the frigate, HMS *Andromeda*. The aircraft carrying 8 Troop had to turn back in mid-flight for technical reasons, so only the one troop actually dropped on that first mission. Each man wore a diver's dry suit, carried swimming flippers and had a flare strapped to his wrist so that he could be located once in the water. It was classed as an operational drop, one of very few to have been carried out by the regiment since the campaign in Malaya, and several men in the troop were only recently 'badged'. Over the DZ, the pallets containing stores, the men's Bergens and their personal weapons were pushed out, and then Soldier 'I' led the way:

I was number one in the stick, standing on the edge of the tail-gate, adrenalin-charged, aching for release. It's fearsome, being number one: you see everything in front of you – and worse, everything below you. When you are three or four in the stick, all you see is the pair of shoulders and 'chute of the guy in front of you. You can shuffle forward almost with your eyes closed, as easily as a blind man being led over a cliff.

I was in the ready position: right hand gripping the parachute static line, my left hand resting on top of the reserve. Far below was the grey wash of the sea. I moved closer still to the edge. The deafening roar of the aircraft slipstream made all conversation impossible. My head was raised and turned to the right, watching, waiting for the red warning light to turn to green. My rear leg was braced, ready to launch me over the edge of the tail-gate.

The light changed and out went Soldier 'I' followed by the rest of the troop. All the parachutes deployed properly, the reserve chutes were jettisoned and then the men were in the sea, inflating life-jackets and struggling into their flippers. The water was bitterly cold, freezing exposed hands and faces as the stick bobbed around waiting for the rigid raider craft launched from the frigate to pick them up. Soldier 'I' was the last one to be collected, having spent half an hour in the water and nearing the end of his resistance to exposure and exhaustion. Even then his ordeal was not over, as one of the pallets had gone missing and he and another troop member spent several unpleasant hours on deck as the ship plunged through the grey night looking for it.

On 25 May the various commanding officers from the task force were summoned to an Orders Group by the Brigadier on his floating command post, HMS *Fearless*. The successful landing had been inhibited by frustrating delays in getting sufficient stores ashore to break out from the bridgehead, the main problem being the chronic lack of helicopters – which was exacerbated when the *Atlantic Conveyor* was sunk by Exocet missile with the loss of three Chinooks. Colonel Nick Vaux, commanding 42 Commando, stated in his book *March to the South Atlantic* that he was buttonholed by Mike Rose after the meeting and taken off to the SAS command post, which he described as 'a brigand's cave of specialist weapons and technological devices, where menacing individuals muttered quietly into unfamiliar radio sets, or pored over strange maps and diagrams'. According to Vaux, Rose told him that the SAS surveillance patrols had reported that Mount Kent, overlooking Port Stanley, was only lightly held and perhaps it would be a good idea if 42 Commando were to seize it.

Rose had already taken certain steps and Cedric Delves with an advance party from D Squadron had been inserted on to the position to prepare for the rest of the squadron, which by then had been transferred to the landing ship, *Sir Lancelot*. The SAS flushed out a number of enemy patrols as they skirmished in the dark around the craggy mountain area, and after frustrating delays caused by the lack of airlift capability, K Company of 42 Commando was flown in on 31 May together with three 105mm. artillery pieces and a couple of mortars. They were accompanied by Rose, Vaux and the journalist Max Hastings, who had somehow managed to smuggle himself on to the mission. The task force thus had a small but powerful force on the dominating high ground overlooking Stanley, as a base to receive 3 Para. and 45 Commando who had been yomping across the desolate landscape. The following night the Commando brought in a further company and small detachments of the SAS squadron moved out to explore the neighbouring hilltops, clearing them of enemy patrols. Inevitably, John Hamilton's mountain troop was in the thick of the chilly manoeuvring from crag to crag, before the bulk of the squadron was relieved and flown back to *Sir Lancelot*, where the food was stated to have been excellent.

Covert observation patrols were still out in force at various locations, concentrated around the hills overlooking Stanley, and on the island of West Falkland on which there was still a considerable enemy garrison at the settlements of Fox Bay and Port Howard. Those forces had been masked by SBS patrols who had called down regular doses of naval gunfire, and there were two resident patrols from G Squadron, which were relieved by men from D Squadron on 5 June. Again, John Hamilton was in command, but on 10 June even his incredible luck ran out. He had only been in the SAS since January but had brought with him considerable mountaineering experience. He and his signaller were surrounded by an enemy patrol while manning a forward observation post on open ground overlooking Port Howard. Hamilton was mortally wounded, but ordered his signaller to make good his escape while he, unable to move, gave covering fire. The citation for his posthumous award of the Military Cross read:

In the action which lasted some 30 minutes, Captain Hamilton displayed outstanding determination and an extraordinary will to continue the fight in spite of being confronted by hopeless odds and being wounded. He furthermore showed a supreme courage and sense of duty by his conscious decision to sacrifice himself on behalf of his signaller.

At about the same time a strong fighting patrol from D and B Squadron elements was inserted on to West Falkland after it was rumoured that the Argentines intended to send in three Hercules loaded with reinforcements for a parachute drop from the mainland. A total of sixty well-armed men were flown in the dark to a reception party and deployed on high ground overlooking the presumed dropping zone. In the end, the enemy never arrived but the men still had to wait in cover until the following night to be relieved.

On the night of 9–10 June Captain Hugh McManners took his naval gunfire support team on to Beagle Ridge, six miles north of Port Stanley, with orders to observe activity in the town and to call down fire from warships as required. His four-man party was flown in to a reception committee from D Squadron which had been patrolling in the area for some time, while gradually the main force assembled along the line of hills to the west of the town, ready for the final attack. The flight in was a hair-raising experience, as he described:

As we sat in the Sea King, screaming along in total darkness veering from side to side, pulling up suddenly and swooping down to avoid hills and follow valleys, the perspiration caused by the loading of the Bergens became a chilled dampness. The cold began to permeate the layers of clothing. The rear side-door was open and the wind swirled and buffeted. The darkness outside suddenly became a hill with sheep running in all directions away from the sudden presence of the helicopter.

On the night of 11–12 June, D Squadron arrived in the area, tasked to mount a raid in support of the main action and commanded by Cedric Delves in person, who led from the front at all times. Initially they cleared the surrounding area of any stray enemy, and on the afternoon of 13 June the squadron commander issued his orders, a meeting that was described by Hugh McManners:

The 'O' group took place in a small, clear area between the rocks in a snowstorm. Cedric knelt on a sleeping mat and tried to keep the wind from blowing his notes and map away. We had all emerged from holes in the rocks and were blinking like badgers caught in car headlights.

The people fresh from the ships had smooth faces and rosy cheeks and the remainder of us were sallow-faced and sunken-eyed, with bearded faces smeared with old cam cream and dirt.

While struggling to keep a badly rolled cigarette alight, he explained that the idea was to give the enemy the impression that a major amphibious assault was being launched at the same time as the main attack went in from the west. Part of the squadron was to march south to Blanco Bay where they would meet up with four rigid raider boats manned by Royal Marine coxwains. The boats would take them across the mouth of the Murrell river; they would land on the other side and attack a known enemy position, backed up by fire support from the rest of the squadron.

D Squadron plus a troop from G moved off at last light, and the amphibious party made their rendezvous with the rigid raiders, which embarked them together with the necessary weaponry. As they neared their landing point, however, they were heavily fired upon from shore positions, and as they attempted to withdraw, the Argentine hospital ship anchored there illuminated the scene with searchlights – which under the accepted rules of war, it most certainly should not have done. Although all the boats were damaged and two men injured, the raiding group made it back safely into Blanco Bay. In the meanwhile, the other two troops disconcerted the enemy in their target area, making sufficient commotion to divert attention from the 2 Para. assault on Wireless Ridge.

It became apparent that the enemy no longer had the will to fight. Mike Rose and a Spanish-speaking marine, Captain Rod Bell, had been conducting their own band of psychological warfare on the enemy via the local medical radio network for several days. On Monday 14 June Rose was informed that General Menendez was ready to discuss surrender terms. In the early afternoon, a Gazelle helicopter landed behind Hugh McManners's observation post and Rose, Bell and an SAS signaller got out. They chatted for a while to McManners, who pointed out to them various features in the town, while the crew attached a wire with a large white flag underneath the helicopter. Weighed down with a lump of rock, the flag fluttered as the machine flew off and landed in Port Stanley, some distance from its destination, Government House. The negotiators had to scramble through gardens and hedges to get there, but later that evening the Argentine commander formally surrendered to Major-General Jeremy Moore.

There remains one aspect of the Falklands campaign as waged by the SAS which remains tantalizingly opaque: the expeditions to the mainland of Argentina. One possible reason is the fact that Britain went to war to regain control of the Falklands and was not, officially at least, at war with Argentina. Operations within that country, had they become compromised, of which there was always a risk, could well have hampered diplomatic efforts to maintain the moral high ground internationally. Yet there is a considerable body of evidence which points to the fact that such operations were carried out and I have been told by someone involved, 'Of course we were bloody well there.' It would have been surprising if the SAS had not been there, bearing in mind the almost total lack of hard intelligence that Britain possessed at the start of the conflict. The evidence points to a number of clandestine missions, probably for the purpose of providing an early warning of enemy aircraft taking off. There is no evidence to suggest offensive raiding; wrecked aircraft littered over Argentine airfields would certainly have attracted attention, if not at the time then after the conflict had ended.

It became well known that the wreckage of a British helicopter from one of the squadrons attached to the task force was discovered in southern Chile. On 20 May, the day before the main amphibious landing at San Carlos, a burnt-out Sea King was abandoned and its crew of three turned up several days later at the British Embassy. The official version was that they had experienced difficulties while on patrol and had sought refuge in the nearest neutral country. All three received high gallantry awards in the subsequent honours list, far and away above what one would expect for crash-landing a helicopter. Whether they were on a mission that failed or not remains unknown, but there is a further possibility, which will be discussed below. It is also significant that the diesel/electric submarine *Onyx* arrived to join the task force in late May. British nuclear submarines are far too large to work in shallow inshore waters inserting special forces patrols.

The greatest single threat to the survival of the task force as a whole came from the air-launched Exocet missiles of the type that sank HMS *Sheffield*. It was known that Argentina could deliver them from their Super Etendard aircraft, but at the time there was uncertainty over the actual number of missiles available. In fact there were only four and the last one was fired on 30 May, missing its intended target. Militarily there would have been a strong case for eliminating that capability and there is no reason why an experienced SAS team could not have done so by destroying the aircraft on the ground. Four Super Etendards from the Argentine Navy's 2nd Fighter and Attack Squadron were based at Rio Grande in the extreme south, according to the well-researched book, *The Air War*, by Rodney Burden. No losses are quoted for that squadron during the course of the war.

In 1990, the Insight team from the *Sunday Times* published a short article which claimed that two Hercules took off during May from Ascension with a full SAS squadron on board. Their mission was to land on the enemy airfield at Rio Gallegos, which was also in the south and was nearest to the Falklands. The men were to pour out, destroy as many aircraft as possible and then make their escape overland. According to the article, the mission was aborted in mid-flight as it was feared that the plan had been discovered. As authority, the authors cite 'SAS soldiers who took part in the mission', and state that the leader was Ian Crooke, of whom mention has already been made in this book. At that time he was second in command and operations officer of 22 SAS and would have been the natural choice, as Mike Rose was with the task force in the South Atlantic. As B Squadron arrived at Ascension on 20 May, according to Soldier 'I', they were presumably tasked to carry out the raid, if the Insight article is correct. Soldier 'I' makes no mention of this, but I have quoted his account above of an aborted mission to crash-land on Stanley airport, when in fact they did not actually take off.

The article goes on to state that the job of the crashed Sea King was to insert a reconnaissance patrol twenty-four hours ahead of the main raiding party, and it was the discovery of the wreck that caused the plan to be aborted. The whole idea would have had to be discussed and approved at the very highest level: the War Cabinet. It is tantalizing to speculate about what might have happened, although we have seen that the Super Etendards were not actually based at Rio Gallegos. There was a very good chance that the Hercules would have managed to land and, faced only by air-force personnel running an airfield, the squadron could have achieved a vast amount of mayhem. It is also certain that they would have sustained heavy losses, and that others would have been captured while trying to escape. The newspapers would have applauded their daring, however, and the government would have done its best to weather the inevitable diplomatic storm – which might well have brought other South American countries into the war on the side of Argentina.

As far as the SAS was concerned, and the same applies to other special forces units, the Falklands War was highly successful. As Max Hastings wrote, 'few British campaigns in this century have been fought with a lower level of military data about the enemy'. As a result, the information provided by special forces teams on land was vital to those whose task it was to plan operations. Afterwards, the SAS was criticized for its failure to correctly estimate the size of the enemy garrison at Goose Green and Darwin, although now it is known that reinforcements were flown in at the last minute from the Mount Kent area. Corporal Trevor Brookes commanded an observation team that kept watch there for sixteen days, and was awarded the Military Medal for his efforts. Had he been at fault, such a decoration would hardly have been suggested. In truly appalling weather conditions, the SAS and SBS teams became the eyes and ears of the task force commanders, as well as providing a reliable raiding force. Their success was reflected in the awards which were made in the special honours list.

Cedric Delves, who had been in the thick of it with D Squadron throughout, received the DSO. In addition to John Hamilton, Captain Timothy Burls who commanded the D Squadron boat troop, was awarded the Military Cross, as was Captain Wight of G Squadron. There were two Military Medals and a considerable number of mentions in dispatches including one for the commanding officer, Mike Rose. Three out of four squadrons had been deployed, the largest concentration of the regiment at any one time and place since the Malayan campaign.

13
Selection and Training

The preceding chapters have shown the wide variety of operational situations in which the regiment has been involved since 1947, ranging from steaming tropical jungles to the blizzard-swept mountains of the Falkland Islands and the deserts of Arabia. What is evident is the adaptability required: all ranks must be able to cope with whatever may be flung at them, often at short notice. A troop can be pulled off a mountain in Norway, flown back to Hereford, re-kitted and be on its way to the Oman, in twenty-four hours. Of course there will be griping from all concerned, but that is endemic to all armies. The SAS, however, will simply make the best of things, work out what needs to be done and then get on with it.

There is no such animal as the typical SAS man – whether officer, sergeant or trooper – and they vehemently deny that they are in any way supermen. By the very nature of the job they do, they tend to lead somewhat restricted lives, ever wary of publicity, but they also get married, have children, buy houses and pay tax. The regiment has thrown up remarkably few absolute rogues, has its own ways of weeding out the potential undesirable, and fosters a strong sense of internal loyalty. The SAS is élitist but does not need to brag about the fact, and in ethical terms it could be likened to the medieval war band in which allegiance was based upon ability, mutual trust and the feeling of being part of a 'family' – nobody can lead except by example.

The regular regiment recruits from those already serving within the British Army, while the territorial regiments find their members from the civilian population. Having said that there is no typical SAS man, certain generalizations can be made, based upon empiric observation. What is certainly called for is a high degree of individuality and self-reliance, coupled with the ability to get on with others in both small and large formations. He has to be able to sit in a hole for three weeks with two or three colleagues, with little chance of movement, and not harbour murderous thoughts about someone else's annoying habits. Very few lengthy orders are given – a problem is stated and it is up to the individual to sort out how to solve it. He must be able to operate entirely alone without waiting for an officer or an NCO to tell him what to do. He must of course be extremely fit, but not necessarily in the muscle-bound sense. A form of mental toughness and a highly developed strength of will is needed; a determination never to give up. Coupled with that, a balanced psychological profile is essential to provide a man who is even-tempered and unlikely to get in a panic when things start going wrong. He needs to trust his mates and they need absolute confidence in him in any circumstances.

There is no room in the regiment for the thug or the gorilla – violence and the ability to kill are part of the job, but that is all. An officer who had commanded the SBS once told me that he had only had to get rid of one man because he had developed an unhealthy interest in killing people. The SAS do not brawl around the pubs and brag in bars about their exploits – anybody who does is a candidate for immediate RTU. Many of those I have met have an intellectual curiosity, a high degree of intelligence coupled with a practical approach to life and an irreverent sense of humour. Small, stocky, wiry men, they have watchful eyes, droopy moustaches and the restfulness often associated with advanced practitioners of martial arts. David Stirling, an aristocrat by birth, envisaged the SAS as a classless society, which is what it has become, where position in the pecking order is determined by ability rather than by the automatic respect due to rank.

The process of selection laid down by John Woodhouse in the 1950s has only changed in detail since. Essentially it involves a number of hikes of ever-increasing length over difficult terrain, advanced map-reading skills, referred to as 'land navigation', and the carrying of heavier and heavier loads, to prove an individual's stamina and powers of endurance over a three-week period. Both officers and other ranks undergo the same ordeal, although for the former there is an extra week at the end, when those who have successfully completed the first part have to prepare and explain a variety of tactical situations – to an often sceptical audience which will include experienced NCOs. In the past, the course has been criticized for being over-physical, but that is the system which has worked well for the SAS. The failure rate is immensely high – a figure of around 80 per cent has been quoted – and the regiment has always resolutely refused to water down its standards for acceptance. Over the years, several men have died from exposure up on the hills, but that is a risk that is accepted as the price of excellence. Once through basic selection, the potential recruit faces several more months of continuation training when he can still be sent back to his parent formation at any time. Only then is he 'badged' and admitted to a squadron, yet still on probation.

The outsider may well ask: why do it? The average recruit is in his mid-twenties, has a good military record and is already an NCO, although he will revert to the rank of trooper when he tries for the SAS. The regiment does provide information and gives presentations to various army units, but it is up to the individual to make the effort to apply for selection, which takes place twice annually in the formidable range known as the Brecon Beacons, in Wales. Participants on the winter course face the hazards of mist, snow and almost continual dampness, while those who opt for the summer have to cope with the sweaty heat.

Owing to their part-time status, selection for the TA candidate is spread out over a longer period, but is just as gruelling; they are not second-class SAS. Many are looking for a sense of adventure and personal challenge which they find lacking in a normal army environment – there are no great financial inducements.

A man has to be recommended by his commanding officer, who generally is unwilling to lose a promising young soldier so can make difficulties about processing the application. The soldier himself has to weigh up the potential risk to his career by trying for the SAS and then failing, as well as the risk to his marriage of having to spend up to eight months in every year separated from his family. Today the British Army is in the process of retrenchment, which means that skilled personnel are in even greater demand as older and more experienced men are made redundant. Against that, although reverting to the ranks, the soldier in the SAS will receive extra pay, and after his probationary period can expect to be enrolled as a permanent member, spending the rest of his career with the regiment. Many senior NCOs take commissions later on in their careers and can serve as officers in a variety of capacities.

An officer too has to consider his career when thinking about applying. The Army as a whole looks with favour upon a tour with the SAS but individual regiments and corps may think differently. Service with the SAS has not hindered certain officers, for example General de la Billière, from rising to extremely high rank, and on acceptance there is the reward of promotion to captain, as there are no subalterns in the regiment. Some officers who join are content with a tour as a troop commander and then go on to different things, but others, obviously bitten by the bug, return as majors to command squadrons and then aspire to a regimental command as a lieutenant-colonel.

On arrival at Hereford equipped with the necessary approvals, each potential recruit is given a thorough medical check-up and has to pass the standard British Army Fitness for Battle test – which, surprisingly enough, means a 10 per cent reduction in the numbers on the course right from the start. The really determined ones will have been working on their own intensive fitness programme for weeks or months in advance. They come from a variety of parent units, but there is said to be a preponderance of men from the Parachute Regiment and the Light Infantry. G Squadron still recruits from the Brigade of Guards, although it is no longer exclusive, and there will be others from the Artillery, the Engineers and the other army formations. There is no shouting of orders and the candidates have to sort themselves out to a large extent. They are issued with basic kit and told when to report and where – if they are not there, the trucks leave without them and they receive a railway warrant back to whence they came. There is no 'bull', standing to attention by beds, marching along shouting slogans or being 'beasted' over assault courses by screaming NCOs.

The staff of the Training Wing, according to accounts, can be quite remote and cynical – almost detached from the process, as if they simply do not care. What they are doing, however, is carefully assessing how each man is doing, judging not only his level of stamina but whether he will 'fit in'. Much of the first week is taken up with instruction in land navigation, for many of the recruits come from units where such skills are not normally practised. In the SAS, map references have to be memorized for security reasons and maps must be carried folded along the original creases to avoid giving the enemy any indication of the operational area. The rest of the time the men work as a group on a series of graduated hikes across the hills to build up their level of fitness.

During the second week the pace hots up, the loads and distances increase, as does the amount of time each man has to spend out on the hills. This inevitably takes its toll: more and more men are either rejected or resign voluntarily. There are also those who have to be put aside on medical grounds, but they at least can come back and have another go. The day starts at four o'clock in the morning as sleep-drugged men, still aching from the previous day, hump their Bergens and rifles on to the trucks which will drop them off at intervals in the hills. They will not finish until late that evening, when there is just enough time to tumble into bed for three or four hours. What were termed 'sickeners' used to be built into the course: for example when the men arrived at the final rendezvous for the day they would see the trucks driving off. They were then told there had been a mistake and they must march another ten miles, which inevitably caused a few waverers to jack it in. Those who simply carried on without grumbling would discover that the trucks were actually parked only a mile or so away. More recently the emphasis has been on encouraging trainees to pass rather than trying to put them off.

By the beginning of the third week, which is known as test week, the intake has probably been roughly halved as more and more red lines are drawn through the faces on the board in the Training Wing. During test week the men have to swim naked across the River Wye carrying their rifles, Bergens and clothes, as well as ascending and descending the fearsome mountain known as Pen-y-Fan, three times non-stop. Nearly 3,000 feet high, it is a formidable obstacle for an experienced fell walker to climb once, but three times with a loaded Bergen weighing by that stage around 40lbs., a rifle that has no sling and has to be carried all the time, and ammunition pouches, calls for a very special type of endurance. To finish the course within the set time limit a man has to jog wherever possible, uphill and down. An added refinement is that he will be on his own against the elements, without the companionship and mutual support of a four-man patrol.

The final endurance march is known as Long Drag, and those who embark upon it are already half dead of exhaustion from the previous days. It entails covering a distance of forty miles in twenty hours over some of the most difficult terrain possible, loaded up with 55lb. in the Bergen. To complete it, a man has to keep going all the time, stopping only to snatch some high-energy food. More potential recruits will drop out during the course of the ordeal, and in February 1979 there was a well-known death: that of Mike Kealey, the hero of Mirbat. He had returned to 22 SAS as a major to command a squadron and opted to put himself through the selection process to prove that he was still up to scratch after a period of deskwork. The weather was appalling, with driving snow, high winds and sleeting rain, yet Kealey opted to march in light order without a layer of windproof clothing and carrying a Bergen weighted with bricks. This resulted in hypothermia as his normal clothing became soaked with rain and drained away his body heat. A couple of hours into the march, some of those on the course noticed that he had slowed down, but as they decided to seek shelter lower down the hillside, he was seen plodding on over a route which he knew well. Others encountered him from time to time, his condition worsening, and finally, after seven hours of exposure, he was discovered, only just alive by a captain and a corporal. The latter dug a snow hole and tried to use his own body temperature to keep Kealey warm, while the captain went down the hill to get help. Kealey died of hypothermia and it took hours for rescue parties to find him. Suspicions were raised about the cause of his death in a recent sensational book by the explorer, Ranulph Fiennes, as we shall see in the next chapter.

Long Drag is a fearsome ordeal even for the fittest of men. You are on your own, with map, compass, watch and a memorized map reference which you must not forget. Every loss of direction means extra distance to be covered and if the mist sweeps in, you have to trust your compass. At that stage there is still a competitive edge among the remaining trainees and a great urge to beat any officers who are on the course. Michael Asher, who passed through it as a Territorial volunteer, described each pace as like 'sitting in a fridge with a hundred-pound barbell on my back'. His book, *Shoot to Kill*, contains a most penetrating description of the whole selection process during the 1970s:

I can try to replace myself on that last hill, already far beyond the normal bounds of exhaustion, still alone after trekking through snow and wind for almost a day. My feet are a raw and bubbling mass of blisters, especially where my pinched toes have rubbed together, despite the gauze inside my boots. I dare not stop to remove the boots, since I know that my tortured feet will instantly swell up like sausages and I will never be able to get them on again. If I sit down and rest, I may just fade off into unconsciousness and be found the next morning frozen to the ground. There are deep galls on my shoulder now and around the kidneys where the Bergen has rubbed against the flesh like sandpaper. The sweat is cold under my shirt, but I dare not stop to put on my sweater. The heavy wool will draw more precious salt out of my pores and slow me down more rapidly. My feet, hands and face are raw with cold. I might be alone in this shapeless night. Perhaps everyone else has reached the RV hours ago. Time is running out. Perhaps my bearing is wrong. A wild blackness of hysteria and misery waits to engulf me.

For the lucky few there are the trucks waiting at the end and helping hands from the instructors to remove Bergens. Mugs of hot sweet tea and cigarettes. Most sleep in the jolting wagons all the way back to Hereford, knowing that their reward is a long weekend at home. The initial selection has weeded out many, and those who return for continuation training know full well that they are still only there on sufferance.

Continuation training lasts for about four months, and since many of the candidates come from specialist branches of the Army, they have to be taught the basic infantry skills, including advanced weapon training and tactical movement. There is also a week each of medical knowledge, signals procedures and demolitions to be passed, interspersed with initiative tests and the ever-present need to keep fit. All this time the candidate is constantly being watched: part of the aim is to weed out anyone who was fit enough to get through the basic selection period but is an idiot when it comes to using his brains. Skills training is followed by a lengthy spell of combat survival and resistance to interrogation.

Combat survival involves learning about edible plants, how to skin and prepare animals and to live off the land by eating fungi, seaweed and roots. It is all about being hunted by others, hiding and camouflage. The basic skills today are refinements of those learnt during the Second World War by aircrew who managed to escape. The trainees learn how to deal with dogs and how to move through country while at the same time covering their tracks. For the final exercise they are let loose after a thorough body search, with nothing but their basic clothing. Their task is to make their way to a rendezvous through countryside infested with other soldiers out looking for them. If caught, they will be taken to the 'pen' and interrogated; and if they make it they will suffer the same fate anyway. The basic techniques of interrogation were learnt in Western armies from men who were captured during the Korean War and others who were later prisoners of the Vietcong. The techniques that are practised on SAS trainees are those which were condemned by international courts when used on suspects in Northern Ireland. A man who is captured must be able to resist as long as possible in order not to compromise the operation he is on or the lives of his mates who may still be at large, so the exercise must be realistic.

As the essential tool of the interrogator is sensory deprivation, the captives are kept hooded and bound with no means of knowing what the time is, or even which day it is. They are permitted only to reveal their name, rank and number and date of birth. Even an innocent 'Yes' or 'No' can mean failure. The interrogator will offer inducements, such as cigarettes, food or comforting words, and will try to appear as a friend. Alternatively he may threaten a beating, or worse. The captive, who may be stripped naked to increase the sense of humiliation, will be kept for long periods spreadeagled against a wall he can touch only with his fingertips and on tiptoe, which is extremely painful. If he slackens his position, he will be kicked or given a thumping. He has to maintain that position for hours on end while he can sense his guards drinking beer, and smell plates of bacon and eggs. He may well hear sounds of snarling dogs or someone being beaten and screaming. In fact no real brutality is used as that is felt to be counterproductive, but some of the toughest of candidates have failed at the interrogation stage.

The interrogation is reckoned by many to be the nastiest experience of the whole course, and it is followed by six weeks learning basic jungle skills in Borneo: tracking through the forests, mounting ambushes and mastering survival in a strange environment. The final stage is completion of the basic army parachuting course.

Having successfully completed selection and continuation training, the handful of remaining candidates are called before the commanding officer and given their beige beret and badge, which means that they are members of the regiment, having fulfilled all the basic requirements.

They are then assigned to a squadron and can opt for their specializations, both troop and individual, on the basis that they are still virtual beginners. It is said that it takes two full years of hard graft to train an SAS man, who will spend the rest of his time with the regiment still training.

Those deciding on freefall parachuting go on a series of courses which will equip them to drop from 25,000 feet into a low-level canopy opening – the HALO, or high altitude low opening, technique. They have to be able to free-fall into a narrow Norwegian valley while presenting a minute radar image, loaded with their kit, and land ready to move off instantly. The mountain troop men will be taught the techniques of climbing on rock and ice anywhere in the world, plus the peculiarities of warfare in that environment. The boat troop volunteers will train with the SBS in all the various specialities of amphibious warfare – exiting from submarines and landing craft, navigating Gemini inflatables on to beaches, placing underwater charges and swimming with breathing apparatus. For mobility troop members it is off to the deserts of the Gulf sheikhdoms to learn the skills of navigating their Land Rovers with the sun compasses, extricating them from sand dunes and surviving in the aridity of the sun-baked landscape.

If that were not enough, the newly badged member must also master his own personal skill within the four-man patrol module. Some will learn advanced signalling with the latest sophisticated equipment, while the medics have to master even basic surgery in the field, studying in hospitals. Those with a talent for languages find themselves back at school dealing with the grammar of Malay dialects, different versions of Arabic and, one could conjecture, today Serbo-Croat. The fourth member is the weapons and demolition specialist who will learn to deal with every conceivable firearm, both British and foreign, and will have to pass through the CQB wing.

Having mastered the skills necessary to become accepted as a fully trained member of his squadron and troop, after about two years the 'new boy' will settle down to the routine of duty CRW squadron, tours in Northern Ireland, trips abroad and further individual training. Each man must study the rudiments of the specialities of the others, so that if one is injured the others can carry on. There are also cross-postings between squadrons so that the boat troop man has a chance to gain experience in mountaineering or desert navigation. The regimental motto has been corrupted to read, 'Who Trains Wins'.

Michael Asher, the thinking ex-Para, summed up his experience which might well be that of any SAS man, regular or Territorial:

> No, you can never quite recapture it in words. And to say you walked such and such a distance, carrying such and such a weight conveys nothing. Whenever subsequently I have tried to explain in a few words the agony of SAS selection, and why these marches on the hills should be the basis for choosing members of the best unit of its kind in the world, my words have evoked responses like, 'That doesn't sound much!'. . . . SAS selection is one of those things which 'doesn't sound much' until you try it. Like the SAS itself, it is simple, direct and deadly effective. But pain and agony fade quickly to become dim memories and pleasure alone remains. I can only say this: some of the strongest, most determined, most resilient men I have ever met were SAS, and I never found a single one amongst them who found selection easy.

14
Past, Present and Future

The purpose of this chapter is to tie up a few loose ends and bring the story of the post-war SAS Regiment to a close, although it will continue to excite, and sometimes exasperate, the public appetite for information for a long time to come. Political events in recent years such as the liberation of Eastern Europe and the end of the threat of the Third World War have no doubt meant changes in the strategic thinking of those responsible for the training and eventual deployment of SAS units. Sadly, the sole constancy is the continuation of the conflict in Northern Ireland. So far the SAS does not seem to have been affected by the planned reduction in the size of the British Army, although it must be assumed that a new role will have to be discovered for the two TA regiments. One can only surmise that there will be a small delegation from Hereford keeping a watchful eye on events in the former Yugoslavia and that the Kremlin will have a good stock of maps of the area.

The last time that the SAS went officially to war was in the Gulf, and thanks to the memoirs of General Sir Peter de la Billière, whose name has featured several times in this account, we have some idea of the regiment's activities in that conflict. When Saddam Hussain's troops invaded Kuwait on 2 August 1990, few imagined that the outcome would be the deployment of some 45,000 British service personnel as part of a huge coalition army. During the build-up of that force there were dire predictions about casualties running into the thousands, body bags being flown home, poison gas and even the nuclear option. In the event, the expulsion of the Iraqi dictator from Kuwait was achieved with remarkably few casualties and the 'Mother of Battles' which had been promised turned out to have been bluff.

Sir Peter, shortly before his retirement, was appointed to command British forces in the Gulf and arrived in Saudi Arabia in early October where he was confronted by a number of immediate problems. One was the lack of intelligence about the enemy, just as in the Falklands War, and another was the presence of large numbers of Western civilian hostages in Iraqi hands. Saddam Hussain was threatening to imprison them at strategic sites around the country to deter attack by coalition forces. There was in fact an SAS unit in the United Arab Emirates, D Squadron, officially on a training exercise, and it was earmarked for an eventual operation to free those hostages. In a mission that could be likened to the disastrous American attempt in 1980 to release their diplomatic personnel from the embassy in Teheran, the SAS would have had to infiltrate Iraq and bring out as many as possible to a rendezvous in the desert from where they could have been flown to safety. Although the various intelligence agencies co-operated with the SAS planners to build up a picture of where the hostages were being held, the operation was never mounted, and the captives were released for Christmas.

By doing this, Saddam Hussain gave away a vital trump card; Sir Peter himself admits that they could hardly have expected to bring out more than half, if that, of the numbers held. Had they done so, it is quite probable that the rest would have been murdered as a reprisal. As late as 11 November there seemed to be no other useful mission that special forces could perform, but in December, with the hostages freed, they were ordered to plan deep penetration missions into both Iraq and Kuwait. It seems that General Schwarzkopf, the American commander, was not convinced that special forces had any useful role to play and that targets could be eliminated by use of air power or armour, but by the second week in January that position changed, as a result of a presentation made by the SAS at headquarters in Riyadh. It was agreed that they could cross the border on the day the air war started. To reinforce the numbers available, B Squadron was flown out from England, straight from a spell as CRW standby team.

At that time D Squadron was still stationed 'somewhere in the Arabian Peninsula'. When war broke out officially on 17 January 1991 they had to be moved, with all their vehicles and equipment, 1,500 miles to a base north of Riyadh. That redeployment was carried out by Hercules aircraft and they were ready to start operations on 20 January. There was, at that stage, a level of controversy about the methods of insertion, with some patrols wishing to be dropped by helicopter to operate on foot, while others preferred to drive in by Land Rover and motorcycle. Taking vehicles meant that heavier weaponry could be carried and that the patrol would have a high degree of mobility, but opposed to that was the risk of detection from the air in terrain which offered little cover. The action radius of foot patrols was limited and they would have no means of escape if detected, but they could conceal themselves far more easily.

In the end it was left to patrols to decide for themselves, and as an additional task they were asked to provide three observation posts to keep watch on the Iraqi supply routes. Some opted to work on foot; others drove in. In terms of communications they were vastly better served than they had been in the Falklands and each patrol even carried a portable satellite navigation aid which could pinpoint their position to within a few metres in often featureless desert. Once over the border, however, and settling into position, the mission was drastically altered when the first Scud missile was launched against Israel. While the diplomats exerted the strongest pressure to keep that country out of the war, the mobile Scud missile launchers became priority number one for the SAS as they proved difficult to locate from the air. Moving around an area of several thousand square kilometres, the patrols scored some amazing successes against the launchers, both by calling down air strikes and by direct attack with their Milan anti-tank rockets. They also concentrated on communications facilities and managed to capture an Iraqi artillery officer complete with his sets of maps. Sir Peter claims that the SAS war against the Scud launchers was so successful that after 26 January no further effective launches were made against Israel, as the rockets and their crews had been driven back into the hinterland of Iraq, out of effective range. In May 1991, John Major, the British Prime Minister, stated: 'I'll tell you who destroyed the Scuds. It was the British SAS. They were fabulous.'

The area in which the men were operating was a high rocky plateau in the west of Iraq, which at night became bitterly cold, the effects of which had been underestimated. It seems almost unbelievable that in Iraq the

SAS suffered from snow, hail and frost, and had to light fires under the fuel tanks of the vehicles to stop the diesel from freezing. Yet they operated right round the clock, carrying out pin-prick raids which led the enemy to believe that considerable forces were involved. The SBS were also carrying out clandestine operations, and on 23 October destroyed a considerable stretch of the main communication cable running from Baghdad to the front-line units. They were flown in in two giant Chinook helicopters, did the job and were all safely extricated.

In war, though, there is always a bitter price to be paid, and one of the foot patrols, Bravo Two Zero, was discovered shortly after having been inserted by Chinook, on a mission to hunt for Scud launchers and to cut communications cables along the MSR, the main supply route running west from Baghdad. In all eight men were known to be missing, and there was naturally the worry that if they were captured they would be paraded on television, with consequent distress to their families who did not even know that they were inside Iraq. If, however, the next-of-kin were to be informed, there was the risk that SAS involvement behind the lines would leak out. In the event it was decided to inform the families and swear them to secrecy.

Sir Peter gave an outline account of what happened to that patrol, but in a recently published book, *Bravo Two Zero*, its commander, Sergeant 'Andy McNab', has told the full story, which corrects his boss's version in a number of ways. This is the first time that a detailed account of a modern SAS operation has been recounted in such depth so soon after the event with expletives undeleted, a rich black humour, and typical modesty.

According to McNab, the patrol was inserted by mistake right in the middle of an Iraqi troop concentration. After a day hidden up near an Iraqi anti-aircraft battery the patrol was spotted by an Arab goat-herd, who gave the alarm. The men decided to move off, but when they emerged into the open they were confronted by Iraqi troops and a battle developed. Hampered by their Bergens, which weighed in the order of 100lbs. each, the men abandoned them and managed to reach cover without sustaining any injuries. They had no alternative but to walk for their lives and the nearest frontier was the Syrian, 120 kilometres away. After making a feint to indicate to pursuers that they had headed south for the Saudi border, they moved north, and in seven hours covered sixty kilometres, which brought them back to the Baghdad–Amman road.

In the lead was Corporal Chris. As one of the men, Sergeant Phillips, was showing signs of exhaustion, they shared out his belt equipment and weapons between them and placed him second in the column. The road itself was flat and the valley some three miles wide, so the corporal led across it at a fast pace, but when he reached the high ground on the other side he realized that five of the patrol were missing. Apparently they had heard an aircraft and had stopped to try to contact it with their search and rescue beacons. The three remaining men pressed on through the night, with the problem ahead of them of being caught out in the open in daylight. Eventually they found themselves in an empty tank shelter scooped out of the sand and lay down in one of the ruts made by the tracks. When dawn broke, it started to snow, and the three lay there, unable to move, frozen and soaking wet throughout the day.

That was the start of what was to become a remarkable feat of endurance for the corporal known as Chris. The three set off when darkness fell, minus the satellite navigation set which had been with the rest of the patrol, but the exhausted man, unable to carry on, had to be left behind and subsequently died of exposure. Down to two, they staggered on through the night and at daybreak managed to find a shallow wadi in which to shelter. During the morning, they were found by an Arab, who urged them to go with him to get some food. The corporal declined, but the other went off, only to be led straight to an enemy position. On his own, tormented with hunger and thirst and with his feet in a desperate state, the corporal struck off towards the distant frontier. His ordeal was to last eight nights and seven days during which he existed on two packets of biscuits and some contaminated water. Eventually, near death and hallucinating, he crossed the frontier and was given food and water in a peasant hut. After further tribulations he was finally handed over to the British Embassy and sent home.

The five men who had originally become separated suffered appallingly from the effects of the cold, which led to advanced hypothermia as they too trekked towards the border. They made it to the metalled road that ran between Baghdad and Syria, where they hijacked a vehicle at gunpoint, which turned out to be an ancient New York yellow cab. They left the driver and his two passengers beside the road. The men drove along quite merrily for several hours, but were caught up in a vehicle checkpoint only a few miles away from freedom and had to shoot their way out. They became separated and were rapidly running out of ammunition for their Minimi light machine guns and Armalite M16 rifles. Andy McNab was finally caught only four kilometres from the border, holed up in a culvert, totally exhausted and with only his fighting knife left.

According to Sir Peter's account, four SAS were killed in the Gulf War, though afterwards allegations surfaced in the press about others having been tortured to death. It had been stated in the *Daily Express* on 3 August 1991 that a party of six dressed as Arabs had infiltrated Iraq to capture part of a nuclear device. Two had managed to escape but the other four – Sergeant Vince Phillips, Corporal David Tenbury, Trooper Bob Consiglio and Trooper Steve Lane, according to an unnamed 'source' – had been captured and murdered. We know that Consiglio, Lane and Phillips were members of Bravo Two Zero and were not dressed as Arabs except that they were wearing the *shamag* headdress which is standard for the SAS in desert conditions. Vince Phillips died of exposure and his body was handed over to the Red Cross at the end of the war. The other two patrol members were killed in action and their bodies were also recovered. Tenbury was presumably on a different mission. As Sir Peter stated that all special forces personnel were accounted for after the war, it is unlikely that anyone was simply done away with.

What is certain is that those men who were captured were badly beaten. McNab's story of his time in captivity makes grim reading and is remarkable testimony to his courage and that of his mates. His Iraqi interrogators behaved with callous brutality, which ceased only when it began to dawn on them that they were losing the war. On 4 March the Iraqis handed over their first batch of British captives, among whom were two men whose names had never been released as missing in action. They were seen briefly on television and were named in the press, before being spirited away, and the authorities refused, quite rightly, to say anything about them. McNab and 'Mark' came out two days later and were smuggled out of the aircraft into an ambulance.

The other patrols meanwhile continued their deadly work behind the lines and a column of vehicles drove into Iraq on a resupply mission. In a display of bravado the Warrant Officers' and Sergeants' Mess held a formal meeting in the open desert at which decisions were reached and minutes taken. The SBS had also been busy: they went into Kuwait City on 27 February. The following day a troop abseiled down from a helicopter on to the roof of the British Embassy and officially re-occupied it. In various newspaper accounts, many of which may have been flights of fantasy, other operations were hinted at. There were persistent reports that before the air war started an SAS team had captured the tracking device of an Iraqi surface to air missile, or had helicoptered out the entire rocket and its crew. There were also reports that SAS men disguised as Arabs had been inserted in and around Baghdad, guiding the Allied bombers to their targets. Whatever the truth of such statements, the fact is that special forces in general, including a large American contingent, made a very substantial contribution to the eventual success of the campaign and thoroughly vindicated the decision to deploy them.

When the SAS goes to war, both in regular conflict and in the fight against terrorism, it does so with a broad spectrum of public approval and it is only a small minority of anarchists, Trotskyists and assorted left-wingers who persist in seeing the regiment as some sort of governmental Praetorian Guard opposing the interests of the 'working classes'. However much it may shun publicity, the regiment is often thrust into the limelight by the activities of its members once they have left the Army. In an earlier chapter I alluded to certain extra-curricular adventures with which David Stirling and others were involved, and it was his company, Watchguard, which was the forerunner of a number of other private security ventures. It was the exposure in 1987 of the nefarious dealings of a certain colonel of the US Marine Corps, Oliver North, that subjected companies which employed ex-members of the SAS to the mercies of public scrutiny by hostile journalists.

Stirling himself lost interest in Watchguard International in 1972 following its exposure in the press, and spent the following years involved in a number of organizations which were set up to combat left-wing influence in government, the Civil Service and the trade unions. That period coincided with the growth of international terrorism, and thus a market was created for such services as bodyguarding, kidnap protection and security in general – in which SAS training was a marketable commodity. The government too required, from time to time, specialists to undertake certain tasks with which it was unwilling to become officially identified. On average, a professional soldier in the British Army serves an engagement of twenty-two years and thus retires at around 40 years of age with a pension, but still needs some form of occupation or second career.

Two things that anyone who has served in the SAS has to sell are his expertise and the mystique of the regiment itself. Some manage to market their skills in a purely civilian environment, by running Outward Bound type courses for business executives. In that field one only has to think of Lofty Wiseman, who has made a successful career as an author and broadcaster on the subject of survival based on the success of his book, *The Official SAS Survival Handbook*. A few others have ventured into print, although that has never been encouraged. 'Soldier I' was none too popular with the powers that be when his memoirs were published a couple of years ago. Many of those who leave the regiment seem quite happy to start new careers as landlords of pubs, salesmen, or owners of small shops. Quite a few find employment in the security industry. There is nothing wrong with that, and many simply join the ranks of ex-policemen who work in a purely civilian environment, responsible for such mundane matters as crowd control at big events, vetting personnel and advising management on security matters in general. A relatively small number of men are recruited into one of the state-run intelligence agencies, the Secret Intelligence Service (SIS) or MI5.

One of the main problems that many men face is organizing the abrupt transition into civilian life. Trained to the peak of efficiency and enjoying the privileges of relatively senior rank after half a lifetime of service, it is difficult simply to put on civilian clothes and thus become a 'civvy'. One man who has spent almost all of his military career in the SAS told me recently that the greatest problem was the necessary readjustment of thought patterns. In the Army in general, a man knows his place in the command structure, is given clear instructions about the job he has to do and is then expected to carry it out. He is not paid to trouble himself about the wider implications, possible political connotations or where the money is coming from. If he requires a particular piece of kit, he demands it from stores, and if the issue is justified, he will get it. In civilian life, however, there is the need to adjust to lateral thinking, to take ultimate responsibility for one's actions and to sell oneself to potential employers. Income tax, VAT and a whole horde of other commercial implications intrude, and have to be dealt with in a businesslike way.

A small number of private security companies, run by people who have served in the regiment, give rise to frequent accusations in the press about mercenaries and hired guns. These firms absorb the talents and expertise of what is essentially a pool of freelance operatives, who enter the market-place on leaving the SAS. These men sometimes form small companies themselves, perhaps going into partnership with a friend and hiring an office somewhere. Others simply let it be known that they are available for assignments, and such is the close-knit nature of the fraternity that their abilities are graded by their peer group. There are the Sabre squadron men, who are backed up by various personnel who have served in the support arms of the SAS such as signals experts, vehicle specialists, computer technicians and medical people.

Freelance operatives who are employed on a contract basis by such private security firms fulfil a variety of tasks. By far the most common is bodyguarding, or 'close protection', for which there is seldom a lack of clients. That type of work can be on an individual basis, or based on the provision of a team of men who work in shifts around the clock. Such assignments can be on a long-term basis or purely for a couple of days when a particularly vulnerable person happens to be in the United Kingdom. Ex-SAS men are especially adept at such work, as they are expert shots and are well trained in risk assessment. As the SAS does not encourage thugs and braggarts, it follows that they are eminently suitable to accompany VIPs, being able to fade into the background, wearing dark suits, quiet ties and evening dress when required – with weaponry kept discreetly out of sight.

In addition to bodyguarding there is the entire field of covert surveillance, commercial investigation and intelligence-gathering, at a level far higher than that normally offered by the local private detective agency. This sort of work can be offensive or defensive; in the latter case, a company often needs the services of experts to 'sweep' its premises against electronic eavesdropping. This type of assignment can often degenerate into morally grey areas, and even some which are downright black. Industrial espionage is one example, and it is extremely prevalent in commercial life. It is not against the law and a company that feels threatened by a competitor, for example, can apply legitimate means to counter action being taken against it. The definition of legitimate means, however, is often somewhat nebulous. After all, Spy Catcher Peter Wright, employed by the government, 'burgled and bugged his way around London'.

The degree of industrial espionage that is discovered is only the tip of the iceberg. The cases that make headlines can well lead to appearances in court, where the fact that the defendants may have served in the SAS adds spice to the story. The fact is, of course, that we live in violent times, and those who can pay for it have the right to protect themselves from unwarranted intrusion, threats against their executives and possible danger to their families from kidnappers.

After Watchguard International was quietly liquidated in 1972, the next such company to appear was Control Risks, which was formed in 1973 to advise the insurance industry on asset protection and risk assessment, especially in the field of potential kidnapping of business executives. The board of Control Risks has included ex-commissioners of the Metropolitan Police, Field Marshals and other luminaries, and it subsequently became a subsidiary of the insurance brokers, Hogg Robinson. It has provided ransom negotiators in kidnap cases and there is no evidence that it has engaged in paramilitary activities, despite the occasional allegations that have surfaced.

Far more controversial has been the company known as Keeni-Meeni Services or KMS Ltd, the name deriving from the undercover patrols carried out by the SAS in Aden. Formed in 1974 as a subsidiary of Control Risks by a former SAS officer, Major David Walker, its brief was to win government contracts for security work. In 1977 Walker staged a management buy-out and took control. He was joined by Colonel Jim Johnson who had managed the Yemen operation for David Stirling, and the company base was moved to Jersey. For the first ten years of its existence, KMS remained decently in the shadows, mainly occupied with lucrative contracts to train and equip the Sultan of Oman's special forces. It procured arms and special kit, and supplied ex-SAS personnel on contract. There is no reason to suppose the government had any objections, as Oman was regarded as a friendly power. In 1983 KMS also became involved in a training mission in Sri Lanka with the blessing of the British government, which had been asked to provide an SAS contingent to help local forces suppress the uprising by the Tamil Tigers. Unwilling to antagonize the Indian government, the British temporized by passing the contract to KMS, which was deniable. The Foreign Office frequently stated that it had no contact with the company, but under pressure the government did once admit that it had hired bodyguards for diplomats abroad from KMS.

The Sri Lankan contract went badly wrong: without KMS' knowledge the trainees set about torturing and executing opponents of the regime. The original SAS contingent had endeavoured to teach their 'hearts and minds' approach, which was undermined when an aggressive Israeli contingent arrived on the island, some of whom were determined to sell weapons. This resulted in mass resignations from the team by men, several of whom were Fijians, who were disgusted by what was going on, and these activities were highlighted in a report by Amnesty International. In an attempt to salvage the contract, Walker and Johnson brought in ex-soldiers from ordinary regiments and ex-Rhodesian SAS, whose racist attitudes antagonized the trainees.

Walker's downfall, however, was caused by his links with Oliver North, which had started in 1984 when Congress refused further funding to support the Contra rebels in Nicaragua. It was alleged in the US Congress that Walker offered to organize a team to infiltrate the capital Managua to destroy the government's Soviet-made Hind helicopters, and also alleged that KMS supplied men to train the guerrillas, and provide some helicopter pilots. Neither Walker nor Johnson admitted this. The company's involvement came to light when a sketched flow-chart prepared by North was found. When the story broke in 1987, every investigative journalist scented a juicy story and a horde of articles about Walker and Co. were written. That June, Walker and Johnson handed over the day-to-day running of KMS to two former SAS officers, and much of the work was passed to a subsidiary company based in London. From time to time during 1987, other stories surfaced about KMS, alleging that they were training the guerrillas in Afghanistan at the behest of the CIA.

In the paramilitary security world, when KMS faded from view it left the field largely free for Defence Systems Ltd, which was founded by Major Alistair Morrison in 1981. DSL has been occupied with a contract in Mozambique, training government troops to fight South-African-funded MRN guerrillas, and has also been active in guarding mines and communications in Angola. In spite of the expenditure of a vast amount of journalistic time, the allegations about ex-SAS 'Dogs of War' proved to have little substance and most of those that were discovered were Rhodesians. No great scandals rocked the British government to the core and the vast majority of security work is perfectly legitimate. If a wealthy Arab feels the need for skilled and expensive guards for his racehorses, then who can blame an ex-member of the regiment for taking on the job?

In 1986 David Stirling re-entered the security business when he formed KAS Enterprises, operating from his offices in South Audley Street in London. By sheer coincidence the number of the building was twenty-two, which in numerals could be expressed as 22 SAS. He appointed as his managing director Ian Crooke, who had left the Army as a lieutenant-colonel and whose last posting had been as commanding officer of 23 SAS. A small team of men with excellent records in the regiment was recruited, but business was hard to come by, despite Stirling's contacts, and overheads were high. By then, however, Stirling's health was beginning to fail and he spent less and less time in direct control of the company. According to his biographer, Alan Hoe, his reasons for this last business venture were threefold, and one prime motivation was financial: he wished to make some money to set up a trust fund for the younger members of the Stirling clan. Beyond that, though, he saw danger looming for one or two African heads of state who were under threat from coups, and the vulnerability of industry to extortion by terrorists and criminals.

Banking upon his reputation in Black Africa from the days of Capricorn (see p. 82) Stirling provided assistance to at least one president who was an old friend, by sending experts to advise on security. KAS may also have been active in the Philippines on behalf of the government there, and it set up a subsidiary company to provide anti-poaching patrols along Scottish salmon rivers. It was in the field of rhino and elephant poaching, however, that KAS became involved in a fascinating adventure that sadly ended up in controversy and recrimination.

During 1987 Prince Bernhard of the Netherlands, President of the World Wildlife Fund, was extremely disturbed by the increase in rhino poaching in Africa. The Geneva-based organization had produced a whole raft of costly reports, but seemed powerless to stop the poaching, which was threatening the extinction of the species. Prince Bernhard's concerns were shared by Dr John Hanks, the WWF programme director for Africa. Quite independently, a fund-raising appeal on behalf of the endangered rhinos arrived one day in the post at the offices of KAS, where it was read by David Stirling's secretary. There was some discussion about the problem and the chairman, with his passionate interest in Africa and in wildlife conservation, became extremely enthusiastic about doing something. As money was in short supply as usual, he proposed to offer the services of KAS to provide direct help. An approach was made to the Prince via Hanks, and a discreet meeting was arranged on 13 November 1987, at which Stirling and Crooke argued their case for action. The Prince too became enthusiastic and agreed to finance a preliminary report out of his own pocket, bypassing the WWF bureaucracy. What he wanted was proof of collusion on the part of governments in Africa with which he could confront them. Thus Project Lock was born out of idealism and genuine concern.

The preliminary phase, which took up much of 1988, was essentially an intelligence-gathering operation concerned with black rhino horn poaching, but it extended into white rhino and elephant ivory as well. The aims were:

to identify the organization and individuals involved in the poaching trade;
to identify the smuggling routes to the intermediate and final destinations;
to collate all available intelligence in order to provide an accurate perception of the scale of poaching;
to produce recommendations by which the activities of the poachers could be reduced.

David Stirling, whose faculties were as sharp as ever, realized that the only long-term solution was to reduce the demand for horn and ivory, for which there were two main markets. The first was the Yemen where men carried traditional ceremonial daggers, the handles of which were made from ivory horn. The second was the Far East where rhino horn was believed to have aphrodisiac properties and where ivory was traditionally carved into trinkets. His team concluded that on the ground in Africa they should target the buyers of illegal horn and ivory by entrapment, as well as encouraging the training of paramilitary game wardens.

The active phase of the operation got underway in January 1989. Ian Crooke and a team of a dozen ex-SAS members established themselves in South Africa, where they organized a safe house and set up computer database containing their accumulated intelligence. It was then that their problems really began. The team established cordial relations with various South African agencies based on mutual self-help, which immediately made them suspect to Black Africans. Apart from a couple of Fijians, all the team were white, which hampered their movements in countries such as Zambia and Zimbabwe and elaborate cover stories had to be invented. Even worse were the jealousies their presence provoked among certain vested interests on the ground who saw them as a bunch of gung-ho cowboys. Lastly, there was the problem of endemic corruption in high places: in a number of countries, government officials and army officers worked hand in glove with the poachers.

In July 1989 the whole operation was blown wide open, allegedly as a result of Ian Crooke's indiscretion. A local Reuters correspondent issued a report which insinuated that Project Lock was an undercover operation designed to destabilize certain Black African states, funded by South Africa and using as operatives ex-SAS mercenaries. The respected magazine, *Africa Confidential*, went further, mistaking the initials KAS for KMS and linking the firm with the North affair. Stirling sued for libel and won, but by then the damage had been done and a well-known figure who had been prepared to donate a large sum of money withdrew his offer. As most of the money put up by Prince Bernhard had been spent, Stirling and a London businessman associated with the project put considerable sums of their own into the kitty because they both believed passionately in what they were trying to achieve. By the autumn, however, the financial situation was desperate and regretfully they had to cease operating as they could no longer even afford the payroll. In February 1991, three months after the death of Stirling, KAS was finally wound up.

On the positive side, much had been achieved, especially the setting up of a successful training base for game wardens in Namibia. The very presence of the team had concentrated minds in a number of countries, and much valuable intelligence had been gained. On the negative side, the termination of Project Lock resulted in wild allegations, documents being leaked to the press and an ex-employee threatening to take Stirling to an industrial tribunal. Part of the problem lay in the increasing illness of the chairman and the lengthy communications between London and South Africa. There was also a certain level of incompetence in the field and a lack of rapport between the London staff and Ian Crooke.

In the 1990 New Year Honours List, David Stirling finally received the long overdue knighthood, but in November he died, missing the fiftieth anniversary of the regiment he had founded in the Western Desert. Controversy continued to dog Project Lock, with press allegations of financial improprieties, and also press accusations that Prince Bernhard had been ripped off. These culminated in a police investigation that uncovered no evidence of illegal activities.

The last few months of Sir David's life had been soured when in June 1990 allegations of a different nature were made against KAS. According to newspaper reports, the firm had been engaged by the chief executive of National Car Parks to spy on a rival company and had infiltrated a former woman army officer into Europarks as a secretary. At the time of writing, this matter is still *sub judice* and is for the courts to decide. But tacky industrial espionage would have been out of keeping with the rest of Sir David's life, committed as it was to personal integrity.

Shortly after David Stirling's death Ranulph Fiennes's *The Feather Men* was published. Fiennes, the well-known explorer, had been an army officer attached to but not a member of the SAS during the war in Dhofar in the early 1970s. In *The Feather Men* he alleged that four men, two of whom were members of the SAS, were killed by a mysterious organization called the Clinic, which had been hired by an Arab sheikh to avenge the deaths of his sons in the conflict. The fifth victim was to have been the author himself, but he was rescued in the nick of time by an equally mysterious group known as the Feather Men. Fiennes, whose book used reported speech but otherwise purported to be factual, stated that the Feather Men had been founded by Stirling as a sort of upmarket vigilante group to avenge those who had in some way been wronged.

In the previous chapter I referred to the death of Mike Kealey from exposure in the Brecon Beacons. This appeared to be perfectly straightforward, yet the book states that he was murdered by the Clinic by an injection of insulin. The other supposed SAS victim was Corporal 'Mac' McAuliffe, who had been invalided out of the regiment after being blown up by a land mine in 1975. As a result of his injuries he had suffered from chronic epilepsy, and he died of a fit at his home in

Hereford. That too, allegedly, had been engineered by the mysterious assassins.

The accuracy or otherwise of this book remains shrouded in mystery. There has been no flurry of writs but naturally the SAS has denied involvement. The detail in the book is quite impressive; it seems unlikely that the author can have made it all up and hoped to get away with it. Fiennes states quite categorically that he was 'authorized' by the Feather Men to write the story, which would clearly have been difficult without their co-operation – if, indeed, they existed.

In 1991 the SAS Regiment and family celebrated its anniversary with a series of events which brought together a horde of members past and present for banquets, a church service and jollifications. Security was tight and the various events passed without untoward notice in the press. Yet in spite of the nostalgia that such occasions evoke, those responsible for British military planning inevitably have to look towards the future of special forces as a whole. During the 1980s the scope of the directorate was enlarged to include the Royal Marines SBS, which provides the deputy commander under an SAS brigadier. Closer co-operation between the two forces was unavoidable after their joint experiences in the Falklands.

During the 1960s it was government policy to disengage from commitments outside Europe and to rely on a nuclear deterrent capability supplied by the Americans. Yet, paradoxically, on both occasions that this country has officially gone to war since then, we have been obliged to project considerable forces over large distances into theatres over which we possessed little intelligence in advance. In both cases, the Falklands and the Gulf, special forces provided a considerable amount of vital intelligence for a relatively small cost in terms of equipment and manpower. As Britain gradually withdraws from Germany and reduces its armed forces, there are many who state that it may end up with insufficient manpower to meet its international commitments. In the future these could involve the defence of British interests overseas and taking part in United Nations or European 'peace-making' operations. It may well be that the SAS and other such units will find a ready-made field of employment within multinational forces, especially as other European countries tend to look to their police to provide counter-insurgency expertise.

Many of those who attended the celebrations in Hereford in 1991 will have paid a visit to the regimental plot in the graveyard beside a church on the outskirts of the town, where many who 'failed to beat the clock' lie buried. That expression is used to denote those whose names are inscribed on an ornamental clock tower at the barracks, who died in action or through accidents. There they rest, under normal headstones, overshadowed by gentle trees in a very English setting – far from the heat of the Oman and the freezing seas of the South Atlantic. The need for anonymity past, their names, service numbers and parent regiments are neatly inscribed under the winged dagger badge.

Most people admire the SAS and are glad that they are there. A few hate them as instruments of an oppressive government. Enemies certainly have cause to fear them, the men with droopy moustaches and names like Taff, Jock, Chalkie, Spike and Snapper. From a shaky re-start in 1947, the regiment has refined itself, learnt from its mistakes and, above all, has been able to adapt to changing circumstances – in a democratic society that is traditionally wary of military élitism. Yet the lessons of history demonstrate that such societies, once they lose the will to defend themselves, often on ethical grounds, are easy prey for the terrorist, the dictator or the demagogue. May the regiment continue to serve our society, imperfections and all, for as long as it is needed.

The Organization of the SAS

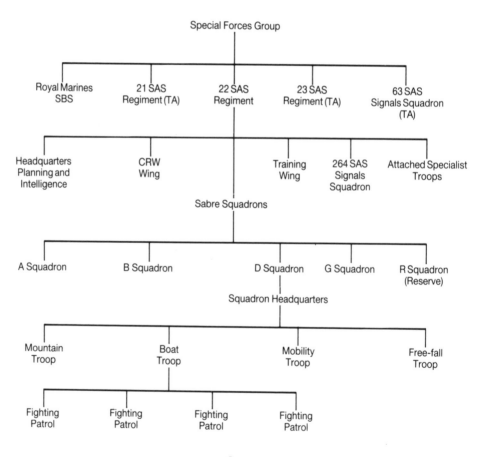

Abbreviations

BAOR	British Army of the Rhine
BATT	British Army Training Teams
CCO	Clandestine Communist Organization (Borneo)
CLF	Commander Land Forces
COBRA	Cabinet Office Briefing Room
CQB	close quarter battle
CRW	counter-revolutionary warfare
CTs	Communist terrorists (Malaya)
DL/AW	Directorate of Land/Air Warfare
DLF	Dhofar Liberation Front
DSL	Defence Systems Ltd
DZ	dropping zone
GPMG	general-purpose machine gun
HALO	high altitude low opening
HE	higher establishment
Int.	Intelligence
Int and Sy	Intelligence and Security Group (Northern Ireland)
JOC	Joint Operations Centre (MoD)
JRRU	Joint Reserve Reconnaissance Unit
KAS	security company founded by Sir David Stirling
KMS	Keeni-Meeni Services Ltd
MRF	Military Reconnaissance Force (Northern Ireland)
NCO	non-commissioned officer
OCTU	Officer Cadet Training Unit

OP	observation post
PFLO	Popular Front for the Liberation of Oman
PIRA	Provisional Irish Republican Army
REME	Royal Electrical and Mechanical Engineers
RFA	Royal Fleet Auxiliary
RHQ	Regimental Headquarters
RTU	return to unit
RUC	Royal Ulster Constabulary
SAF	Sultan's Armed Forces (Oman)
SBS	Special Boat Section
SIS	Secret Intelligence Service (MI6)
SLR	self-loading rifle
SOAF	Sultan of Oman's Air Force
SOE	Special Operations Executive
SSM	Squadron Sergeant Major
TA	Territorial Army

Bibliography

Adams, James, *Secret Armies*, Hutchinson, 1988.

Adams, James, Morgan, Robin, and Bambridge, Anthony, *Ambush. The War between the SAS and the IRA*, Pan, 1988.

Akehurst, John, *We Won a War: The Campaign in Oman 1965–75*, Michael Russell, 1982.

Arkless, David C., *The Secret War. Dhofar, 1971–72*, William Kimber, 1988.

Asher, Michael, *Shoot to Kill*, Viking, 1990.

Ballinger, Adam, *The Quiet Soldier*, Chapman, 1992.

Barber, Noel, *War of the Running Dogs: Malaya 1948–1960*, Collins, 1971.

Billière, Gen. Sir Peter de la, *Storm Command*, Collins, 1992.

Burden, R.A. *et al. The Air War*, Arms & Armour Press, 1986.

Buxton, David, *Honour to the Airborne. Pt. II*, Elmdon, Solihull, 1985.

Cole, Barbara, *The Elite: The Story of the Rhodesian Special Air Service*, Three Knights, Transkei, 1985.

—— *The Elite – Pictorial*, Three Knights, 1987. Photographic supplement to *The Elite*.

Cooper, Johnny (with Anthony Kemp), *One of the Originals*, Pan, 1991.

Cramer, Chris and Harris, Sim, *Hostage*, John Clare, 1982.

Daly, Lt.-Col. Ron Reid, *Selous Scouts. Top Secret War*, Galligo, South Africa, 1982.

Deane-Drummond, Anthony, *Arrows of Fortune*, Leo Cooper, 1992.

Dewar, Michael, *The British Army in Northern Ireland*, Arms & Armour Press, 1985.

Dickens, Peter, *SAS: The Jungle Campaign – 22 Special Air Service Regiment in Borneo*, Arms & Armour Press, 1983.

Dillon, Martin, *The Dirty War*, Hutchinson, 1990.

Fiennes, Ranulph, *The Feather Men*, Bloomsbury, 1991.

—— *Living Dangerously*, Macmillan, 1987.

—— *Where Soldiers Fear to Tread*, Hodder & Stoughton, 1975.

Fleming, J. and Faux, R., *Soldiers on Everest*, HMSO, 1977.

Fox, Robert, *Eyewitness Falklands*, Methuen, 1982.

Geraghty, Tony, *Who Dares Wins*, Arms & Armour Press, 1980; Fontana paperback (with additional material) 1983; new edn, 1992.

—— *This is the SAS*, Arco, New York, 1983.

Hastings, Max and Jenkins, Simon, *The Battle for the Falklands*, Michael Joseph, 1983.

Hoe, Alan, *David Stirling*, Little, Brown, 1992.

Horner, D.M., *Phantoms of the Jungle*, Unwin, 1989; Greenhill Books, 1991.

Jeapes, A.S., *SAS.: Operation Oman*, William Kimber, 1980.

Kemp, Anthony, *The Secret Hunters*, Michael O'Mara Books, 1986.

—— *The SAS at War, 1941 to 1945*, John Murray, 1991.

Kennedy, Michael Paul, *Soldier 'I' SAS*, Bloomsbury, 1989.

Kitson, Frank, *Bunch of Fives*, Faber & Faber, 1977.

Ladd, James D., *SAS Operations*, Robert Hale, 1986.

Large, Lofty, *One Man's Special Air Service*, William Kimber, 1987.

Macdonald, Peter, *The SAS in Action*, Sidgwick & Jackson, 1990.

McManners, Hugh, *Falklands Commando*, William Kimber, 1984.

McNab, Andy, *Bravo Two Zero*, Bantam Press, 1993.

Murray, Raymond, *The SAS in Ireland*, Mercier Press, Cork, 1990.

Niven, D. M., *Special Men, Special War. Portraits of Dhofar*, privately published, n.d.

Philip, Craig and Taylor, Allan, *Inside the SAS*, Bloomsbury, 1993.

Rennie, Frank, *Regular Soldier*, Endeavour Press, Auckland, 1987.

Rivers, Gayle, *The Specialist*, Guild, 1985.

Seale, P. and McConville, M., *The Hilton Assignment*, Temple Smith, 1973.

Seymour, William, *British Special Forces*, Grafton Books, 1985.

Shortt, J. *The Special Air Service*, Men-at-Arms Series No. 116, Osprey, 1981.

Smiley, David and Kemp, Peter, *Arabian Assignment*, Leo Cooper, 1975.

Stokes, Brummie, *Soldiers and Sherpas*, Michael Joseph, 1988.

Strawson, John, *A History of the SAS Regiment*, Secker & Warburg, 1984.

Sunday Times 'Insight' Team, *Siege*, Hamlyn paperback edn, 1986.

Thompson, Leroy, *The Rescuers. The World's Top Anti-Terrorist Units*, Paladin, 1986.

Urban, Mark, *Big Boys' Rules*, Faber & Faber, 1992.

Vaux, Nick, *March to the South Atlantic*, Buchan & Enright, 1986.

Warner, Philip, *The SAS*, William Kimber, 1971; Sphere Books paperback edn, 1983.

Wiseman, John, *The Official SAS Survival Handbook*, Collins Harvill, 1986.

Note on Sources

The first book in this two-volume series, *The SAS at War 1941 to 1945*, was based largely on documents freely available in the Public Record Office, London, and was annotated accordingly. These were supplemented by a series of interviews and selected material from secondary sources.

For the present book I have had to rely far more heavily on secondary sources, as British official archives are made available only after the lapse of thirty years. I have, however, made use of the limited amount of official documentation available on early campaigns, as listed below under PRO classifications.

War Crimes Investigation: WO 209, WO 235, WO 261/71, WO 311, and TS 26.

The Malayan Emergency: DEFE 11.

Borneo: DEFE 13.

Jebel Akhdhar: WO 337 and WO 305. (Note: some documents have been 'retained' by the Ministry of Defence.)

In addition, there are files on general policy regarding special forces during the 1950s in DEFE 11, WO 193 and WO 218.

Wherever possible I have endeavoured to indicate a source but have refrained from giving footnotes, as these would have been applicable only to the earlier chapters.

Although I have enjoyed the benefit of many hours of discussion with men who have served in the post-war SAS, I have not betrayed any confidential information and the only names mentioned are those which have already been published, for one reason or another. The book is in no sense an 'official' history and any mistakes of fact are mine alone.

Index